Praise for
EAGLE DOWN

"Afghanistan is one of the most dangerous countries in the world, and US Special Forces are one of the most secretive groups in America's military. That Jessica Donati managed to crack both and write a book that is both brutally honest and deeply compassionate about this elite group is a journalistic triumph. It is beautifully written, impossible to put down, and deeply terrifying for anyone who has worked in that country. She's one of those writers who makes me deeply proud of my profession."

—Sebastian Junger, *New York Times*–bestselling author

"*Eagle Down* is a powerful, important, and searing—and at times uncomfortable—account of the extraordinary missions our special operations forces have undertaken in Afghanistan in recent years. It captures vividly the challenges, accomplishments, and issues faced by those on the bleeding edge of the latest campaigns."

—General David Petraeus, US Army (Ret.), former commander of the surge in Iraq, US Central Command, and US and Coalition Forces in Afghanistan, and former director of the CIA

"In this courageous, moving account, Jessica Donati shows us that the war in Afghanistan never really ended—and may keep going. She brings us an unprecedented look into the world of secretive US special operations forces, who continue to fight and die in a war that the American public knows little about. The stories are heart-rending and hard to put down. This is the most important book I've read on this latest phase of our never-e̶ never-ending tragedy."

*No̶
D1041888*

"*Eagle Down* is a must-read for anyone interested in American foreign policy. Donati shows how US Special Forces ended up fighting the past few years of the endless forgotten war in Afghanistan with little leadership, muddled orders, and few resources—in other words, with no real hope of success, however that's now defined in the war-torn country. Along the way, Donati catalogs the human toll of a conflict that barely registers on Americans, from those killed in action to those seemingly betrayed by their own government."
—Kim Barker, author of the bestselling *Taliban Shuffle*

"This book takes you from the Special Forces soldiers on the front lines in Afghanistan to the corridors of power in Washington, DC, where politicians and military leaders far removed from the battlefield make decisions impacting the fate of a nation and the lives of those who step up to wear the uniform. In a powerful book that is equally inspiring and tragic, *Eagle Down* reminds us that the true cost of war is always paid, not just by those who raise their right hands to defend the nation, but by their families whose resilience in the face of overwhelming adversity is a true testament to the American spirit."

—Jack Carr, former Navy Seal and
New York Times–bestselling author of
The Terminal List and *Savage Son*

"Fighting long after the fires of 9/11 had cooled, and most of their nation had lost focus on their fight, these Special Forces soldiers reflect both the courage and cost of combat. An important read to understand that wars don't always end just because we stop watching."

—General Stan McChrystal,
US Army (Ret.), author of *Team of Teams*

"A sobering story about what was happening behind the scenes as groups of American warriors attempted to carry out their duties in Afghanistan during the waning days of the Obama administration while dealing with an undefined mission, the fog of war, a belief their military leaders didn't support them, and Washington politics. Their courage and strength are remarkable to this day."
—Cami McCormick, CBS News correspondent

"Donati's on-the-ground account—and it's clear that she put herself in constant danger to tell the soldiers' stories even as American officials dithered about how to deploy those troops—is sometimes as hallucinatory as *Dispatches* and as taut and well-written as Mark Bowden's now-classic book. Exemplary journalism and a powerful argument for not putting soldiers in harm's way unless we're sure we know why." —*Kirkus* (starred review)

"Skillfully interweaving big-picture policy analysis with frontline reporting, Donati shines a stark light on this shadowy conflict. The result is a distressing yet vital update on America's longest war."
—*Publishers Weekly*

EAGLE DOWN

DOWN

AMERICAN SPECIAL
FORCES AT THE END OF
AFGHANISTAN'S WAR

JESSICA DONATI

PUBLICAFFAIRS

New York

Copyright © 2021 by Jessica Donati
Preface copyright © 2022 by Jessica Donati
Cover design by Pete Garceau
Cover image copyright © XM Collection/Alamy Stock Photo
Cover copyright © 2022 by Hachette Book Group, Inc.

Hachette Book Group supports the right to free expression and the value of copyright. The purpose of copyright is to encourage writers and artists to produce the creative works that enrich our culture.

The scanning, uploading, and distribution of this book without permission is a theft of the author's intellectual property. If you would like permission to use material from the book (other than for review purposes), please contact permissions@hbgusa.com. Thank you for your support of the author's rights.

PublicAffairs
Hachette Book Group
1290 Avenue of the Americas, New York, NY 10104
www.publicaffairsbooks.com
@Public_Affairs

Printed in the United States of America
Originally published in hardcover and ebook by PublicAffairs in January 2021
First Trade Paperback Edition: May 2022

Published by PublicAffairs, an imprint of Perseus Books, LLC, a subsidiary of Hachette Book Group, Inc. The PublicAffairs name and logo is a trademark of the Hachette Book Group.

The Hachette Speakers Bureau provides a wide range of authors for speaking events. To find out more, go to www.hachettespeakersbureau.com or call (866) 376-6591.

The publisher is not responsible for websites (or their content) that are not owned by the publisher.

Print book interior design by Six Red Marbles.

The Library of Congress cataloged the hardcover edition as follows:

Names: Donati, Jessica, author.

Title: Eagle down : the last special forces fighting the forever war / Jessica Donati.

Description: First edition. | New York, NY: PublicAffairs, Hachette Book Group, 2021. | Includes bibliographical references and index.

Identifiers: LCCN 2020036573 | ISBN 9781541762558 (hardcover) | ISBN 9781541762572 (ebook)

Subjects: LCSH: United States. Army. Special Forces—History—21st century. | Afghan War, 2001– | Special forces (Military science)—United States.

Classification: LCC DS371.412 .D66 2021 | DDC 958.104/78—dc23

LC record available at https://lccn.loc.gov/2020036573

ISBNs: 9781541762558 (hardcover), 9781541762572 (ebook), 9781541762565 (trade paperback)

LSC-C

Printing 1, 2022

CONTENTS

THE SPECIAL FORCES (GREEN BERETS)

THERE ARE FIVE active duty Special Forces Groups in the US Army. Historically, each has a primary geographic area of responsibility:

1st Special Forces Group: Asia Pacific
3rd Special Forces Group: Sub-Saharan Africa
5th Special Forces Group: Middle East and Central Asia
7th Special Forces Group: Latin America
10th Special Forces Group: Europe, North Africa

The National Guard has two Special Forces Groups:

19th Special Forces Group
20th Special Forces Group

Each active duty Special Forces Group is made up of four battalions.

Operational Detachment Alpha or A-Team

An Operational Detachment Alpha (ODA) is the twelve-man team that makes up each building block of the Special Forces. There are usually six ODAs in a Special Forces company. Each team member has a specialized role, denoted by a number and letter, often described as below:

Team leader (18A): captain, or detachment commander
Team sergeant (18Z or "Zulu"): executive officer implementing plans, advises captain on operations and intelligence

Warrant officer (180A or "Whiskey"): senior enlisted member of the detachment, oversees operations and personnel

Intelligence sergeant (18F, or "Fox"): intelligence collection and analysis

Two weapons sergeants (18B, or "Bravo"): specialized in a range of weapon systems

Two engineer sergeants (18C, or "Charlie"): combat and construction engineering

Two medical sergeants (18D, or "Delta"): trauma and routine medical care

Two communications sergeants (18E, or "Echo"): radio and other communication

Operational Detachment Bravo or B-Team

The Special Forces team that commands and supports the ODAs or A-Teams in the company.

Operational Detachment Charlie or C-Team

The Special Forces battalion headquarters that commands and supports the companies in the battalion.

MILITARY ACRONYMS

Useful acronyms to know in Afghanistan:

ANA-TF: Afghan National Army Territorial Force

AOB: advanced operations base, the headquarters for an area

CONOP: concept of operations, the plan for the mission

GFC: ground force commander, the commander of all forces involved in an operation

IED: improvised explosive device

NDS: National Directorate of Security, the Afghan intelligence agency

ODA: Operational Detachment Alpha, the twelve-man team that makes up the fighting blocks of US Special Forces

OFS: Operation Freedom's Sentinel, the unilateral US counterterrorism mission in Afghanistan

RPG: rocket-propelled grenade launcher

RS: Resolute Support, the US and NATO mission in Afghanistan

SOF: US Special Operations Forces, includes US Air Force, US Army, US Marine Corps, and US Navy Special Operations Forces

SOJTF: Special Operations Joint Task Force, leads US and NATO Special Operations forces in Afghanistan

SOTF: Special Operations Task Force, leads US Army Special Forces in Afghanistan

VSO: Village Stability Operations, a US military program that ran from 2010 to 2014 that tasked Green Berets with raising village-level militias to fight the Taliban

CHARACTERS AND PLACES

Parts One and Two

Military Characters

US Commanders
Gen. John F. Campbell: US and NATO forces commander in Afghanistan

Maj. Gen. Sean P. Swindell: Special Operations Joint Task Force–Afghanistan (SOJTF) commander

Brig. Gen. Tony Bauernfeind: Special Operations Joint Task Force–Afghanistan (SOJTF) deputy commander

1st Battalion, 3rd Special Forces Group (Airborne)
Lt. Col. Jason Johnston: 1st Battalion commander

Kunduz

Charlie Company, 1st Battalion, 3rd Special Forces Group (Airborne)
Maj. Michael "Hutch" Hutchinson: Charlie Company commander

ODA 3111, Camp Pamir, Kunduz
Josh Middlebrook: Delta

Benjamin Vontz: Echo

ODA 3133, Bagram Airfield, Parwan
Patrick Harrigan: captain

ODA 3135, Camp Morehead, Kabul

Helmand

Alpha Company, 1st Battalion, 19th Special Forces Group (Airborne)

Maj. Ronnie Gabriel (pseudonym): Alpha Company
    commander

ODA 9123 (Attachment from Bravo Company, 1st Battalion, 19th
Group), Camp Antonik, Helmand
    Caleb Brewer: Fox
    Chris Clary: Bravo

ODA 9115, Camp Morehead, Kabul
    Andy MacNeil: captain
    Dan Gholston: team sergeant
    Matthew McClintock: engineer
    Jordan Avery: Bravo

ODA 9114, Camp Brown, Kandahar
    Jeffrey McDonald: captain

Civilian Characters

Médecins Sans Frontières (Doctors Without Borders)
    Dr. Evangeline Cua: surgeon, Kunduz Trauma Hospital
    Dr. Masood Nasim: medical director, Kunduz Trauma
        Hospital
    Guilhem Molinie: country director, Kabul

National Security Council
    Susan Rice: national security adviser (2013–2017)
    Peter Lavoy: South Asia director (2015–2017)
    Fernando Lujan: Afghanistan director, South Asia director
        (2015–2017)

State Department (US Envoys for Afghan Peace)
    Rick Olson: special representative for Afghanistan and
        Pakistan (2015–2016)

Parts Three and Four

Military Characters and Places

US Commanders

Gen. John W. Nicholson: US and NATO forces commander
in Afghanistan (until 2018)

Gen. Austin "Scott" Miller: US and NATO forces
commander in Afghanistan (2018 onward)

3rd Battalion, 1st Special Forces Group (Airborne)
Lt. Col. Joshua Thiel: 3rd Battalion commander

ODA 1331, Camp Blackbeard, Nangarhar
David Kim: captain

Civilian Characters

National Security Council
H. R. McMaster: national security adviser (2017–2018)
Lisa Curtis: South Asia director (2017 onward)

State Department (US Envoys for Afghan Peace)
Laurel Miller: acting special representative for Afghanistan
and Pakistan (2016–2017)
Zalmay Khalilzad: special representative for Afghanistan reconciliation (2018 onward)

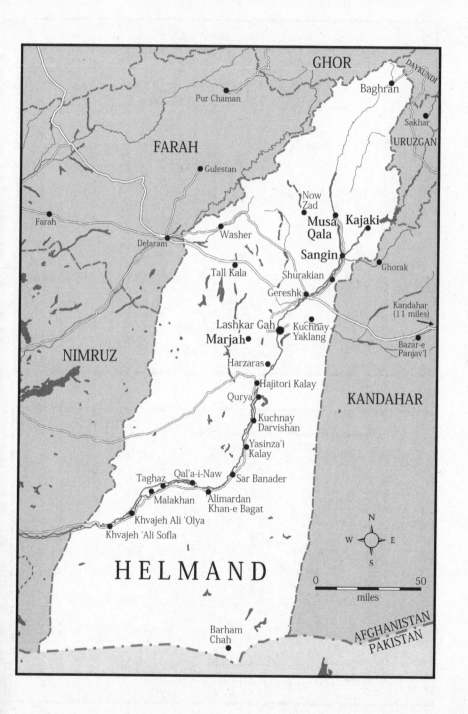

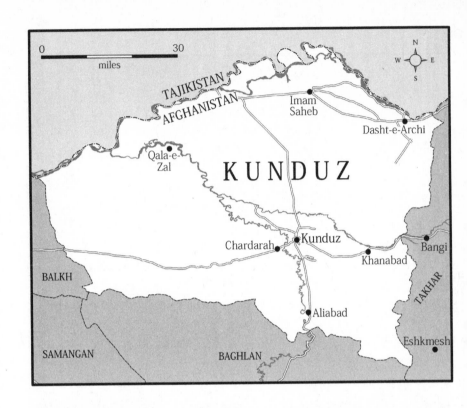

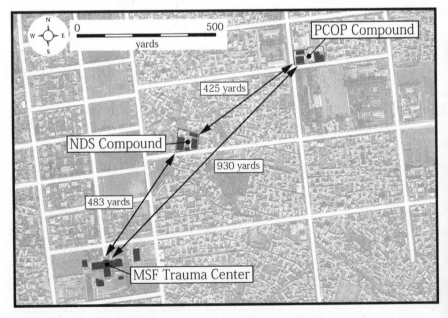

PREFACE TO THE PAPERBACK EDITION

THIS BOOK offers an intimate portrayal of the lives of US Special Forces soldiers deploying in the final years of the Afghan war, from 2015 onward. It aims to provide a window into the covert war that was fought for years during the Obama and Trump administrations long after the United States had pulled most troops from Afghanistan. The cost was borne by a handful of American soldiers and thousands of Afghans, who perished far from the media spotlight as the world moved on.

At the time of this writing, the Taliban had seized power in Kabul after a stunning summer offensive that began as the United States was pulling all US troops out to meet the Biden administration's August 2021 deadline to withdraw. Most of the country fell in less than a fortnight with minimal fighting. The Kabul administration fled without warning one Sunday morning, ruining a last ditch, US-backed plan to negotiate a peaceful transition in Doha, Qatar.

The US suddenly found itself operating in a country controlled by its enemy of two decades. It abandoned its vast, heavily fortified embassy compound while thousands of American troops were sent back in to oversee a chaotic and desperate effort to complete the evacuation of remaining troops, US citizens, allies, and local Afghans at risk. To the US government, and the rest of the world, the speed with which Kabul fell was a shock. It shouldn't have been.

If Washington had been open about the extent to which US Special Operations were propping up the Afghan government, the vacuum in which the Taliban was able to establish control would have been obvious. As vividly depicted by the lives of the soldiers profiled in this book, the United States for years relied on its most highly trained forces, supported by airstrikes and the world's most advanced military technology, to keep Afghanistan from collapse.

President Barack Obama began this mode of covert warfare in Afghanistan in 2015 as part of an effort to deliver on a campaign pledge to end forever wars. Although he announced the end of combat operations and the start of a new training mission to prepare the Afghan government to take full control, what he actually did was turn the losing battle over to US Special Operations, who could operate in near-total secrecy and with virtually no accountability to the US public.

President Donald Trump inherited this mode of warfare and ramped it up to address the deteriorating conditions on the ground. Like his predecessor, he struggled to extract himself from the Afghan war, partly due to resistance in the national security establishment, whose members warned that leaving Afghanistan could cause it to collapse, exposing America to the risk of another large-scale terrorist attack.

I lived in Kabul during the first years covered in this book, working as *The Wall Street Journal*'s Afghanistan bureau chief. I moved to Washington, DC, in 2017 to cover foreign policy for the paper. The book follows years of policy changes that led to a growing role for elite US troops and worsening security conditions in Afghanistan until the Trump administration's signing of an exit deal in February 2020.

Under the terms, the US agreed to withdraw within fourteen months as long as the Taliban met certain conditions. But the agreement was vaguely worded, and provisions, such as certifying that the Taliban had broken ties with al Qaeda, seemed subjective at best. The agreement was accompanied by a secret addendum, not released to the public, which added to confusion about how to interpret the terms of the deal. There was no provision requiring Afghan parties to reach an agreement to end the conflict. It seemed the war could drag on for years longer, perhaps even forever. Indeed, some hawks in Washington called for the US to stay indefinitely.

But President Joe Biden, who in 2021 became the third US president to inherit the war, decided in April, after a short deliberation period, to withdraw without preconditions, essentially scrapping the deal. The White House fell silent on key matters such as air or logistical support, and city after city fell without a fight as Afghan government forces lost hope.

With the Taliban surrounding Kabul by mid-August 2021, Biden officials tried one last time to strike a face-saving agreement with the Taliban to set the stage for an orderly transition. Under the terms, the Taliban would avoid entering Kabul, and an Afghan delegation would be dispatched to Doha to negotiate its defeat while the US completed its withdrawal. But that never happened. President Ashraf Ghani and a close circle of advisers fled without warning, and the Taliban marched into Kabul later in the day.

During the US military's last two weeks in the country, the world watched in horror as a chaotic evacuation effort took place. Thousands of Afghans massed at the Kabul airport gates trying to escape; some clung to airplanes and fell to their deaths from the sky. With days to go, a suicide bomber at Abbey Gate killed thirteen US forces and almost two hundred Afghans. In a final act of the twenty-year war, the US carried out a drone strike the next day, mistaking an Afghan man who was a longtime US aid worker for a terrorist, killing ten members of his family, including seven children. It took the United States more than two weeks to admit the error.

How did things go so wrong? The US ended up believing its own narrative about handing over the war to a government it had propped up for years. US intelligence agencies missed the many indicators that pointed to an urgent need for a change in policy, from soaring civilian casualties to widening Taliban control across the countryside. In the final months of the withdrawal in 2021, the CIA and others rapidly revised predictions for how long Kabul would survive without support, but none anticipated that the government would fall before US troops had left.

To understand how the United States was able to miss the signs of a rotting establishment, one must look back to 2014.

President Obama had announced that the Afghan war was over, and he promised to deliver on a campaign pledge to end the costly engagement in Afghanistan. He scheduled all remaining troops to return home within two years after completing a training mission that would transition the Afghan government to full control. But less than a year later, the Taliban swept into the northern city of Kunduz and captured its first province. It was a stunning defeat for the US-backed government and should have been a sign that drastic change in policy was needed.

It showed the flaw in the plan to turn over the war to the Afghan government and extract the United States from the long conflict. For too long, the reconstruction effort had empowered local warlords and made an industry out of corruption. The government was weak, and injustice fueled the Taliban insurgency. US Special Forces and Afghan commandos were dispatched to save Kunduz. Although the province was saved, nothing was done to address the root causes of the conflict and the rotting state of the Afghan government. As security worsened and more places risked falling, US Special Operations became the solution for everything.

To some extent, the justification was provided by concerns that things would be even worse without US troops there. An Islamic State affiliate was taking root in the east, and Iraq was a lesson that loomed large. President Obama had ordered a unilateral withdrawal of US troops from Iraq in 2011, which accelerated the country's descent into chaos and gave rise to the Islamic State. The extremist group inspired one of the greatest movements of jihadists the world had seen in years and soon drew US troops back to Iraq and into neighboring Syria. An abrupt US exit from Afghanistan also raised the specter of the civil war of the 1990s, which had taken place after the Soviet withdrawal and had led to the rise of the Taliban in the first place.

As a foreign correspondent in Afghanistan, I found reporting on the role of US Special Operations in the conflict at this new stage in the war to be my greatest challenge, even as it became increasingly apparent to me that these elite forces were the only thing preventing the country from complete collapse. At the *WSJ* bureau in Kabul, I worked with a team of two great reporters: Habib Khan Totakhil and Ehsanullah Amiri. Habib and Ehsan were both in their twenties, passionate about journalism, and remembered watching the US invasion as children, when they were living as refugees across the border in Pakistan. Our bureau was located in a house that must have once belonged to a wealthy Afghan family; we shared it with the *Washington Post*'s Kabul bureau to save costs. Our offices were in rooms at the back of the garden, and I converted the garage into a gym, where we had an old Chinese treadmill that would stop dead during power outages and later return to life, displaying indecipherable Chinese script on its screen.

The US military rarely granted embeds with US Army Special Forces, known as the Green Berets. The few reporters that were granted access were based in Washington, DC, and even then, embeds were limited. Foreign correspondents never got to embed, probably because we were too critical of the mission. But as I discovered, there was another way to get in: through the Afghan forces who operated as the Green Berets' partners, fixers, and translators.

US Special Forces worked with a range of Afghan partners, depending on the circumstances and the location, from ragtag village groups to elite Afghan army commandos. If we wanted to find out what was going on in the east against the new Islamic State affiliate, we traveled with village militias in Achin or Kot district. When Kunduz fell a second time, we embedded with the Afghan commandos who partnered with Green Berets to recapture the city in 2016.

It was a riskier way to work. The US military used helicopters to shuttle personnel among their many bases, including those located barely a mile apart in different locations in Kabul. Afghan forces generally moved by road and expected us to drive to them, no matter how remote the location. Hitching a ride on an Afghan army helicopter was possible, but rare. Our Afghan hosts often displayed extraordinary bravery and hospitality, but they necessarily had a cavalier approach to safety, adding to the dangers we faced during embeds.

We prepared for trips as best we could. Information was critical. The same highway might be under police control between ten a.m. and four p.m., and then under Taliban control at night. I would sit in my blue burqa in the back seat of the vehicle, typing away under the folds of the flowing fabric. My Afghan colleague, Habib, was more likely to be stopped by the police than by the Taliban. He had long, jet-black hair and a beard, and he towered over six feet. He looked like a Taliban in the pale blue salwar kameez that he wore for such expeditions, with large, dirty, white sneakers. The advantage of traveling like this, of course, was that we had much greater freedom and flexibility than any closely controlled embed with the US military.

As the war worsened, so did the anger and frustration of the Afghan soldiers and villagers who spent time with us. Insider attacks, in which Afghans turned on their US or coalition partners, were common and never far from our minds. In 2014, an Afghan policeman had fired at two Associated Press colleagues in Khost province just before the presidential elections, killing photographer Anja Niedringhaus and severely wounding reporter Kathy Gannon. Increasingly, Afghan soldiers and police turned on their fellow brothers in arms, after switching sides, as fewer foreign troops were exposed.

As we sought to deepen our understanding of the role that US Special Operations played in propping up the government, Kunduz fell a second time. The US military once again secretly dispatched teams of Green Berets to help the Afghan commandos rescue the province and halt a possible ripple effect across the rest of the northeast.

At *The Wall Street Journal* Kabul bureau, we knew that US Special Forces had played a role in the critical operation to recapture the city. Reporting on how that battle had played out would reveal the truth behind the White House's claim that the United States was no longer in combat, and the story was worth the risk of getting to Kunduz to investigate. It became the story that motivated me to write this book.

Habib obtained papers granting us an embed with the Afghan army's 10th Special Operations Kandak. Over the course of a week, we got to know some of the Afghan commandos, and a few US soldiers too, and patched together the story of how they had recaptured Kunduz. Two teams of Green Berets had fought alongside the Afghan commandos in the city for days, backed by US airstrikes. Kunduz was under government control again, but everyone cautioned that it wouldn't be for long. The Afghan government was as corrupt as ever, and Afghan commandos were abandoned on frontline posts for weeks without resupply.

The US and Afghan soldiers were preparing for a night raid to kill or capture a local Taliban commander when we left to return home. A few days later, when we were back in Kabul, news broke that the raid had gone horribly wrong. The soldiers had gotten trapped in the village of Boz-e Kandahari and fought all night to get out alive. An AC-130 gunship attacked the village to help them escape, killing thirty-three civilians, including many children. Two American soldiers and three Afghan commandos were dead, and many others wounded. In the morning, angry villagers paraded the children's tiny, bloodied, dusty bodies in the streets.

The Pentagon, still refusing to discuss the role that Special Forces had played in saving Kunduz, provided no explanation for the village raid, which the soldiers had told us aimed to capture or kill a local Taliban commander. The whole thing was framed as a training mission. "The service members came under fire during a train, advise and assist mission with our Afghan partners to clear a Taliban position and disrupt the group's operations in Kunduz district," a statement said. I looked at the footage of the grieving families carrying their dead children and found it hard to square with the kindness we had seen from the US soldiers in Kunduz.

The Wall Street Journal published the Kunduz story soon after, describing the role played by Special Forces in the recapture of the city and in the broader fight to save several other provinces also on the brink, such as Helmand, Uruzgan, Farah, and Baghlan. The newly elected president, Donald Trump, we predicted, would be faced with a tough choice: escalate the secret war, or allow Afghanistan to slip out of grasp.

A few days later, I received a letter from the grieving mother-in-law of one of the US soldiers killed in that raid, Captain Andrew D. Byers. Her daughter had opened the paper and read our article, which was dated November 18, 2016. The two had been married for seven years. The mother-in-law wrote:

> Andy is a casualty of a policy without clear purpose, in a seemingly endless war. It is easy to want to make heroes out of people in this circumstance. The term hero is too strong. What is worth noting is that there are men and women who choose to serve, and in many ways, give up their freedom by serving. Andy was a soldier, doing his job with honor. He embodied respect, responsibility, and hard work. These qualities are becoming more difficult to identify in a world where being a victim is esteemed.
>
> Thank you for the commentary that highlights the need for those who govern to consider the impact of the war. What a sad way for our country to lose good people.
>
> —Laura Crites

Back in Afghanistan, we felt the losses at home as well. Toryalai, one of our drivers, lost his twenty-one-year-old brother, who had worked with the National Directorate of Security, the Afghan intelligence agency, in Kunduz. The kid was ordered out on a mission and shot dead by a sniper. I visited their family home with the *WSJ* bureau staff and went to the women's side with our cleaning ladies, known as khalas, or aunties, to meet the grieving mother and sister. Everywhere, women were wailing. The khalas immediately started crying as well. The war had taken a toll on everyone. The cries coming from the women weren't about a single loss. They contained all their losses, the decades of war, and the losses to come—the helplessness of it all.

I thought about the number of Afghan forces killed in the war that year—was it five thousand? Or eight thousand? I tried to imagine the grief that I was witnessing in our driver's home, multiplied a thousand times, day after day, year after year. How could one country contain so much grief?

I thought about how the US military officials and diplomats informally called the casualty rates among the Afghan army and police "unsustainable." This one death seemed unsustainable to me. Casualty figures in Afghanistan had become a closely guarded secret to avoid hurting morale. But in the first four years of the new mission that was launched in 2015, some forty-five thousand Afghan army troops and police officers were reportedly killed.

Most Americans have forgotten the war in Afghanistan. But to the soldiers I write about in this book, who have served multiple deployments in service of the War on Terror, Afghanistan was like a second home. Special Operations kept the country intact, providing just enough support through airstrikes and joint operations to prevent the Taliban from seizing major cities. Their sacrifices, such as they were, remain unsung.

The White House called the Special Forces "advisers" instead of soldiers and describes battles like the ones fought in Kunduz as "training missions." A handful of American soldiers gave their lives each year in the same places: Nangarhar, Kunduz, Helmand, Kabul. The low number of American body bags kept the war out of public debate while little thought was given to the Afghan forces and civilians bearing the brunt of the violence year after year.

It's not just Afghanistan. Historically, US Special Operations have been deployed all over the world, from Iraq and Syria to Libya and Yemen. A little-talked-about Special Operations mission continues in the African countries of Niger and Mali against extremist groups linked to Islamic State, al Qaeda, and others. In all these battlefields, the complexity of local dynamics undercuts the simple good-versus-evil narrative. The conflicts are often fueled by scarcity of resources, tribal disputes, and long-standing ethnic rivalries left over from colonial eras. We in the media never question the counterterrorism argument, and so the wars continue in shadows with no end in sight.

"A perpetual war—through drones or Special Forces or troop deployments—will prove self-defeating, and alter our country in troubling ways," President Obama said in a 2013 address promising to end the war in Afghanistan the following year.

But that's exactly what he started. US Special Forces led the invasion in 2001 to oust the Taliban and chase down the leader of al Qaeda, Osama bin Laden. Green Berets were the first to arrive in Afghanistan with the Central Intelligence Agency that year, riding over the mountains on horseback alongside Afghan warlords. Twenty years later, they were the ones left on the front lines of the war.

—Jessica Donati, Virginia, January 2022

PART ONE

WITHDRAWAL

CHAPTER 1

Back to War

HUTCH

Major Michael Hutchinson was at 3rd Special Forces Group (Airborne), Fort Bragg, North Carolina, preparing to deploy to Afghanistan in the summer of 2015. He was thirty-five and, with fair hair and blue eyes, still fresh-faced. The other soldiers called him Hutch. This would be his fifth combat deployment, counting three tours in Afghanistan and one in Iraq. He'd spent the last year in California, completing a degree in unconventional warfare at the Naval Postgraduate School in Monterey, where he wrote academic papers converting his experiences in Afghanistan into theory and passed easily. He had felt renewed after his time on the sunny California coast with his family. Now, however, he felt apprehensive about the upcoming deployment.

He had been promoted to commander of Charlie Company, 1st Battalion, 3rd Group. He was in charge of seven Special Forces teams. He thought of all the men that would depend on him on the battlefield and felt unsettled. Did he still have it in him to fight after having left the war behind? In California, he had focused on his family for the first time in years, bonding with his two daughters, who barely recognized him at first. He took them on trips to Hawaii and the Grand Canyon. They had a family membership at the Monterey Bay Aquarium and went shopping at farmers' markets on the weekends.

He was glad the girls would have lasting memories of him, in case anything happened. But did he really still have the ability to act decisively in the fog of war? He always prepared for the possibility that he might not return and had made all the usual preparations. He had updated his will and had written letters to his wife and daughters in the event of his death. As he sat at the table at Green Ramp, Pope Army Airfield, playing cards with the family, he tried to push his thoughts away and concentrate on their last moments together. But the disquiet persisted.

He had promised his wife, Tina, that this deployment to Afghanistan would be different from the years of hardship he'd spent at remote outposts. US Special Forces were deploying as part of the new Resolute Support training mission, and they were expected to have very limited exposure now that the combat role was officially over. The soldiers were there to support the handover to Afghan forces before all remaining US troops withdrew the following year. Still, a familiar scene was playing out in the waiting area, where families and friends spent their last moments together until the loudspeaker called their flight. Infants cried, and mothers bounced them on a hip. Some wives and girlfriends looked tearful. It was a matter of odds; there was always someone that didn't make it back.

He was known in the battalion for leading a Special Forces team, a unit known as an Operational Detachment Alpha (ODA),* during the Village Stability Operations (VSO) at the war's peak in 2010–2012. He was the captain of ODA 3325, which operated out of Firebase Shkin in a remote part of Paktika province near the border with Pakistan. It was located at seventy-seven hundred feet over an infiltration route for the Taliban, accessible only by dirt track. Soldiers compared it to a Wild West fort. His team identified itself with a patch bearing a Viking braid and the Greek letter lambda, the symbol worn by the Spartans, which reflected both ferocity and

---

* In movies and popular culture, a Special Forces team may be better known as an "A-Team."

endurance. And just about everyone had it tattooed on themselves somewhere.

The team's job was to recruit friendly militias to fight the Taliban in Paktika and to secure an economic corridor to offer an alternative to violence. Hutch had to immerse himself in local tribal dynamics. The US military's chosen partner was a local warlord known as Commander Azizullah, who had been named chief of police. Their first major battlefield success came by mistake, after they got lost in the mountains in April 2010, only a few weeks after arriving.

Hutch stopped the convoy, which was led by one of Azizullah's men, and examined his GPS-enabled Blue Force Tracker map that was supposed to identify friendly and hostile forces. He mapped a route through the thick forest back to their camp. The trucks resumed moving single file, and drove directly into a clearing where men were setting up a camp. Some were in Adidas track pants; others wore the traditional Afghan tunic known as a salwar kameez. There was a group lighting a fire and another setting up a tripod for mortars. Taliban.

Before he could give orders, his men opened fire in all directions, chasing down fleeing Taliban with their trucks. It was chaos. Hutch was almost shot by one of his own soldiers. The group's favored weapon was a dual-mounted M240 machine gun, fed by two belts and affectionately called "the Twins." He counted eleven dead Taliban when the battle was over, including some carrying foreign passports: Uzbeks and Tajiks, who had likely reinforced the locals for the summer. The rest were Afghans.

News of their success ran up the chain. Generals cited it as an example of how the VSO was supposed to work. The program aimed to secure rural areas by winning the support of villages in remote areas, where conventional forces did not go. Working with native forces was exactly what Special Forces were designed to do.*

---

* But in Afghanistan, military alliances are fickle. The VSO program was effective in some places but fueled long-standing grievances in others. A short

To Hutch, serving during the VSO was more than just a job. Over three years of back-to-back tours in Paktika, he began copying the gestures of elders in village *shuras* (meetings or consultations). When they prayed, he bowed down too. He wasn't a Muslim, but he felt part of the community. When it was time to leave, like many other soldiers, his sense of self was skewed. He felt foreign at home and as though he was simply going through the motions of family life. It took him a long time to leave the mud-brick Afghan villages behind, but he'd done it.

Awaiting departure at Fort Bragg in 2015, Hutch roused himself from his memories. After the long break in California, he didn't know if he could do it all over again. But, he thought, conditions in Afghanistan were different now. He'd spend most of his time at a desk or in meetings in Kabul, far from the battlefield, ensuring that the teams ran smoothly and major infrastructure remained under government control. Combat operations were banned. The war was over.

HUTCH'S WIFE, TINA, who sat across from him with her long, dark hair sweeping over her shoulders, looked down at the cards in her lap, and tried not to think too hard. They had started playing Texas Hold 'Em as a family during power outages in California, and it had become a ritual. Other families sat around them, wives and children waiting for soldiers to deploy. She was eager to get out of there.

She hated lengthy goodbyes. It was like she and the other moms were playing a game of chicken to see whose child would cry first. The soldiers took off for remote corners of the world, and the women were left with a chorus of wailing toddlers, not knowing if or when their husbands and boyfriends would come back. Their daughters were six and eight now, old enough to understand how long an eight-month deployment really lasted.

---

timeline further undercut the mission. The UN and other rights groups recorded a catalog of abuses linked to US-backed militias, including the militia led by Azizullah and trained by Hutch's team.

Tina had refined the process of waiting into a fine art, and the girls would have to learn too. She planned to fill the time with activities, trips, and school events, breaking down the June-to-February deployment into increments, like a relay race. She felt extremely sad and tired but chalked it up to moving home and their time in California coming to an end. It was the longest she and Hutch had spent together since college.

She had met Hutch in his second year at West Point, at a formal ball, before the concept of war had seemed real to either of them. The cadets attended in uniform, and their dates wore fancy dresses. She had gone with a friend as someone else's blind date, but Hutch immediately fell for her. She was dressed in black and looked incredibly exotic to him. Friends had warned her that he was an excessive partier, so she resisted his advances as advised and refused to surrender her phone number.

Hutch was enamored with the idea of warrior culture at West Point, which involved drinking, partying hard, and fighting to the death, though at that point neither he nor his classmates had ever seen a war. After much persuasion, he finally managed to extract Tina's AOL messenger handle and spent six months wooing her before he managed to get her phone number. She made him laugh. He was hooked. The next time they met, with a group of friends at a dive bar in Manhattan, they spent the night deep in conversation, oblivious to everyone else.

Hutch watched the September 11 attacks happen on live TV while he was in class at West Point. He had just attended the Affirmation Ceremony, a rite of passage for cadets that committed them to at least five years of military service. He later watched the invasion of Iraq while sitting on Tina's couch; she was in college, and they weren't yet married. It hadn't meant much then. It still wasn't real. He hadn't even decided to try out for the Green Berets at that point.

He graduated from West Point with a degree in Middle Eastern Studies and Arabic, and deployed to Ramadi, Iraq, soon afterward. It didn't take long for him to abandon his romantic notions about war—that happened during his first deployment in 2004, when it seemed that their only strategy was to drive around and wait for something to hit them so they could fight back. When he tried out his Arabic on the locals, they would look perplexed or run off to find the guy that had lived in Germany and spoke some English so they could communicate.

He learned that shrapnel and bullet trajectories didn't follow the rules he'd studied in class. One soldier survived a bullet that shot clean through his helmet but barely grazed his head, while another was decapitated by shrapnel—from a bomb blast that didn't even hit his vehicle. The soldiers were afraid. Deaths and injuries whittled down their numbers, and fighting alienated the people they were supposed to be securing.

After the bitter experience in Iraq, Hutch decided to give military life another chance and try out for the Green Berets, which he hoped would allow him to train in a foreign language and use his understanding of local culture and history to be more effective. He hadn't even known that Special Forces really existed until meeting some of their members at West Point. They were a legendary division that inserted behind enemy lines and worked alongside native forces in small, independent teams. Tina encouraged him to apply. He wanted the freedom to make decisions and interact with local populations.

He went through Special Forces Assessment and Selection, one of the most grueling selection processes in the army, alongside one of his classmates from West Point. They competed against each other at every step. Hutch admired him for his sharp mind and athleticism. Hutch was sure that his classmate would make the cut. He wasn't so sure about his own chances. But the soldiers were separated into two groups at the end—pass and fail—and Hutch saw his classmate standing next to him.

"Thank god," he thought. "If he's standing here, I must be through."

The Special Forces Qualification Course, known as Q-Course, included foreign-language training and took up to two years to complete. It was a multistage program for entry to the US Army Special Forces. Hutch graduated from the captain's career course and was assigned to 3rd Group. It was historically oriented toward Africa but had turned to the Middle East and Central Asia to cope with the demands of fighting the wars in Afghanistan and Iraq.

Hutch had found his place in the Green Berets. He'd been interested in the military since childhood. He had read about every war in his father's *Encyclopaedia Britannica* and had joined the military book club at thirteen, absorbing everything from military manuals to war-related literary classics. The scale and drama of war seemed so powerful, beyond any other human experience. The people and battles that shaped the fate of nations seemed much more exciting than anything on offer in his hometown of Peoria, Illinois.

His father, an accountant, was strict with money. The family's only extravagances were sending Hutch and his brother to a private Catholic school and indulging in some travel between school terms. The family's history of military service was limited to Hutch's grandfather, who had been drafted against his will during World War II and sent to fight the Nazis in Europe. When Hutch announced plans to go to West Point, the prestigious military academy, both his parents protested against him joining the army.

His father relented eventually and took him to spend the night at West Point to try out life as a cadet. Hutch was thrilled. He submitted his application to the local congressman, and recruiters asked him just one question during the physical test: How many pull-ups did you do? Pull-ups happened to be his greatest strength. He had done twenty-three. The aides put him at the top of the list.

He called it one of many times that luck had prevailed in his life.

At Pope Army Airfield that summer afternoon in 2015, as the plane waited on the tarmac, Tina said goodbye. She and Hutch were among the few couples that had survived the steady pace of deployments through the years. She was used to him leaving but realized that she felt sadder than usual this time. When he was finally called to board, she hugged him, kissed him, and took the two girls back to the car. Kate, the youngest, started crying and didn't stop for the entire twenty-minute journey home.

Hutch was off, heading first to Jordan and then assigned to another military flight bound for Bagram Airfield in Afghanistan.

CHAPTER 2

The Helmand Job
CALEB

CALEB BREWER was excited about the upcoming trip to Afghanistan. It would be his first combat tour as a Green Beret, and he had just qualified as an intelligence sergeant. Although he was new, it was a senior position on the team. He was almost thirty, with light brown hair and blue eyes, and he looked more like a surfer than a soldier. He knew his work wouldn't change the course of the war, but he was eager to make a difference and help the Afghan commandos.

Caleb's team was part of the National Guard's 19th Group. They trained in Utah's Rocky Mountains, and, like him, many of its members were experienced climbers. The high altitude and cold weather created conditions similar to those found in Afghanistan's vast Hindu Kush mountain range. When they found out they had been assigned to Helmand as part of a last-minute reshuffle, the group of climbers laughed. They were going to a part of Afghanistan with no mountains.

Helmand was a vast, mostly desert province fed by a large river that irrigated farmland used to grow poppies, and it held a deep emotional significance for the US military, particularly the US Marine Corps. It was the focus of the eighteen-month surge authorized by President Obama, which had brought the US presence in Afghanistan to a peak of one hundred thousand troops in 2011. The surge aimed to turn the tide against the Taliban after the insurgency had made gains while the US was focused on Iraq. But the Taliban fought hard to control the narcotics-smuggling routes that sustained the insurgency. By the time the last US troops left the province in 2014, more than 450 US Marines and soldiers had died in battles for the villages running along the Helmand River.

Despite US efforts to curb poppy farming, output in Helmand province alone exceeded that of the entire country of Myanmar, the next major producer after Afghanistan. By mid-2015, Helmand was mostly under Taliban control once again. The local government had a presence in the provincial capital and district centers but exerted little control over the population and was widely believed to profit from the booming narcotics trade in the province.

After four months of preparation for the mission, including three at Camp Williams in Utah and a final month of collective training at Fort Bragg in North Carolina, a serious rift had emerged between team members and leadership. Some of the more experienced team members complained that the team's leaders were ignoring their input, and that the training scenarios were poorly designed and would put them in danger. They also warned the lack of cultural training could put them at risk of an insider attack, when Afghans turned on their American partners, sometimes for as little as a perceived slight against their honor.

Caleb was concerned, but he said nothing and focused on his role of gathering intelligence to prepare his team for the deployment. He was an optimist by nature and tried to focus on the positive. He had become a Green Beret to make a difference, to operate at the tip of the spear, and this was his chance. In Afghanistan, each team was tasked to work with a partner force of elite Afghan commandos, or with one of the specialized police units, and was expected to function with minimal supervision to achieve its goals for the campaign.

Caleb's team, ODA 9123, belonged to Bravo Company, based in Utah, but they were deploying as an attachment to Alpha Company, based in Washington State. Alpha Company was short of complete teams. The National Guard companies of the US Army Special Forces were always short-staffed because the soldiers led civilian lives and sometimes fell behind on their certifications or had other commitments.

Alpha Company commander Major Ronnie Gabriel was their new boss. Caleb happened to know Maj. Gabriel from the Special Forces Qualification Course. He didn't discuss his concerns about unity on the team out of loyalty to his teammates. The team was handpicked for the deployment, and dynamics were best handled internally. ODAs, or A-Teams, were the building blocks of the Special Forces, and there were usually six to a company. Each one was coded with a four-digit number, and every job on the twelve-man team was coded with a number and letter. The intelligence sergeant was the 18F or "Fox."

Caleb felt like everything in his life was falling into place after a succession of experiments, including a trip to Iraq with the US Army, a stint in the police, and two unfinished college degrees.

When he departed his home in Tucson, Arizona, Caleb found it hard to say goodbye to Ashley, his wife, and their daughters. The youngest was barely six months old. He tried not to think about all the milestones he'd miss. Ashley was a force of nature. She had resolved to be independent at an early age. She studied engineering, got a job straight out of college, and had bought a house by age twenty-one. Even with Caleb gone for most of the year, she felt confident about juggling two small children and a job. There wasn't a problem she couldn't solve. It was just how she operated.

Caleb said that he knew from day one, the moment he saw Ashley in the hallway during their senior year in high school, "Yep, she's the one." Their first date was dinner at Red Lobster, after which they went back to her house to watch *Super Troopers*. Caleb got a job at the same pizza place where she worked, just to have the opportunity to flirt with her and show off. It worked. Ashley joked that he didn't know how good-looking he was when they started dating. Caleb teased that she only liked him for his car: a '67 baby-blue Mustang. They married in Hawaii several years later.

Ashley hadn't worried much about Caleb's tour in Iraq because he wasn't on the front lines. This new assignment was a different story. Even so, she had supported his decision to join the Green Berets and his recent talk of transferring to active duty. Caleb found it hard to hold down a day job and keep up with the long list of 19th Group premobilization requirements. There were medical training, language proficiency, close-air-support certification, and a zillion other things. He had to travel from their home in Arizona to Utah for each training. At least if he was an active duty soldier, his family could live near the base, and the steady paycheck would help.

In August 2015, Caleb flew with his team to Kandahar Airfield in southern Afghanistan and spent the night there before traveling to Camp Antonik in Helmand province for the handover with 7th Group. US Special Forces maintained an on/off presence at Camp Antonik; officially, the mission didn't exist, because the United States was supposed to have left Helmand a year earlier. The old US military headquarters, Camp Leatherneck, once home to forty thousand people, was now a ghost town. The Afghan army didn't have the resources to maintain the base.

The 7th Group soldiers seemed dismissive. Caleb thought they respected his team less because they were part of the National Guard. The handover operation, also known as the relief in place, should have lasted several days, but it was over in hours. He got a thirty-minute briefing with their Fox, the intelligence sergeant, who answered questions and then left for Kandahar Airfield. Caleb's takeaway from the conversation was that things were going badly and were expected to get worse.

In the spring, the Taliban had made sweeping gains in several districts. They had surrounded the provincial capital, Lashkar Gah. In Kajaki, they were encroaching on an unfinished $260 million

USAID* project to expand an existing hydroelectric dam. In Sangin, they had come close to seizing the governor's office, and in Musa Qala, they had set the district headquarters on fire. The Taliban had captured the district center of Now Zad and raised the white Islamic Emirate flag over the administrative buildings only a month prior to the arrival of Caleb's team.

Morale was low among Afghan security forces. The Taliban dictated when and where battles took place. The Afghan army, unable to rely on conventional forces or the police to hold ground, instead pushed the elite commando units out to the checkpoints. But without US air support, casualties among the Afghan commandos, who were partnered with US Special Forces, were surging as well, and the commandos resented being used like cannon fodder. The Fox warned Caleb to watch out for an insider attack, fueled by resentment.

Caleb thought the situation in Helmand resembled a giant game of Risk. He wasn't surprised that the calculations for the Afghan commandos had changed. Their fate didn't align with the Americans' any longer; their allegiance was to their families and their tribes. He didn't blame them for feeling abandoned. His optimism was already beginning to drain. The province had refused to be pacified by twenty thousand US Marines. What was one ODA spread across all of Helmand supposed to do?

Nor was Caleb surprised when the team's captain announced that Camp Antonik in Helmand was to be their permanent home, and there would be no more trips back to Kandahar Airfield. The US Army Special Forces battalion wanted them to keep an eye on things. There were serious concerns that the Taliban could capture Helmand before the end of the year. Camp Antonik had been stripped of basic amenities because it was meant for expeditionary missions only, not as a permanent base. It was missing key resources like reliable generators and working vehicles, so getting it up and running was their first, and urgent, task.

---

* USAID stands for the United States Agency for International Development, an independent agency of the federal government responsible for administrating civilian and foreign aid.

CHAPTER 3

Gridlock in Washington

PETER LAVOY had worked at the White House as senior director for South Asia at the National Security Council since April 2015. He was a tall, polished man who favored tailored suits, a rarity in Washington, brightened with a red or pink tie. He came from the intelligence community and had recently worked out of CIA headquarters in Langley, Virginia, at the National Intelligence Council.

At the White House, he had the unenviable task of coordinating the various government agencies on US policy in South Asia, a region that included Afghanistan. He considered himself something of a veteran in policy-making circles, and yet the disunity among the departments and agencies over the White House's plan to bring all US troops home surprised him. He made it his goal to get everyone to agree on the way forward and began to prepare a review of the policy.

President Obama had mapped out the US timeline for Afghanistan in a Rose Garden address the year prior. He said the United States would decrease its presence to ninety-eight hundred troops by 2015, reduce that number by around half during the year, and reach a normal, embassy-only presence in 2016. The Department of Defense was making a case for delaying the withdrawal, and the CIA and State Department were also pushing for some form of expanded presence. The national security adviser, Susan Rice, was strongly opposed to any idea that did not constitute withdrawing all US troops before the president left office.

Lavoy had worked on Afghanistan intermittently during his career in the intelligence community and at the Pentagon, and he took the view that the terrorist threat—the reason the United States had invaded in the first place—was still strong enough to warrant a continuation of the mission. He was especially concerned by the rise of militants linked to Islamic State, who pledged allegiance to the main group in Iraq and Syria. The United States had withdrawn all its troops from Iraq in 2011, and swaths of the country had fallen under Islamic State control.

The timeline for Afghanistan was supposed to give local forces enough notice to adjust and take over the war against the Taliban before the United States pulled out, but there were clearly serious flaws in the plan. It was shaping up to be the worst year for the Afghan government since the start of the war: the new rules limiting US operations on the battlefield had a devastating impact on the capability and morale of government forces.

The Taliban maintained a network of powerful commanders or "shadow governors" installed in every province. Poppy crops, which funded the insurgency, were at a record high, despite eradication efforts that had cost Washington over $8 billion. The United States had tried everything, from eradication to crop substitution to education, but nothing worked. The Taliban's annual spring offensive, launched after snow melted in the Hindu Kush, was in full swing and driving a rise in violence. Afghan forces were fast losing ground as both sides realized that the United States was holding back its airpower and forces, leaving the Afghan government to fight on its own.

The US military, prohibited from combat operations, allowed offensive strikes in a very limited set of circumstances: to protect US forces and to target known members of al Qaeda. Every strike had to be reported to the White House. In certain cases the United States could strike to save Afghan lives when they were in grave danger, but the onerous requirements for approval meant the US military often watched the Taliban bulldoze over Afghan checkpoints without being able to help. As an added restriction, some high-level counterterrorism strikes required sign-off in Washington, by which point the opportunity had often passed.

Lavoy sympathized with the Pentagon's case for retaining offensive authorities and holding off on the drawdown of troops on the basis that the timeline and the cap on troop numbers were arbitrary and undermined the mission. The Pentagon viewed the restrictions on US force levels as politically motivated, a strategy to enable the White House to say that "fewer than ten thousand" troops were left in Afghanistan. In line with his defense and intelligence background, Lavoy also saw the merit in the CIA's case for maintaining its bases along the Afghan border with Pakistan, where the agency tracked militants in an area that for decades had been a training ground for al Qaeda and other such groups. Those bases provided an early warning of militant incursions into Afghanistan from Pakistan, sometimes intercepting high-profile attacks planned for Kabul.

IT MADE NO SENSE, Lavoy thought, to cling to preset deadlines that appeared timed for the US electoral cycle without giving the president an opportunity to weigh the views of the various departments and agencies, all of which favored continuing the mission. He set to work on a new strategy for Afghanistan and tasked Fernando Lujan, the National Security Council's Afghanistan director, with mapping out policy options. Lujan was a Green Beret on loan from the Pentagon who had worked at the council for nearly a year and had just started dating a prominent CNN news anchor.

Lujan had served three tours in Afghanistan and was deeply invested in the country's fate. He advocated stepping up US SOF operations to contain the Taliban insurgency. He thought that the strict restrictions on US operations in the country were causing the army and police to get slaughtered, and that an increase in US support would at least halt the Taliban's advance. The second component of the strategy involved setting the goal of negotiating a political settlement to end the war.

US efforts to negotiate with the insurgents had stopped and started since at least 2011. The Taliban had opened a political office in Doha to start talks in 2013, but it was forced to close down almost immediately due to a dispute with then president Hamid Karzai. Since then, the closed Doha office had continued to serve as the de facto embassy, and its Taliban members met with foreign governments, aid groups, and others in Doha from time to time. In 2014, the State Department, through Qatar, had successfully negotiated the release of Private First Class Bowe Bergdahl, the only US prisoner of war, in return for five senior Taliban commanders at Guantánamo Bay. There were hopes that the prisoner swap might revive a peace process, but the parties remained deadlocked over sequencing. The Obama administration insisted that any process had to include Kabul. The Taliban insisted on talks with Washington first.

To break the deadlock, Lavoy proposed leveraging the US relationship with Pakistan to bring the Taliban to the table for talks. Islamabad had played a double game from the start, acting as a US ally but also providing the Taliban leadership with shelter. Like many in the US government, Lavoy saw ample evidence that Pakistan was supporting the group with training, weapons, and medical care. If Pakistan was under pressure, it could force the Taliban's leadership to engage in talks. He drafted a two-page concept note and scheduled a meeting with Susan Rice.

The document outlined three different options for the way forward in Afghanistan that Lavoy hoped would initiate an interagency review of the plan to withdraw in light of the deteriorating security conditions.

Option one outlined the Kabul-centric mission that President Obama had promised the public: dropping to a normal, embassy-only presence. It would reduce US leverage to push the Taliban to negotiate. To maintain security, the United States would fly in troops from Central Asia to conduct counterterrorism operations (which was one of the ways the United States was already quietly circumventing the cap on troop numbers), a costly and ineffective approach. Option two was a far more expansive US troop presence than the White House had promised the public. Option three was a "Kabul-centric-plus" plan: keeping a small number of US troops across Afghanistan's regions beyond 2016 to prevent major territorial losses, and working on a negotiated settlement to end the war.

The meeting with Rice did not go well. She went "ballistic" when presented with the proposal, according to Lavoy. She was opposed to a discussion about how the mission was going or any strategy that did not align with President Obama's plan to draw down to zero troops and maintain a US embassy–only presence in Afghanistan by the end of his term.

"I can't do this; I can't condone this process," he recalled her telling them. "What don't you understand about Kabul-centric?"

The Department of Defense, however, continued to work on its own recommendation for President Obama, and it did not align with the plan to withdraw.

SINCE TAKING OVER THE PREVIOUS SUMMER, General John F. Campbell, the top US commander in Afghanistan, had made holding off the drawdown to fifty-five hundred troops that year his main goal. The reduction would have entailed closing Kandahar Airfield, the launching point for operations in the south, where Helmand was on the brink of collapse. White House officials slow-walked the process in response, dragging out the discussion by drilling into the minutiae of the military's recommendations, scrutinizing and arguing over practically what every individual in the force package would be doing.

Gen. Campbell, undeterred, sat through the endless meetings with Washington with a digital clock over his head displaying the local time in Kabul in large numbers. The meetings often ran as late as two or three a.m. He was frustrated with the White House's fixation with numbers, which hamstrung the mission. But since there was no way around it, he thought the United States should keep at least eighty-six hundred troops in Afghanistan to preserve the military's regional commands, which operated across the country: Bagram Airfield in the north, Forward Operating Base Gamberi in the east, and Kandahar Airfield in the south. Decades earlier, Gen. Campbell had served in 5th Group, and he saw value in what relatively small numbers of highly trained SOF could achieve if the US maintained a presence across Afghanistan.

In the media in Washington, retired American generals and diplomats were given bandwidth to warn against the withdrawal. The line of argument was that al Qaeda and other terrorist groups in Afghanistan still posed a threat, and the United States should protect its investment. There was never a discussion in the media of the evidence showing that these groups existed in significant numbers, nor of the long-term plan for the war. Nor was there much effort to examine why US forces had to be in Afghanistan when militant groups flourished in ungoverned spaces all around the world.

Retired general David Petraeus and foreign-policy expert Michael O'Hanlon published one of many such op-eds in the *Washington Post* in July 2015, in which they warned against President Obama's plan to draw down to an embassy-only presence in Afghanistan. They maintained that the withdrawal could have serious consequences for national security, and the right approach for the Obama administration was to keep military forces there beyond 2016. "We can schedule an end to our role in that nation's conflict, but we cannot schedule an end to the war there or an end to the threat from al-Qaeda, the Islamic State or other extremist elements of the global jihad," they wrote. "Moreover, the Afghan political leadership and public overwhelmingly want us to stay. But all is not lost. Far from it. Kabul is much safer than most cities in war zones—and for that matter, a number of cities in Latin America."

But things in Kabul were about to get much worse.

THAT SAME MONTH, as the Pentagon wrestled with the White House over troop numbers, the State Department was initiating a plan to leverage Pakistan to get the Taliban to engage in talks while the United States still had a troop presence, and therefore influence, in Afghanistan. Washington had seesawed for years over the issue of how much weight to give Pakistan. There were questions about the level of influence Islamabad had over the Taliban, and how helpful it was likely to be in the process. Skeptics took the view that Pakistan was unlikely to sever ties with the Taliban because it nurtured relationships with a host of unsavory groups as a hedge against India. Others recognized the risks but still thought leaning on Pakistan to kick-start talks was worth a try.

The US ambassador to Pakistan, Rick Olson, was skeptical that Islamabad would break ties with the Taliban, but he also believed that getting Pakistan's leaders on board was a necessary component of the process. He was trying to get the Inter-Services Intelligence, Pakistan's powerful spy agency, to strong-arm the Taliban into a meeting with the Afghan government. That effort had borne the first fruits of success earlier in the year. An initial, secret meeting was held between Afghan and Taliban representatives in Urumqi, China, in May 2015. A month later, Afghan government officials met again with members of the Taliban in the resort town of Muree, Pakistan, this time with the United States and China attending in the capacity of observers.

Despite these promising developments, questions remained about the authenticity of the meetings. The Taliban did not officially acknowledge that talks with the Afghan government had taken place, and the political office in Doha said the meetings in China and Pakistan were unauthorized. More generally, the Taliban had long rejected the suggestion that Pakistan had enough sway over their leadership to push them to engage in talks. But US officials and observers noted that the Taliban's chief of staff, Latif Mansur, was among the participants in Pakistan, an indicator that the Taliban's leadership had signed off. It seemed plausible that Pakistan might have enough influence to deliver other high-level Taliban in a future process.

Ambassador Olson was on his way to meet Pakistan's intelligence-agency chief, Lieutenant General Rizwan Akhtar. He had scheduled the meeting to plan for a second round of talks between Afghan and Taliban representatives following the meeting in Muree, Pakistan.

He still hoped that the talks in Pakistan and China might lead to a more formal process, as it was critical to get political negotiations on track while US troops were still in the country.

While Olson was on his way to the meeting, Afghanistan's intelligence agency, the National Directorate of Security (NDS), dropped a bombshell. It announced that the Taliban's supposed leader, Mullah Mohammad Omar, had died in 2013, over two years earlier. Lt. Gen. Akhtar had prepared a PowerPoint presentation for the meeting and was going through the slides when the news broke. He was shocked. Mullah Omar had a legendary reputation among the Taliban, who had given him the honorary title of Amir ul-Momineen: Leader of the Faithful. It would be hard to replace him. Lt. Gen. Akhtar and Olson pressed ahead with the meeting, even though both knew that the news would kill the peace process before it truly began.

The Taliban was forced to confirm the Afghan intelligence agency's announcement. The news sent shock waves through the insurgency. Mullah Mansour, the Taliban's deputy leader, had conspired to keep the death secret, known only to a small handful of inner-circle members. Not even Mullah Omar's closest relatives, including his eldest son, were informed. The Taliban claimed that the deception was necessary to avoid losing battlefield momentum as US and NATO troops were drawing down. But Mullah Omar's family and many battlefield commanders felt betrayed, and soon a splinter faction broke away from the main Taliban group. (Its leader was named months later as Mullah Mohammad Rasool, a former Taliban governor who had fought alongside Mullah Omar during the anti-Soviet jihad.)

US officials hoped the discord would weaken the movement on the battlefield. Instead, the reverse proved to be true. Mullah Mansour, moving swiftly to consolidate power, ordered a massive series of attacks in Kabul. About a week later, just past midnight, the whoosh of an immense blast wave swept across the capital, rattling windows for miles. The first truck bomb to detonate inside the city since the start of the war, it exploded in a poor area of Kabul known as Shah Shahid on August 7, 2015. The Taliban, believed to be responsible, didn't take credit, likely because the bomb had detonated early and missed its target, harming only civilians.

The blast left a crater several meters deep, killed fifteen people, and wounded hundreds with injuries from broken glass and shrapnel. It demonstrated that the insurgency was capable of bringing thousands of pounds of explosives undetected into the city; officials could only imagine the damage it would do outside a crowded government building or foreign embassy, the likely targets of the attack. In the afternoon, the Taliban struck again, carrying out a devastating suicide attack at a police academy that killed and wounded at least fifty cadets.

That wasn't all. In the evening, a group of Taliban fighters rammed a car bomb into the gates of Camp Integrity, the US Special Operations headquarters, the third major bombing in Kabul in less than twenty-four hours. The explosion leveled the gates, and a number of gunmen breached the compound. The soldiers inside ran to defend the base, and a firefight ensued before all the attackers were shot dead. At least eight Afghan contractors were killed.

Hutch had only just arrived in-country when Kabul was hit by the triple attack. His former team sergeant based at the camp gave him a rundown of what had happened there. First Sergeant Andrew McKenna, a Green Beret with 7th Group, was killed in the firefight. McKenna had completed five tours in Afghanistan and one in Iraq and was days away from going home.

The bloodshed was an indication of how rapidly government control around the capital was slipping. The city was protected with security belts of checkpoints—through which insurgents had been able to drive several thousand pounds of explosives. It sent a powerful message about the insurgency's capabilities and the threat posed to Kabul. The final tally that day: 355 casualties in the capital, including 42 deaths and 313 injured. It was the worst violence that Kabul had seen since the start of the war.

CHAPTER 4

"Insider Attack! Insider Attack!"

CALEB was still excited about the tour as he settled into their new home at Camp Antonik in Helmand in August 2015. They had six months to make a difference, and there was a lot of work to be done. The small base had fallen into disrepair. The towers and walls were run-down, and everything was coated in a film of powdery dust that had blown in from the surrounding desert. The logic for restoring a permanent presence at Camp Antonik after the United States had supposedly withdrawn from Helmand a year earlier was unclear to them. The US drawdown was expected to continue, and there were even rumors that Kandahar Airfield, the launching point for all US operations in the south, would close.

Caleb was also disconcerted to find that the local soldiers around them, their supposed partners for the tour, were hostile. The Afghans wore tired green uniforms and long, straggly hair, mirroring their fatigue with the war and contempt for the latest batch of US forces. They wore their Kalashnikov rifles carelessly slung over their shoulders and drew their weapons on the Green Berets whenever the team drove through checkpoints to the Afghan-controlled side of the base, where the airfield was located. At every gate or barrier, they demanded codes in order to let them pass. The Green Berets were ordered to travel in armored trucks inside the Afghan army base, but there was a shortage of appropriate vehicles. There were just three armored trucks left at Camp Antonik, and all of them needed maintenance. The rest of their vehicles were unarmored, which meant team members and their attached personnel often had to travel in soft-skin vehicles despite the regulation.

Caleb barely had a handover with the outgoing Fox, so he was especially grateful when the combat controller, Matthew Roland, an air force captain with the 23rd Special Tactics Squadron, offered to go through all the maps with him and point out where enemy forces were located. Combat controllers were often attached to Special Forces teams and were responsible for establishing air control and providing combat support to the ODA.

Matthew had extended his tour to make sure the handover went well and was the only operator who stayed behind to help them settle in. A redhead, he had a goofy sense of humor and made the most of life on the camp. He had earned the team's appreciation for introducing them to his signature cocktail: a mix that was equal parts Gatorade and Rip It, an energy drink. It was designed to keep one both awake and hydrated through night shifts. The team had to make frequent trips to the airfield to collect supplies and travel to meetings. Matthew showed them how to navigate the area. The base was located inside an Afghan commando base, which in turn lay inside the Afghan army's 215th Corps headquarters, the unit responsible for Helmand.

"A bull's-eye," Caleb joked. They were a tiny green dot in a sea of red. They all questioned whether the surrounding and palpably hostile Afghan soldiers could be trusted not to attack them in the middle of the night.

Within days of their arrival, a second district, Musa Qala, veered toward collapse after the loss of Now Zad a month earlier, and a spotlight fell on Helmand. The team received word that Lieutenant Colonel Jason Johnston, the 3rd Group battalion commander, had been dispatched from Bagram Airfield to get a handle on the situation. He was due to meet with the Afghan army's 215th Corps and the powerful police chief in Kandahar, General Abdul Raziq, whom he knew from previous deployments, to see what could be done. At Resolute Support headquarters in Kabul, officials suspected that the army and the Taliban were cutting deals and trading bases without a fight, allowing vehicles and vast stocks of weapons to fall into enemy hands.

On the day of Col. Johnston's arrival, Caleb was away with a teammate to meet the CIA at another base. Matthew volunteered to lead the convoy from the airfield back to Camp Antonik because he knew the routes through the Afghan army's 215th Corps base well. Matthew's replacement was arriving on the same flight as Col. Johnston, and he was looking forward to going home to his girl-friend, Rose Chapman. Her name suited her. She had rosy cheeks, straight blonde hair, and round blue eyes.

Rose was annoyed about the delay. She was also in US Air Force Special Operations and scheduled to deploy to Afghanistan in the coming weeks. Matthew's sense of duty was interfering with what little time they had together. She was among the few women who flew U-28s, light, fixed-wing aircraft that were used to gather intelligence and that often flew in support of SOF missions. They required crews of two pilots and two system operators and had a wingspan of just over fifty feet. They flew faster than drones and could talk to ground troops without needing a satellite.

Matthew had spent a long time chasing Rose, and they had been friends first. She had a long-distance boyfriend when they met but he insisted on getting her number, and they started to hang out. They were on opposite deployment schedules, but they spent time together between trips. He would crash at her apartment at the end of a night out, and she would make him sleep on the couch. Inevitably, some time later, she would hear a knock at her bedroom door.

"Rose, can we cuddle?" he would ask. "I promise I won't do anything!"

"Go back to bed, Matthew!" she replied every time.

Even after Rose broke up with her boyfriend, Matthew remained in the friend zone. Then they ended up on a deployment together in Africa, where they spent a ton of time with each other. At first, it was just the usual after-work griping about frustrations on the job. Then Rose started to notice a flutter in her stomach when she was around him. She was careful about dating, especially someone at work, but it felt different with Matthew. It was so easy. They got serious, and he soon met her brother and sister. Her younger brother instantly looked up to him as a role model.

It was hard being apart, but they were used to it. They had big plans for the holidays. They would spend Christmas with his family in Kentucky, and New Year's with her family at a rented cabin in Vermont. To celebrate his return, she had bought them tickets to see Taylor Swift. She had spent a fortune, but it would be worth it. He loved Taylor Swift, and they didn't have long together. She worried about her upcoming deployment to Afghanistan, concerned that her squadron might deploy early and she'd be gone before Matthew got back.

COL. JOHNSTON landed in Helmand on August 26, 2015, on a packed flight. Along with Matthew's replacement, there was also a team to fix communication problems at the camp and a 3rd Group ODA that had a strike mission planned with an elite unit of Afghan commandos from Kabul. The newcomers took in their surroundings. The former British-run airfield in Helmand had once been the epicenter of the war in southern Afghanistan. The dozens of abandoned and crumbling buildings and parking lots were a ghostly reminder of the thousands of young US Marines that had passed through on their way to places like Sangin and Marjah during the surge, many never to return home. It was eerie. The heat and dust instantly clung to uniforms, and everyone started to sweat.

The VIPs were led to the armored trucks, while the others, including the visiting ODA and their attached personnel, were directed to board the passenger bus. The precautions were taken to hedge against the risk of an insider attack. The Afghans might be their partners in the war, but trust between them was low. Once the convoy was ready, Matthew steered the bus off the airfield and headed back to Camp Antonik. It was a familiar route for him by this stage of the deployment. The armored trucks formed a line behind him. Around them, Afghan soldiers milled about in their green, dusty uniforms, some eyeing the large American convoy driving past. The Afghan army had not been issued desert camouflage uniforms, a mistake that someone up the chain in the US military had made a long time ago and that had never been rectified.

Matthew's replacement, Forrest Sibley, sat near the driver's seat, and they caught up. They had met on previous deployments. Matthew led the convoy through two checkpoints and finally pulled the bus up at the gates to the Afghan commando base. The interpreter jumped out to talk to the soldiers guarding the gate and ask to be let through to Camp Antonik. There was always a moment of tension at checkpoints. The Afghans sometimes argued about access, and there would be a holdup while someone went to fetch someone more senior or made a call. At first, no one thought anything when the interpreter started to sprint toward another building without looking back. But suddenly, one of the Afghan commandos aimed his assault rifle at the bus, less than fifteen feet away, and opened fire, shooting straight through the window at the driver's seat, where Matthew was sitting.

"Insider attack! Insider attack!" Matthew yelled over the radio, frantically slamming the bus into reverse.

It was too late. He slumped in the driver's seat, blood trickling out from under his helmet. The bus was trapped. The gate ahead was still closed, and the rest of the convoy blocked the rear. The commando continued to spray a volley of bullets through the windows, toward the passengers sitting behind Matthew, who dived into the shattered glass that lay on the floor. The bus ricocheted with gunfire as the soldiers inside fired back, dropping the shooter to the ground.

Several soldiers saw a second Afghan soldier move toward the weapon in the guard tower, and they shot him as well. Later, it wouldn't be clear whether he had a role in the attack.

Soldiers scrambled to help the wounded. Forrest had been shot too and was motionless in the seat behind Matthew. They yanked Matthew out of the driver's seat, and someone else took the wheel as others tried to revive him and Forrest. By the time the convoy had started moving and pulled into the gates back at Camp Antonik, it was clear there was nothing to be done. They were both dead. At least four others were wounded at first count; two had been shot in the arms, one had been shot in the face, and a fourth was saved by the plates in his armored vest.

CHRIS CLARY, a tall, gangly junior Bravo from Oklahoma, had just hung up from a call with his younger brother in America. He worked for a civilian aid group between deployments, and it was his third combat tour with Special Forces in Afghanistan. He emerged from his room to a camp in chaos. The interpreter had arrived on foot and told the gate guards what had happened. Later, they would find out he had helped plan the attack. The surgical team was scrambling to get the tent ready for the casualties, unsure how many would arrive and of the severity of their injuries. Chris quickly put on his body armor, grabbed his gun, and went to the gate to receive the convoy.

As the convoy pulled into the camp, it still wasn't clear how many of the Afghan commandos had been involved in the shooting, or whether it was the start of a bigger attack on the base. The attached infantry unit set up a security perimeter. Chris saw that the team sergeant who was supposed to be in command had frozen up. Once the casualties were taken to the surgical tent, the sergeant with the 3rd Group team, which had been on the bus, took control instead. He had been through an insider attack before. He started a head count while the VIPs, including Col. Johnston, moved to the ops center. The request for a medical evacuation was corrected because the initial request, in the chaos, missed key details, including the fact that the wounded were all Americans.

Chris tried to make himself useful. He checked on the guard towers and went to the surgical tent to let everyone know the exact time the medevac helicopters were scheduled to land, which would allow them to work on the patients until the last moment. The two surgeons worked on the soldier who had been shot in the face, while the Deltas, the medical sergeants, dressed the gunshot wounds that the two infantry soldiers had received to the arms. Chris decided to look for Matthew next, to see if he needed help preparing for the medevac. He couldn't find him.

Feeling a sense of dread, Chris approached the bus and peered in. Matthew was still inside and slumped on a row of seats where the other soldiers had tried to revive him. Broken glass and blood-stains were everywhere. A second American also lay in the wreckage. Chris was shocked. It was his third tour in Afghanistan with Special Forces, but he hadn't lost a team member before. He felt a terrible sense of guilt as he prepared to drive the truck to the helicopter landing zone just outside the camp's gate. Matthew and Forrest were zipped into body bags and loaded in.

Two medevac Black Hawks finally landed to collect the dead and wounded soldiers for the short flight to Kandahar, where the regional US military hospital was located. For seriously wounded patients, the hospital was the first stop on the way to Walter Reed in Maryland. Meanwhile, at Camp Antonik, the soldiers were still working on the head count. Josh Wood, one of the communications sergeants, was missing. They discovered him asleep in his room with the door locked shut. He emerged looking confused. He was supposed to have driven the bus to the airfield, but Matthew had volunteered because he was more familiar with the routes. Because of that, Matthew was heading to Kandahar in a body bag. The story of what had just happened left Josh in a deep state of shock.

Maj. Gabriel, the company commander, gathered everyone for a meeting. The attack could have been worse, he told them. The entire battalion staff had been out there. This was an opportunity to show resilience, and Col. Johnston wanted them to regroup quickly. The military usually had a knee-jerk reaction when an insider attack took place: they would order forces to pull back from training and issue another layer of force-protection measures as a response. The situation in Helmand couldn't wait, he told them. Musa Qala district had just fallen to the Taliban. The priority remained to focus on the mission to support the Afghan commandos and prevent the loss of Helmand.

Later that day, Maj. Gabriel and Col. Johnston went to meet senior staff at the Afghan army's 7th Special Operations Kandak as planned, to make a point of showing that the attack would not hold them back. The battalion wanted to send a team out with the Afghan commandos to recapture Musa Qala. The team in Kandahar that was partnered with the Afghan commandos involved in the operation was itching to get out, but headquarters would not approve the mission and authorized airstrikes instead, using a loophole that allowed the United States to carry out strikes against the Taliban.

The United States was supposed to have ended combat operations against the insurgency and shifted to training and advising that year, but there were exceptions that had never been made publicly clear. This was because US forces in Afghanistan operated under two separate missions: the NATO training mission known as Resolute Support (RS), and a unilateral US counterterrorism mission known as Operation Freedom's Sentinel (OFS).

Gen. Campbell, the top US commander, was in charge of both, and SOF could function under either mission. The advantage of operating under OFS rules was that it gave the United States more flexibility to strike. OFS was generally understood to be the mission against al Qaeda and other terrorist groups, but in practice it was used in critical situations against the Taliban. Events later in the year would reveal the blurry lines between the missions.

OFS rules allowed the United States to carry out airstrikes to support Afghan forces that found themselves in grave danger. The Musa Qala strikes were thus approved under the OFS mission. Celebratory footage posted online by Taliban fighters from the center of Musa Qala was likely a motivating factor. That area had once been a focal point of the US military surge in Helmand. Over the next

couple of days, Col. Johnston guided bombs into the village until the
Taliban retreated, melting back into the countryside.

Caleb was at Camp Dwyer, a Helmand base used by the CIA,
during the insider attack. When he returned to Camp Antonik
the following day, he found that the rest of the team was furious
at the indifference of their leadership, who were pressing them to
start planning joint operations with the Afghan commandos to keep
Helmand from falling, as if nothing had happened. The team's only
interaction with the commandos so far had been to get shot by them
at their gates. The team first wanted to revet each commando and
collect signals intelligence to find out if any others had been involved in the attack. The fate of Musa Qala's district center seemed
secondary to many team members. The Kabul government had long
lost any influence there, and in another year all US forces would be
gone anyway.

ROSE WAS ASLEEP in her apartment in Florida, thousands of miles
away. The sun had barely started to rise. It was the height of summer,
and by midday the heat would be uncomfortable. But it was cool
now, and the ringing of her phone had woken her up. It was five
thirty a.m. She groggily reached for the device. She was supposed to
deploy in the next few days, and maybe someone needed help. She
slid her finger across the green answer key on the screen, and the
phone lit up. A man's voice came on the line.

"Captain Chapman?" he said.

It was her commander. Had she done something? She struggled
to clear her head.

"Do you still live at your apartment?" he said.

"Yes," Rose said.

She thought it was an odd question. The squadron was packing
for the deployment, but she wasn't due to leave for a few days. Was
she in trouble?

"I'm here with a few men at your door. We're going to knock,"
he said.

She practically fell out of bed, grabbed a pair of sweatpants and a shirt, and struggled to the door. She still didn't understand. Was this about the deployment? Then why was the captain at her front door at dawn? She half ran to open it. Her commanding officer was in his service dress blues, a row of badges pinned to his chest. The chaplain stood to one side. At the other was a man she didn't recognize. He was also dressed in official uniform and in the red beret worn by US Air Force combat controllers. As soon as she saw the red beret, she knew something had happened to Matthew. She tried to steady herself. He was probably just hurt, she told herself.

"Are you Rose?" the man in the beret said.

She nodded.

"I'm really sorry to have to tell you this, but Matthew was killed last night," he said.

Rose stared. For a few moments, the world seemed to crumble away as each word slowly sank in. Her stomach fell. Her heart stopped. It wasn't possible. She swayed unsteadily.

"No," she began. She was unable to continue.

She heard her breath loud and heaving, as though it belonged to someone else. She felt tears stream down her face. Her officer swooped in and caught her, enveloping her in a huge, bear-like hug.

"I'm so sorry," he repeated.

She felt a tidal wave of sorrow and collapsed into his arms, crying, until a faint light interrupted the fog in her mind. She had to pull herself together and find out what happened. If she could only focus on the next five minutes, she wouldn't have to think about the rest. About the fact that Matthew was gone forever, and nothing would bring him back.

The officers started to explain what would take place next. The military had a protocol for everything, and she tried to concentrate on their words. Matthew was on his way back, on the same flight as another soldier who had been killed in the attack. She could travel to Dover Air Force Base in Delaware to meet him, as long as Matthew's parents gave their approval. Girlfriends did not have the same rights as wives, even though Matthew had added her to his notification papers. She would have to wait for his parents to sign off before heading there. They hadn't met her, unless you counted waving to each other on FaceTime. They were supposed to meet at Christmas.

The notification team, made up of the officer, the squadron leader, and the chaplain, wouldn't leave her alone until someone else had arrived to keep her company. She had to be careful about whom to call, because the military had been unable to contact Matthew's sister. She called one of her best friends, who lived nearby. For the first time, she tried to get the words out.

"Dan," she stuttered, "Ma-Ma-Matthew...died."

She broke down crying again. Dan showed up right away. The notification team left, and Dan helped her call a few more close friends. They arrived at Rose's apartment, sat her in a chair, poured her a large glass of wine, and packed her bag. It was a time-tested routine to cope with loss: stick together, distract, support. At any moment, they expected a call telling her that she was cleared to travel to Dover to meet Matthew's body the next morning. The friend that had introduced Rose to Matthew persuaded her to go to lunch while they waited.

Rose was staring vacantly at the table when her mobile rang. It was Matthew's parents.

"Of course we want you to be there," they told her.

Within hours she was on a plane with two members of Matthew's squadron. They landed around two a.m. and drove to the Fisher House for families of the fallen, about an hour away. Matthew's family was up waiting for her. His mom, dad, and sister enveloped her in hugs. They wanted to know all about her, and they sat her down to talk until they ran out of energy and went to bed.

She woke up the next morning feeling life drain away as reality came into focus. It wasn't a bad dream. It was real. Matthew's family treated her like one of their own. His father pushed her to eat. Fisher House was stocked with every type of food and comfort imaginable, but she couldn't stomach anything.

"Rose, you have to eat something," Matthew's father said.

"I am eating," she said with a weak grin, nudging a bag of gummy bears.

The family of the other air force officer, Forrest, was there too. When the plane carrying them both home got held up in Germany, they all went to the park and lit a barbeque. The strict rules at Fisher House prohibited visitors from disturbing the grieving families. Matthew's and Forrest's friends joined them at the park, told stories, and made toasts over beer. Rose spent the day in a fog, hollow and numb, barely aware of her surroundings.

Matthew and Forrest arrived the following day in identical caskets draped with American flags. The fuselage of the aircraft was otherwise empty, as per protocol. The ramp was lowered and the caskets carried to the waiting vehicles. At the funeral home in Dover, a team was waiting to prepare the bodies for burial. Soldiers often suffered such extensive wounds that their caskets were kept closed to avoid upsetting the families and wrecking the last memories of their husbands and sons. Matthew's family knew that he had been shot. No one had discussed it, but they all supposed that his body was riddled with bullets and horribly disfigured. Rose didn't expect to lay her eyes on him again.

The funeral home called Matthew's parents: an open casket was an option. Did they want to view his body? They hadn't prepared for this. But everyone agreed they needed to see Matthew one last time or they wouldn't believe it was real. At the funeral home, Rose sobbed in the hallway while waiting for her turn to go in. His friends from the squadron were outside. His two-year-old niece approached her with a tissue.

"I think Auntie Rose is crying!" she said.

"I think we're all crying, Mina," Matthew's sister said.

Matthew's parents went in first. Rose heard his mother wailing. She started to panic.

"I can't do this. I can't do this," she told herself.

Someone came to get his sister. Eventually, Matthew's team leader appeared with another teammate and gently led Rose to her feet and into the viewing room. She walked straight to the other side without looking at the casket, getting as far away from it as possible. Seeing him would take her one step closer to accepting that he was really dead. His teammates steadied her, waiting for her to be ready. Finally, she turned around to face him.

Matthew's face was lying below her line of sight, and deep down she knew that he was in there. She forced herself to his side. Then she looked down. It was a shock. His hair had been cut and combed over. He had always had messy hair and a scruffy beard that sometimes caught flecks of dip. Someone had sewn his lips closed. Rose turned to one of his teammates.

"Nate, it doesn't look like him," she said, choking on her words. "They cut his hair, and his hair looks stupid."

"Do you need me to mess it up for you?" Nate asked.

She nodded.

"Okay, Rose, I promise, before we close the casket, I will mess up his hair for you," he said.

She told him that would be perfect. Then they left her so she could be alone with Matthew for a while. She tucked a letter into his pocket along with a small can of dip. A day later, Matthew was buried in Arlington National Cemetery, one of more than twenty-three hundred American soldiers killed at war in Afghanistan.

CHAPTER 5

We'll Play It Safe
HUTCH

HUTCH quickly got into a routine at Camp Duskin, the company headquarters known as Advanced Operations Base (AOB) North, on the outskirts of Kabul. He woke early each morning to work out at the gym or run circuits around the small base. By seven a.m., he was done with breakfast and was reading emails, situational reports (SITREPS), and intelligence in the operations center. He was responsible for a vast area spanning seventeen provinces—half the country—and the seven Special Forces teams under his command were spread out.

His plan was to visit all seven ODAs in his first few weeks there. He had been watching as the security situation declined and felt devastated knowing that so many of his friends had sacrificed themselves to the war in Afghanistan. He knew that his best hope at this stage was to succeed in securing the major infrastructure of the country and avoid losing any major cities. Already, there were two potential crises on his hands.

The Taliban were threatening Kunduz province in the north, where the capital was surrounded and had come under heavy pressure in the spring. The team stationed at Camp Pamir at Kunduz Airfield had little control over the situation because restrictions kept them confined to the base. The 10th Special Operations Kandak commandos, their Afghan partner force, responsible for the north-east, were nowhere to be seen because they were constantly engaged elsewhere. They were spread out across the several provinces, guarding roadside checkpoints or buildings because the government didn't trust the regular army or police. The Taliban were gradually picking them off, and it was contributing to a serious downturn in morale. The commandos, who didn't believe in Washington politics and simply didn't understand the logic for withholding air support, were angry that the Americans had stopped reinforcing them on the battlefield. The dynamic was becoming a real threat to the mission across the country, not just in Kunduz.

The second major problem was in Nangarhar province, in the east, where a group that had pledged allegiance to Islamic State was gaining ground. The team based at Camp Fenty at Jalalabad Airfield was skeptical of this news; they thought it was the same old militants that had just rebranded. The Islamic State affiliate popped up as US troops were leaving in 2014; its brutal punishments and executions near the border with Pakistan made headlines. It was led by former members of a Taliban group in Pakistan known as the Tehrik-i Taliban. But the Afghan government was playing up its presence to draw resources from Washington, where some were already making comparisons to Iraq. The group's influence was limited, but the association with Islamic State in Iraq and Syria was powerful.

Hutch advised the captains to be creative and find work-arounds, to think in terms of economic potential. He privately thought the Afghan army ought to scale back to the key highways and cities it could control. But that wasn't an option. The headline "Afghan Government Cedes Control of 66 Percent of the Country" would not sit well in Washington. Hutch still thought the Special Forces could have impact. Col. Johnston, the battalion commander, had assigned Hutch to AOB-North at the last minute, precisely because of Hutch's intimate understanding of the country's tribes and politics. The south was more violent, but they didn't expect to have teams out on the front lines because of the restrictions on US operations. And ultimately, losing Kabul would be worse.

TINA WAS BUSY unpacking their furniture and boxes into their new home, a detached five-bedroom house in Southern Pines, North Carolina. The picturesque town, set in a forest of tall, slender pine trees, was worthy of its name. An old railway chugged through the center of town. American flags were draped in many front gardens. It was popular with soldiers that were looking to escape the sprawling malls in Fayetteville, which was closer to Fort Bragg.

Hutch was in touch daily. Tina's only stipulation, when he was deployed, was regular check-ins.

"I just need proof of life," she would say.

He could tell her all about the deployment when he got home. She just wanted to know that he was safe, and if he was in danger, she had to know when the danger had passed. It was that simple. Life went on at home without him. The girls were starting their new school soon and complained every day about missing their father.

"I know," she told them. "I miss him too."

Tina had terrible headaches and nausea and was short of patience with just about everything. She knew that Hutch was in deployment mode and tried not to bother him with her concerns. But she hadn't been feeling well for weeks now. What was wrong with her? She had close friends who provided moral support, but nothing seemed to help.

She was a seasoned unpacker. It was a necessary skill in a military wife. But now that she was sick, boxes sat around the house. The furniture waited to be put in position. It was sad not having Hutch around. She had got used to him being at home. Now she noticed all the behind-the-scenes stuff he used to do. Turns out the trash didn't take itself out. How had they managed three deployments in a row?

Tina tried to keep to a schedule of seeing friends. Some of them were in the army, others were outside the circle. It was good to get a break. The moms organized playdates in different places, to keep each other entertained. One day, a friend came over and asked how she was feeling. "Bad headaches, nausea, sadness," Tina said.

"Could you be pregnant?" she asked.

Tina's friend went to the store and returned with a pregnancy test. Sure enough, it showed positive.

They hadn't planned for another baby. It would come as a surprise to Hutch as well. But Tina knew that he was under pressure at work, and she was aware of the life-or-death decisions he might have to make. What was she going to say, "Oh, by the way, I had to deal with morning sickness today"? She was excited to be expecting but decided to wait until Hutch had settled into his job before telling him the news.

BACK AT CAMP DUSKIN, Hutch was absorbed in the question of how to prevent further security losses considering the various challenges they faced—limited troops, ever stricter rules guiding their operations, and a lack of access to financial resources. The ODAs were all on autopilot; many of the guys were on their fifth or sixth deployment. He didn't have to worry about them. But he was frustrated, especially in light of the triple attack in August that had included the truck bomb in the city and the suicide attack at Camp Integrity, the Special Operations headquarters in Kabul.

Col. Johnston visited from Bagram Airfield and sat down with him to review their limited options. Col. Johnston had deployed to Afghanistan more often than anyone—making trips every year since 2002. Hutch could talk to him freely and respected him immensely. The teams also saw the battalion commander as someone they could trust. They agreed that the priority was to secure Kabul's highways to try to prevent the insurgents from bringing in enough explosives for another truck bomb. They would have to renew efforts to get the Afghans to improve security along Highway 7, the heavily trafficked road that ran east from Kabul to Pakistan.

Kunduz was a more intractable problem. One of the Taliban's most successful commanders, or shadow governors, was making rapid gains there, and the battalion was unable to get approval to run missions with the commandos to beat them back. Mullah Akhund Salam, Kunduz province's longtime shadow governor, was among the first field commanders to have pledged support to the new Taliban leader, Mullah Mansour, in August. His backing was crucial at a time when the Taliban was recovering from the embarrassment of admitting that its supposed leader had been dead for years.

Mullah Salam's story was common in a war that had comprised many twists and turns over the decades. The CIA arrested him in a joint operation with Pakistan's intelligence agency in 2010. Pakistan released him three years later as part of a deal to free high-level prisoners to advance peace talks. He returned to his post as shadow governor in Kunduz, despite assurances from the Taliban to the contrary.

In early 2015, Mullah Salam had taken advantage of the void left by the withdrawal of foreign troops to launch relentless attacks in the province's districts, driving army and police forces to retreat to large bases. The Taliban seemed to be consolidating in rural areas around the provincial capital, also named Kunduz, ahead of an assault on the city, the ultimate prize.

The abusive and deeply corrupt provincial government accelerated the Taliban's rise in the province under Mullah Salam's leadership. For example, locals turned to the insurgency to sort out legal disputes because provincial judges were known to be corrupt and could extort bribes for years before ruling on a case. The Taliban demanded a flat tax of around 10 percent from residents who lived under their control, but they did not take bribes. In some parts, they even administered services paid for by the US-funded government, such as education.

The Taliban were also able to capitalize on resentment toward the US-led coalition, which had committed some of the worst errors of the war in Kunduz. In 2009, German colonel Georg Klein called in a US airstrike on stolen fuel tankers, mistaking villagers crowding around the vehicles for Taliban. The airstrike killed over a hundred civilians, including many children.* And local police units set up by US Special Forces during the VSO were problematic. Instead of securing villages, the groups acted like local gangs and were used by their commanders to prey on locals and settle scores.

TINA, back in Southern Pines, waited for the right moment to tell Hutch they were expecting a baby. It was easier to cope with her exhaustion now that she knew about the pregnancy. And communication was so much better now than it had been in the past, when Hutch might have been offline for days. Still, she had to break the news at some point. Once it seemed that Hutch was settled, she decided to announce it.

"So, I'm pregnant," she said, trying to suppress a grin, over FaceTime.

Hutch was too surprised to say anything for a moment. They hadn't planned another pregnancy. But he immediately felt excited. The two girls were growing up fast, and it would be fun to have another baby. Tina's mom and sisters could help out with childcare if necessary, but he'd be home before the baby was due. They chatted excitedly for a while. He wished he could be there with her, to talk everything through in person.

When Hutch put down the phone, he tried not to think about the other concerns that bubbled up. Like what if he didn't make it home?

Tina felt guilty as they hung up. She had a close friend that had been trying to get pregnant without success. It was intimidating, starting from zero again, now that the girls were nearly teenagers. But she was happy. Knowing that Hutch would be home before the birth, she started to feel more relaxed about this deployment. He seemed to be in a safe place for a change. She could get through this. The months

---

* Klein was promoted to general in 2013, despite the grievous error. Lawyer Karim Popal, who represents an Afghan man, Abdul Hanan, who lost two sons in the strike, has taken the case to the European Court of Human Rights. The plaintiffs accuse Germany of failing to adequately compensate the victims, who were paid $5,000 each.

ahead were mapped out until his return: a trip to see her sister in New York, another to go apple picking with the girls, a high school reunion at Christmas—and soon after that, Hutch would be home.

A WEEK OR SO LATER, the team at Camp Pamir called Hutch to report that trouble was flaring in Kunduz. Fractious ethnic divisions in the Kabul administration had been playing out between appointees to the local government. Afghan police who were loyal to one power broker or another were rumored to change clothes at night and attack rival checkpoints. The Afghan commandos were the only force likely to defend the city in the event of an attack.

In recent days, the Kunduz team, ODA 3111, had started to receive reports of a large number of Taliban amassing in the district of Chahar Dara. Insurgents supposedly accompanied by foreign advisers from Pakistan had planned a large-scale attack on the city. The governor was rumored to be out of town after being bribed to let the city fall to the enemy.

"This feels credible," the captain told him. "Something is about to happen."

Hutch suspected the reports of hundreds of Taliban fighters amassing around the city of Kunduz to be exaggerated—experience had taught him to be wary of the local tendency to inflate numbers. It was probably just Afghan math. It was mid-September, too late in the year for the Taliban to stage a significant attack. He thought they would continue to consolidate their position in the districts and position weapons in the city for an assault the following spring. Still, it was best to be cautious.

"Okay," he told the captain. "We'll send another team to reinforce you. It's probably nothing, but we'll play it safe."

He ordered air assets and a team based at Bagram Airfield to relocate to Kunduz to act as reinforcements in case anything happened. The troops arrived at Camp Pamir the following night, with six Romanian Special Forces and nine infantry uplift personnel. By the time the soldiers had landed, the city was already on the verge of collapse.

CHAPTER 6

The Fall of Kunduz

DR. MASOOD NASIM was covering for a vacancy as medical director at the trauma hospital run by the French aid group Médecins Sans Frontières in Kunduz in September 2015. He was a slight man, with dark, piercing eyes and aquiline features, and had worked for the group for four years. He was usually based in Kabul, but his family lived in Kunduz, where his wife taught at the local university. He now regretted not moving them all to the capital.

He anxiously watched his wife and the children squeeze into their Toyota Corolla with his uncle's family. The entire city of Kunduz was in a state of panic, and about a third of the population was on the move. The Taliban were rumored to have gathered huge numbers of forces in the districts and were preparing to attack the city that night. Civilians were packing up their cars and fleeing in droves. Many government offices and police stations had already been abandoned.

He hoped it wasn't too late to get his family to safety. Most people were evacuating to neighboring Takhar province, where aid groups provided tents and food. Dr. Nasim was lucky: his family was from Takhar. He planned to drive his wife, their children, and his uncle's family to stay with relatives there. They locked up the house in Kunduz, not knowing if they'd see it again. He planned to sleep in his office at the hospital when he returned to the city. Médecins Sans Frontières staff had performed more than twenty-three hundred surgeries since the start of the year, a record, and he knew the coming days would be even worse.

Dr. Nasim couldn't remember a time when Afghanistan hadn't been at war. He had been a year old when the Soviets invaded in 1979. He remembered fleeing his home to hide in caves when Soviet warplanes bombed his village. The anti-Soviet mujahideen, backed by the CIA, were just as bad. They killed his father after he refused to let a commander marry one of his young nieces. Then they came back two months later and shot his aunt dead in front of her young son. Now the Soviets were gone, but the Americans were here, and the mujahideen leaders had become fabulously rich taking lucrative posts in the US-backed government.

Still, Dr. Nasim loved his country. It was hard to choose to leave. The latest outbreak of fighting revived a nagging feeling of guilt and a sense that it would be best for his children to start a new life abroad. The Toyota strained with the weight of the women and children packed into the back as he pulled onto the road and joined the exodus of cars leaving Kunduz.

The first checkpoint they encountered was Taliban. The fighter waved them through after glancing at the burqa-clad women and the cluster of children around them. The next one was controlled by Afghan police, who, waving and shouting angrily, stopped the car.

"Where are you going in such a rush?" one of the men demanded, a rocket-propelled grenade (RPG) launcher swinging from his shoulder.

"I have my car full of women," Dr. Nasim told him. "I have to get them out of the city."

The policeman peered into the car and glared at the passengers suspiciously. Ten women and children were squeezed into the back and front seats. He swore loudly but let them pass. The rest of the journey to Takhar went without incident. Dr. Nasim dropped off his passengers at the home of relatives and turned back to Kunduz. It was bad enough leaving the city, but would he be able to return to it without being arrested or shot? He had to try. The hospital needed him.

He spotted an elderly man walking along the road in the direction of the city, and slowed the car. Dr. Nasim would be less of a threat to the Taliban or the Afghan police in the company of an old man.

"Brother, where are you going? Do you need a ride?" he asked.

"Thank you," the man replied gratefully.

The man was trying to get home after checking on family in the districts. The Taliban stopped the car again on the way back, searched them, and let them pass.

Dr. Nasim went home to pick up some toiletries and then drove to the hospital, planning to stay at his office for as long as the hospital remained open or until the fighting stopped. Médecins Sans Frontières' trauma hospital in Kunduz was the only Western-standard facility of its kind in northeast Afghanistan. It offered free, lifesaving treatment to Afghan victims of injuries sustained in war and other traumas. Patients with life-threatening wounds and their families often traveled for days just to be treated there. The hospital afforded their only hope of survival.

That night, patients streamed into the waiting area, overloading the doctors. One of the Afghan surgeons picked up his mobile phone and dialed Dr. Evangeline Cua, an expatriate surgeon who worked at the hospital. It was after one a.m.

Dr. Cua was at the residence for staff, located only a few minutes away. She had her own practice in the Philippines but had taken a break to work at Médecins Sans Frontières in Kunduz over the summer. It had been an intense several months. She wasn't used to seeing children with gunshot wounds or injuries from a roadside bomb. But she learned from her Afghan colleagues, and she felt that she was living her dream of scrubbing up every day as a surgeon to save lives. The call woke her up.

"Hello," she said, worried. "What's going on?"

The Afghan surgeon described how patients were flooding the hospital. They needed her help.

"The city is under attack," he told her.

She was terrified but wanted to help. The French manager at the residence ruled it out.

"It's too dangerous to leave now," she said. "We have to wait until daylight."

Dr. Cua lay back in bed and thought about the seven-minute drive to the hospital. What would happen if the Taliban stopped them on the way there? Would it be better to sit in the car and wait? Or should she take her chances, get out, and run?

She thought about home. She was from a small town in the Philippines and had never imagined being at the epicenter of the Afghan war. She became a surgeon after seeing the impact her mother had as a midwife in poor rural communities. She had wanted to be a surgeon for as long as she could remember. She came into contact with Médecins Sans Frontières when a massive 2013 typhoon struck the Philippines. It was the worst storm in the country's history.

She joined the French aid organization for two months to help deliver medical care, and then applied to join their international staff after being impressed with their work. When they offered her the mission in Afghanistan, her parents objected at first out of concern for her safety. But another Filipino doctor who was already working in Kunduz helped her convince them to let her go. She kept in touch with her family through her sister and posted regularly on Facebook to reassure them that all was well.

Dr. Cua didn't tell her parents how difficult it was to see the war's young victims or about the sense of community that grew among the staff at the hospital. She worked there on weekdays and spent her free time at the Médecins Sans Frontières residential compound. They weren't allowed to go out, so the expats living there found ways to stay entertained, organizing cooking nights, movies, and group exercise. It was a diverse collection of people from all over the world.

Dr. Cua constantly feared being kidnapped by the Taliban on the way to the hospital. The doctors treated every patient the same, no matter what side they were on. She worried that the Taliban would demand preferential treatment. But the longer she cared for them, the more she came to realize that members of the Taliban were just like the other patients. They were afraid, respectful, and had the same kind of concerned relatives as everyone else. The main difference was that Taliban members were often discharged against medical advice, sometimes even before they got to the recovery room, because they feared the government might come for them.

She tried to sleep, knowing she had a long day ahead. But she couldn't stop fretting about the journey to the hospital and what awaited her there.

As THE HOSPITAL BRACED for a flood of patients caused by the Taliban attack on the city, Josh Middlebrook, a Delta on the Kunduz team, was busy taking stock of medical supplies. Josh had been living at Camp Pamir for about a month, and it was his fourth tour in Afghanistan, including two fifteen-month tours as an infantryman. He had never expected to spend so much time there. He had joined the military to go to Iraq after dropping out of college. He wanted to do something meaningful with his life. He had considered journalism but decided the army was the fastest route to Iraq.

The army recruiter told Josh his grades were good enough to try for any job. He hadn't thought that far ahead.

"I want to join the war in Iraq," he said.

"Okay, infantry then," the recruiter told him.

Nine years later, he still hadn't been to Iraq. He was barely aware of the war in Afghanistan before joining the army. But he had grown to love the country in a way that was tied to the hope and loss experienced over years of deployments. The tour had been troubling from the start. Because of the strict rules limiting their operations outside the base, neither Josh nor any of the team had been to Kunduz city. Their mission to train and advise the Afghan commandos was difficult to execute as the elite soldiers were scattered across northeast Afghanistan at checkpoints because government officials didn't trust the regular army and police.

Josh's team initially expected to run missions out of the US Army's northern headquarters in Mazar-e Sharif, but they ended up restoring a permanent US presence at Camp Pamir on the outskirts of Kunduz city. It was located inside the Afghan army's 209th Corps headquarters. As in Helmand, security in the northeast was declining, and US military commanders wanted them to keep an eye on things.

Josh had lobbied the team sergeant to fortify the camp in case of an attack. Like other abandoned American bases, Camp Pamir was a mess. It was supposed to have closed a year earlier and had been stripped down. It didn't even have armored vehicles. Josh was eventually cleared to travel back to Mazar-e Sharif aboard a C-130 transport plane to see what equipment and provisions were available. He took a couple of guys and loaded up the plane with four Humvees and as much ammunition as the pilots would let them carry back to Kunduz.

That was two weeks ago. It was starting to look like those supplies would come in handy. The team had been preparing for the worst since receiving the first reports of contact between the Taliban and government forces in the early hours of the morning. Since then, the Afghan commandos had reported that the police had abandoned the main entry points to the city and were fleeing in droves to the airfield at the 209th Corps base, hoping to make an escape. The thud of mortars and the rattle of gunfire seemed to be getting closer. It sounded like the northern section of the city had fallen, and the rest seemed likely to follow soon. The Afghan commandos were the only force left on the main highway between the base and the city.

As Josh inventoried the medical supplies, one of the team's local interpreters, Ehsanullah, approached him. Looking stricken, he explained that the Taliban were ransacking the city, searching homes for government workers and their families, and separating the men from the women. The interpreter's wife was eight months pregnant and at home with his father, who worked on maintenance at the camp. Once the Taliban figured out that the family was connected to the US military, they were sure to kill them both.

"Holy shit," Josh said. "How much time have we got?"

Ehsanullah looked close to tears. "They're going house to house right now," he said.

Josh hadn't anticipated anything like this and had to think quickly.

"Tell your father to get in a car," he said. "If he can drive to the edge of Kunduz Airfield, I'll find a way to smuggle them onto the camp."

Ehsanullah looked grateful and left to make calls. Josh didn't have a plan, but the Afghan army controlled the outer perimeter of the camp. It was about a three-kilometer drive to the entrance. Josh could drive down to meet the family. The interpreter reappeared a couple of hours later.

"They're heading here right now," he told Josh.

Josh took a truck and drove with Ehsanullah to the gate. As they neared the outer wall, he realized he'd made a mistake. The 209th Corps headquarters was crowded with unidentifiable men out of uniform, many of them carrying big guns. He didn't know if they were soldiers, police, or Taliban. Some of them jeered and pointed their weapons at him.

"Fuck you, America!" they shouted. "Fuck you, America!"

Josh realized that the Afghans were surprised to see an American. They thought the Americans had withdrawn from Kunduz. Seeing him there was a huge insult. If American soldiers had been holed up at the base all along, it meant they were letting the city fall without a fight. American forces could easily stop an attack with airstrikes. Josh wasn't used to being separated from his teammates, and now he was alone in a crowd of angry Afghan men. They all looked like potential Taliban to him. He felt very exposed and far from the safety of the US Special Forces camp.

"Fuck you, America!" they kept repeating.

He didn't know which way to look. There were guns pointed at him everywhere. He was sure that someone would shoot him in the back at any moment. He gripped his rifle, determined not to go down without a fight, and pointed it at the crowd. He could feel their resentment and couldn't blame them. The situation made him angry as well. There seemed to be some commotion at the gate.

"Take the gun, and keep it pointed at whoever has the biggest gun," he told Ehsanullah while heading to the gate. "I'm going to get your family. Don't take your finger off the trigger!"

A Toyota Hilux pickup truck containing Ehsanullah's father and wife had rolled up at the entrance to the base, where it was being held by the Afghan soldiers, who refused to let them in. It was bad enough that the Americans had been sitting on the base doing nothing this whole time. And now they wanted to pluck *this* guy's family out of the battle and leave the rest of them behind?

This is bad, Josh thought.

He had no idea how to negotiate the family's release in his broken Dari and Arabic, but he had to try. Looking inside the Hilux, he could see Ehsanullah's wife in a burqa and her father-in-law in the front. At the checkpoint, everyone was shouting at each other.

A second vehicle appeared behind the Hilux, and more Afghan soldiers jumped out. It was the Ktah Khas, the elite Afghan Special Unit from Kabul. They undertook the most specialized missions, often alongside US Special Operations, and commanded respect from everyone. Josh couldn't believe his luck. The Special Unit joined in the argument about the interpreter's family. It was growing heated, and Josh had no idea what was going on.

"They say you can go," one of the Ktah Khas told him.

Josh didn't stick around to discuss it further.

Ehsanullah jumped into the Hilux with his family and followed Josh's truck back to Camp Pamir, past large crowds of Afghan forces amassing at the 209th Corps headquarters in a variety of uniforms and civilian clothes.

Soon after, around three p.m., Josh's team reported that Kunduz had fallen. Inside the city, a chaotic scene played out. Taliban fighters emptied jails and looted abandoned police and army compounds, seizing stockpiles of weapons, including antiaircraft guns and ammunition, all supplied by the United States. At least thirty

Humvees, forty Ford Rangers, and even two Russian tanks fell into their hands. The thriving jewelry bazaar was ransacked for gold. The building that housed the United Nations, which had already evacuated expatriate staff and told local staff to stay home, was set on fire. Columns of black smoke billowed into the sky through the day as Taliban squads carrying lists of government workers searched residences.

News that Kunduz had fallen traveled faster in the media than through the chain of command. Senior US military commanders in Afghanistan were still unaware of the gravity of the situation by the evening. As the city descended into chaos, the Special Operations Joint Task Force (SOJTF) Afghanistan, which coordinated all US and NATO Special Operations, was focused on a large-scale operation in Helmand. At six p.m., the deputy commanding general for operations, Brigadier General Tony Bauernfeind, was interrupted during a videoconference with a message to call off the Helmand mission because all US air assets needed to be urgently diverted to Kunduz. The US military didn't have enough assets and personnel in Afghanistan to fight in two places at once.

Brig. Gen. Bauernfeind turned around the helicopters carrying US Special Forces to Helmand midflight.

In Washington the loss of Kunduz was an embarrassment. The Taliban had scored their greatest victory since the start of the war, and Kabul's sudden collapse exposed the flaw in the claim that the government could simply take over the war after the United States left Afghanistan. Major news outlets carried photos that the Taliban had tweeted of themselves celebrating in the streets. Many brandished Kalashnikovs with ammunition belts strapped to their chests and wore only sandals on their feet. The city's red-and-white traffic circle, surrounded by cheering crowds, became the symbol of its collapse to the Taliban.

Across the northeast part of the country, other Taliban fighters, seeking to capitalize on the momentum, escalated attacks, laying ambushes on the routes along which Afghan army reinforcements were arriving from Kabul and elsewhere. Suddenly, it seemed possible that other provinces might fall next, like dominos, resulting in the collapse of the rest of the northeast.

President Obama wasn't whipsawed by current events, but National Security Council staff worried that the city's collapse could fuel the arguments in favor of leaving Afghanistan as planned. If the Afghans couldn't demonstrate an ability—or even willingness—to hold ground after the billions of dollars invested there, it seemed as though the time had come for the United States to cut its losses and leave them to it.

CHAPTER 7

Kunduz Clearing Patrol
CONOP

GEN. CAMPBELL, the commander of US and NATO forces in Afghanistan, was irate. The timing of Kunduz city's collapse could not have been worse. He was due to travel to Washington later that week to present his recommendation for US troop levels at a National Security Council meeting chaired by President Obama. The case for an expanded US mission rested on the need to preserve the stability of Afghanistan and avoid a resurgence of al Qaeda and the risk of another terrorist attack on the homeland until the Afghan government was ready to hold ground alone. He was also due to testify at the Senate Armed Services Committee about the state of play in Afghanistan.

Gen. Campbell had worked for months with National Security Council staff at deputies' meetings and at meetings with the principals to present a strong case for holding off the US troop withdrawal. Skeptics of the Afghan war were sure to argue that the fall of Kunduz demonstrated that the government was losing capacity rather than improving, and that no amount of US military support would ever stabilize the country.

The US had spent over $65 billion on the Afghan army and police alone, yet it appeared that a small force of ill-equipped Taliban had overrun a major city. It was unclear how many government soldiers and police were on duty in Kunduz at the time of the Taliban's attack. Some seven thousand were on the US-funded payroll, but a large proportion was evidently missing or dead—or perhaps had never existed at all. The rest appeared to have fled, leaving behind only the Afghan commandos to defend the city.

Reports varied on how many Taliban had participated in the attack, but conservative estimates put the figure as low as a few hundred. It seemed, in short, that the Afghan government had abandoned the city with barely a fight. It was an unpleasant turn of events, but few could claim that it was a surprise. The city had come under repeated attack in the spring, and morale among government forces was low as high-level corruption sapped even basic supplies like food, water, and fuel.

Early reports were still arriving from the field, and Gen. Campbell knew it would be weeks before the full picture emerged. He requested an urgent video teleconference with the leaders of the Afghan army's 209th Corps in Kunduz to hear about their planned response to the crisis. He needed to know that they had a clear plan to regain control before heading to Washington to advocate for continuing the mission.

DR. CUA BARELY REGISTERED the battle outside on the first day. Her scrubs were covered in blood. Her hands were washed raw after she performed many consecutive surgeries without a break. She was dimly aware of the rattle of gunfire and explosions outside. Inside the hospital, it had been a battle against time, triaging the patients in the crowded emergency room waiting area. She couldn't imagine how her Afghan colleagues were coping. This was their home after all. At the gates, hospital staff had worked through the day, steadily admitting patients and relatives one by one, taking names.

Each patient was allowed one accompanying family member, but the rule was difficult to enforce when relatives showed up with multiple children. Many of the patients streaming in wore mismatched uniforms and were assumed to be opposition fighters. The staff at the gates had to explain to each of them the hospital's key rule: no weapons or uniforms inside. The primary goal was to keep the hospital safe. Médecins Sans Frontières treated all victims of war, regardless of their affiliation.

Dr. Cua had been dismayed to find out earlier in the day that the rest of the team at the residential compound had been evacuated. That meant there was no one left to relieve the workers at the hospital in the evening, and it was unclear if they'd missed their opportunity to be evacuated. She was asked what she wanted to do and weighed her options.

There were two factors to consider. One was the chance of actually making it to the airport. The sound of gunfire reminded her of the battle still raging in the streets. Would she get caught in the crossfire, like so many patients, or worse, kidnapped by Taliban? The second consideration was the lives of the patients at the hospital, and all those to come in the days ahead. If she fled now, who would perform the life-or-death surgeries that she could provide? What message would this send to her Afghan colleagues left behind? She didn't see any choice but to stay.

Around six p.m., a white Toyota Corolla pulled up at the gates. The driver was a middle-aged man with a long beard; he carried a modified Kalashnikov, a sign of stature. Three men who seemed to be bodyguards sat in the back. At the far end of the street, a Taliban fighter armed with a Kalashnikov stood guard. A caretaker approached the car to speak to the bearded driver and then ran inside to find Dr. Nasim.

After a few minutes Dr. Nasim appeared. He was distracted by the emergencies piling up inside the hospital. Supplies were low, the hospital staff were terrified, and places to create makeshift beds were running out. He walked briskly to the gate to see what the visitors wanted. He noticed the watchman standing on the corner. So this was somebody important. He peered into the vehicle and immediately recognized the driver. He had a long, black beard and close-set eyes and wore a turban.

It was Mullah Salam, the Taliban's shadow governor of Kunduz province. US intelligence had spent years hunting for him, and here he was out in the open in the middle of the city.

"The area is now under our control," he told Dr. Nasim. "If anyone bothers you, let that man know." He gestured at the watchman on the corner. "We know you provide free health care, and we appreciate it. We want you to keep the hospital running, and we will respect your impartiality," he said.

Dr. Nasim nodded. The car carrying Mullah Salam sped off before there was time to process what had just happened.

In Kabul, Guilhem Molinie, Médecins Sans Frontières' country director, was relieved to hear that the Taliban planned to respect the impartiality of the hospital. His main concern now was that the hospital might be struck by a stray rocket or accidentally targeted in a US airstrike. He contacted the US military to verify, once again, that the hospital's GPS coordinates were on the no-strike list, against which all airstrikes were cross-checked. It included entities or objects protected under international law and the rules of engagement. The US military confirmed that the hospital was on it.

Despite the assurances, Guilhem found it difficult to know whether keeping the hospital open was the right thing to do. The team on the ground wanted to stay. Nonessential staff had been evacuated. Staying endangered the staff, but they had been preparing for an escalation in hostility all summer, and their services were needed now more than ever. The trauma hospital in Kunduz had treated 137 wounded patients, including 26 children, by ten p.m. The majority were victims of gunshot wounds with severe abdominal, limb, or head injuries who would almost certainly have died without immediate medical attention.

Hutch spent the following day in contact with the two teams in Kunduz; he coordinated the moving of reinforcements and assets to help secure the airfield, the Afghan government's last stand in the province. He dispatched three members of a third team, ODA

3135, and a combat controller to Kunduz to accompany a fresh contingent of Afghan commandos normally based at Camp Morehead. It was increasingly difficult to follow the situation from afar, and he realized he had to get to Camp Pamir as soon as possible to take control of the mishmash of US and Afghan forces.

Hutch, the last US soldier to touch down at the airfield, arrived around seven thirty p.m. on September 29, 2015, and went straight into a briefing with the Kunduz team. General Abdul Hamid, the commander of the Afghan army's 209th Corps, appeared just as they were wrapping up. The Taliban had started to attack the northern section of the airfield, he told them. The Ktah Khas unit was responding to the crisis but was unlikely to be able to hold the perimeter indefinitely. The Afghan army was already vacating the airfield, he said, and he advised the Americans to do the same before it was too late.

"Please don't abandon the perimeter!" Hutch exclaimed, dismayed. "My guys will go out there and strengthen the position."

Gen. Hamid looked uncomfortable. It was clear that his force had lost all confidence in the situation, and there wasn't much he could do about it. Hutch turned to the teams and ordered them to head for the perimeter and do everything possible to stop the Taliban from breaching the base. They quickly sketched out a plan, took any vehicles they could find at the camp—most were unarmored—and headed toward the northern gates with the Afghan commandos.

A scene of complete chaos awaited them there. Hundreds of Afghan men in various stages of undress ran toward them in waves. Some were still in uniform, others in civilian clothes, and some seemed to be stripping off their apparel midflight, escaping on foot and in vehicles, dumping their weapons on the way.

"Get back here, you cowards!" others called after them, shouting for them to stay behind and fight.

The Ktah Khas had a truck at the vehicle gate mounted with a heavy machine gun to stop Taliban from breaching the base. The US teams took the control tower and spread out to nearby buildings to reinforce the Afghan commandos, establishing positions at the pedestrian entrances. Nearly everyone was riding in unarmored Ford Rangers or on Kawasaki quad bikes, and exposed to gunfire. One team pushed back a group of fighters attempting to enter on foot through a pedestrian gate. Another tried to take out a Soviet ZPU, an antiaircraft gun, that was firing rounds at the control tower.

The arrival of an AC-130 gunship to support the soldiers battling to save the airfield proved to be the game changer. The gunship was the deadliest in the US arsenal and carried an array of heavy weapons: a 25mm Gatling gun, a Bofors 40mm cannon, and a 105mm Howitzer that could flatten buildings. It had sophisticated sensors, had navigation and fire control systems to visually or electronically identify targets, and could engage simultaneously with different weapons. The Taliban, unaware that any Americans remained at the base, were unprepared for airstrikes, which had become rare following the withdrawal of most foreign troops. The gunship took out a second antiaircraft gun located outside the airfield, and the volley of fire sent the insurgents running for cover, halting the attack.

The US teams, working with the Afghan commandos, fought through the remainder of the night to strengthen the perimeter, convincing the regular army troops that had stayed behind to return to their positions guarding the base. The gunship continued to hunt down pockets of Taliban fighters until it was clear the attack was over. At sunrise, the Green Berets were satisfied that the base was under control, and they returned to Camp Pamir to plan the next step. Afghan forces lining the sides of the road cheered as they passed through.

Hutch gathered everyone together to work on a plan to reestablish a foothold in Kunduz city. The Afghans wouldn't go in without them. The teams were skeptical that the Afghan army was sending reinforcements to hold any ground that was cleared, but they dispersed to prepare for the mission and to refine the CONOP, or concept of operations, that would have to be submitted to higher-ups for approval. Hutch left to join the video teleconference that

Gen. Campbell had requested with the Afghan army's leadership in
Kunduz.

Gen. Campbell wanted to understand the situation before heading back to Washington. There were signs that Kunduz was about
to be the start of a much bigger crisis. Afghan forces were caving in
the northeast. To the south, the Taliban had cut off supply routes
through Baghlan to the capital. The entire chain of command, including Hutch's battalion commander, Col. Johnston, and the
commander of US and NATO Special Operations in Afghanistan,
Major General Sean Swindell, was on the call as well.

Gen. Campbell's forehead was creased into a frown. The top US
commander had little patience for ceremony and dived into questions about how the Afghan army planned to regain control. The
209th Corps commander, Gen. Hamid, hadn't brought a translator
and stumbled over his words. His English seemed to be evaporating
fast. The call was not going well.

Hutch knew that the problem was more than simply a language barrier. He had just witnessed the near loss of the airfield and recognized
that it was difficult for Gen. Hamid to admit that he'd lost control of
the army, or that local forces were refusing to return to the city. He
decided to jump into the discussion before it deteriorated any further.

"Sir, there is a plan," Hutch said. "We're going to move into the
city with them."

He laid it out. The ODAs would accompany the patchwork of
Afghan commando units that had arrived to defend Kunduz, help
them regain control of key infrastructure like the governor's office
and police headquarters, and push outward. He guessed there were
perhaps 150 Taliban fighters in Kunduz city. Once the Taliban realized that American troops, backed by US air support, had arrived
to reinforce the Afghans and were serious about regaining the city,
they would likely disperse.

"I really believe that once the Afghan forces see that the enemy
isn't as strong as they thought, they'll come back and man their
posts," Hutch said, "and we can take the next step as advisers."

Gen. Campbell appeared satisfied and told Hutch to get it done. "We're going with them, and we're going to make sure this happens," Hutch said.

Hutch left the conference feeling as though he had been charged with a vital operation—perhaps the most important operation since a small team of Green Berets had led an alliance of Afghan warlords to victory against the Taliban in 2001. He believed the mission had to happen as soon as possible, and failure was not an option. After experiencing the horrors of urban combat as a platoon leader in Ramadi, Iraq, he knew that only a swift response would save Kunduz city from a drawn-out and bloody battle.

Back at Camp Pamir, Hutch checked on the teams' progress. The lack of armored vehicles was an even bigger problem now that they planned to infiltrate the city. The Kunduz team had only the four Humvees that it had brought from Mazar-e Sharif a few weeks earlier. The other Green Berets, along with their supporting personnel, had all arrived by helicopter, without vehicles. The Afghan commandos that had flown in from Kabul didn't have trucks either.

In the end, the teams scraped together a few unarmored Ford Rangers, open-door ground-mobility vehicles, and Kawasaki quad bikes to carry forty-one US and NATO forces.* These were far from ideal modes of transport into a Taliban-controlled city, but they would have to do. It took several more hours to find vehicles for the various Afghan commando units that had flown in. The Afghan army's 209th Corps had lost many of its vehicles and was unwilling to give up its remaining ones. The US teams also failed to persuade the locally based 10th Special Operations Kandak commandos, who had held out in the city until the last moment, to join the mission. That meant none of the Afghan forces accompanying them had been to the city before.

---

* These included ODA 3111 from Kunduz, ODA 3133 from Bagram, three members of ODA 3135, attached US infantry personnel, air force combat controllers, an explosive ordnance disposal (EOD) team, and Romanian Special Forces.

As the sun went down on September 30, the teams made their final preparations, inventorying weapons and ammunition, checking communications systems, and coming up with work-arounds to make up for the various shortages of equipment. They expected to stay in the city at least overnight since Afghan reinforcements seemed unlikely to arrive soon. They had a single 1:50,000-scale map of Kunduz between them, and the only printer left at the camp refused to produce any more, disgorging large, magenta-colored blobs instead. The Afghan commandos had no radios and would have to rely on cell phones for communication, another disadvantage as mobile networks were unreliable.

Hutch submitted the CONOP, titled "Kunduz Clearing Patrol," under the Resolute Support mission to train, advise, and assist Afghan forces. The plan was to drive into the city of Kunduz along the main highway, which the US military called Route Milky Way, at night. Inside the city, the US and Afghan teams would recapture key administrative buildings and establish a foothold at the governor's office. If the mission succeeded, no one would know about the US role in the mission, and it would look like the government had recaptured the city.

CONOPs had to be signed off on by the entire chain of command. The Special Operations Task Force (SOTF) first approved the plan at the battalion level, led by Col. Johnston. The SOJTF, which included all US and NATO Special Operations forces in Afghanistan and was led by Gen. Swindell, had to sign off next. The SOJTF then shared it with RS headquarters. The mission came back approved under Operation Freedom's Sentinel, the unilateral US counterterrorism mission in Afghanistan to hunt down al Qaeda.

Hutch was surprised: the Kunduz operation had nothing to do with al Qaeda. The SOJTF didn't offer any further guidance except the OFS rules of engagement, which were more offensive in nature. He decided to play it safe and continue operating under RS rules, which allowed them to fire or call in air support only in self-defense. He had one last bureaucratic hurdle to clear. He was waiting for the

Afghan commandos accompanying them on the mission to be approved as persons designated special status, which identified them as an integral part of US defenses on the ground. It was another of the legal loopholes that allowed the United States to carry out airstrikes in support of the commandos.

The teams did some quick rehearsals, and Hutch delegated the mission brief to the Kunduz team. A few minutes before the operation was due to start, their Fox, the intelligence sergeant, approached Hutch with a fresh report from a trusted source in the city.

"He says there are around a thousand Taliban fighters in the city," he said, "and they have set up heavy weapons in defensive lines along the highway."

Hutch was concerned, but he found it hard to believe the Taliban could have so many fighters in the city. He thought there were perhaps 150 at best. But it was clear the teams would run into stiff resistance at least at the start, and most of his guys were riding in unarmored vehicles.

The team captain began the mission brief, illustrating the route into the city using their only map. Hutch's thoughts turned to the pep talk he wanted to give the teams. Some of the younger soldiers had never been in combat before, and this would be the sort of urban battle that few in the group had experienced in their lifetimes. It was the moment when years of training would be tested, and the lives of their teammates would depend on them. He tried to remember what it was like during his first patrol in Iraq almost a decade earlier. It seemed a lifetime ago.

When the brief was completed, Hutch stepped forward to rally the soldiers on the importance of the mission, and how Afghanistan's future was at stake.

"This isn't an ordinary mission to disrupt a threat network," he told them. "The whole world is watching, and I know you will not disappoint. I'm honored to be alongside you. Gladiators, I salute you. Prep the trucks."

The soldiers made final checks and boarded their vehicles. They were then delayed by an hour while looking for fuel for the Afghan

commandos after the 209th Corps initially refused to give up its supply. At eleven p.m., they were finally ready. A small group of Afghan
soldiers waved and shouted encouragement. Hutch wondered if this
was the reinforcement the Afghan generals had promised in order to
hold the city after it was cleared. It wasn't much, but perhaps it was a
good sign. The camp lights faded as they headed into the night.

Hutch saw himself as a philosopher by day, but he was never
more in his element than in the middle of a fight. Combat appealed
to something visceral. He felt invincible while at the same time convinced that each moment might be his last. He was calm, totally focused on coordinating the convoy and its various elements, prepared
to drive into battle. He hoped the pep talk had fired the guys up.
In his experience, the Taliban preferred not to stay and fight when
faced with overwhelming US firepower. An AC-130 gunship circled
above them. He figured that a few examples of its destructive force
would be enough to scare the Taliban off.

The Ktah Khas, riding in the lead trucks, came under fire by a
Soviet-era heavy machine gun as soon as they left the perimeter of
the 209th Corps headquarters. The Taliban had positioned it inside
a captured police compound located several hundred meters away
from the gates of the Afghan army base. The convoy ground to a
halt. Hutch called for an airstrike to take out the gun so the convoy
could move on.

The AC-130 sent two volleys of fire thundering into the darkness, and a giant cloud rose into the sky. The shooting stopped. He
sent the team that had arrived from Bagram Airfield to accompany
the Afghans to assess the damage. Afghan commandos quickly shot
dead two Taliban survivors who crept out of the darkness. The team
reported that body parts were mingled with debris and rubble in the
wreckage, and it was difficult to assess how many had been killed inside. They left two different Afghan units arguing over who should
stay behind to guard the police compound and moved on to their
next objective, a prison run by the NDS, the Afghan intelligence
agency, which had fallen under Taliban control.

About a hundred meters farther down the road, the convoy came under fire from the west. They ground to a halt again. The Ktah Khas returned fire, and the shooting stopped. The Taliban then attacked the convoy from the east. Hutch cleared the AC-130 to fire on a large group of men it had spotted on their flank with its sensors. The aircraft unleashed a volley of fire that cleared their path again, leaving two bodies behind. The convoy at last reached the NDS prison, but it was abandoned when they arrived.

Hutch jumped out, planning to help a team of US and Afghan soldiers establish a command-and-control node there, but the rest of the convoy was ambushed again several hundred meters down the road. He began to think it might be a bad idea to split up the teams and safer to keep everyone together. The Taliban had put up a much harder fight than he had expected, and they were still far from their final objective, the governor's office. The ambush up ahead was getting worse, and the team that had advanced with the Ktah Khas reported that it was pinned down with rocket fire and needed close air support.

The AC-130 identified a group of shooters and opened fire again, killing another eight insurgents. The survivors escaped.

Hutch resolved that it was too risky to divide the teams. He told the team at the NDS prison to rejoin the convoy, and left a group of Afghan forces behind to secure the compound. He began to worry about how to find the governor's office. None of the Afghan soldiers were local to Kunduz or knew where it was.

In the silvery-black darkness the roads looked the same, and the GPS coordinates for the compound seemed to have led them into a maze. Further into the city, the Ktah Khas drove into a roadside bomb, which went off with a huge blast. Hutch felt the shock wave in his chest. He couldn't believe it when the Afghan soldiers inside the truck jumped out, all of them unharmed. He heard gunfire and urged the convoy forward. He was anxious to get to the governor's office before dawn. Getting stuck out in the road in daylight would be a disaster.

The convoy hadn't driven much farther when a second Ktah Khas truck snagged a trip wire and detonated another bomb. A few minutes later, the vehicle's passengers again reported that everyone inside was unharmed. Hutch could hardly believe it. The convoy continued ahead and pulled up to the walls of a compound that seemed to match the GPS coordinates.

It turned out to be a high-end hotel, one that was often used to host government officials and other VIPs visiting the province. The teams continued clearing the buildings around them as the Ktah Khas moved on toward an intersection, where a suicide bomber slipped out of the shadows and rammed an explosives-laden vehicle into the front of the convoy. The explosion sent a pillar of smoke above the square, but engineering triumphed again: the Afghan commandos inside were unscathed.

Several Bagram team members riding an unarmored Ford Ranger also came under fire at the intersection. The rest of the team, riding the quad bikes, moved to back them up and drove into the group of Taliban behind the attack. Both sides opened fire, but the insurgents were no match for the better-trained and equipped Green Berets, who shot five men dead before the others broke contact and vanished into the night.

Hutch checked the time. It was after four a.m. They had been on the road for about five hours, and the sun would soon rise. He gathered the captains to discuss a contingency plan. A nearby cement factory could serve as a last resort to provide cover, allowing them to set up operations for the next day. It had fallen under Taliban control and wasn't an appealing prospect.

"We can't be out here on the street when the sun comes up," Hutch told them.

A couple of the guys offered to scout for the entrance to another large compound near the convoy. It was surrounded with defensive HESCO walls made up of earth-filled containers designed to withstand attacks. They bounded around the corner and reappeared a few minutes later to report that it seemed to be the governor's office. Its entrance lay on the southwest perimeter, and the compound was large enough to accommodate the whole convoy. The trucks proceeded toward the gates and zigzagged through the serpentine barriers at the entrance that were designed to slow down potential suicide attackers.

The slow progress into the compound gave the Taliban one last chance to fire at them, but the rounds missed the unarmored vehicles. Once inside, they realized that it wasn't the governor's office after all. It was the police chief's headquarters. But with four guard towers and a complete HESCO barrier around the perimeter, it could suit their purposes for the time being. The teams placed snipers in the towers facing west, the direction from which the heaviest fire seemed to be coming. The Afghan commandos took the eastern wall and positioned a truck at each corner of the intersections with the road. By six a.m. the sun was up and the US and Afghan forces were settled in.

The resistance they had encountered in the city was greater than anything Hutch had encountered in Afghanistan before. He was starting to doubt, for the first time, that the Taliban would give up the city without a fight.

CHAPTER 8

Battle for Kunduz
HUTCH

DR. CUA was drying her hands after another surgery at the Médecins Sans Frontières trauma hospital when an assistant approached her for help.

"Doctor, can you see the patients at the ER and tell us who should go to surgery first?" he said.

"Now?" she asked.

"Yes, now." She could tell by his voice that something was wrong.

She followed him to the emergency room and stepped back in shock. She had performed hundreds of surgeries over the summer but had never seen anything on this scale. It was like a scene from a horror movie. There were patients everywhere—on chairs, on the floor—all of them in bloody, ragged clothing. The room was filled with their groans of pain and despair. Her first instinct was to turn away and run. One woman was heavily pregnant and spattered in blood. A child who had lost both legs howled as blood gushed out of the wounds.

She was expected to triage the cases—rank them in order of urgency. She steadied herself and moved around the room, checking patients with her colleague. A man grabbed her sleeve as she headed back to the operating room. She started. No Afghan man had tried to touch her before. She turned to face him and saw an old man. He had a gray beard and a kind, deeply lined face.

"Please take a look at my son," he begged, surprising her by speaking in English. "He's a good man, my youngest boy."

He pointed to the black zone, where patients that had no chance of survival were given palliative care before dying. She tried not to flinch when she saw the extent of the young man's injuries. A huge wound to his chest left part of a lung exposed. His eyes were already lifeless and glassy. He had no pulse. She adjusted the man's intravenous line and covered his chest with a sheet, unable to do anything else. The old man looked at her gratefully. She was devastated.

The patients kept coming, with heartbreaking stories, including a family of six that had been trying to escape the city by car when their vehicle was hit by an airstrike at a roundabout. When Dr. Cua saw their three-year-old daughter, she couldn't believe the girl was still alive. The blast had severed part of her chest, completely exposing her liver and right lung. Dr. Cua worked to stop the bleeding even though it was futile. The girl died on the operating table. She wiped tears from her eyes. Her assistant surgeon, an Afghan man with children of his own, was also crying. She had never felt so angry, or so desperate. They managed to save the girl's four-year-old brother, a small comfort.

Back in Kabul, Guilhem Molinie, Médecins Sans Frontières' country director, was under terrible pressure. The organization had prepared for a crisis like this, but he was faced with a moral decision as much as a tactical one. The hospital staff wanted to stay and continue to help the population, but they were all in danger. The hospital normally had 92 beds, but staff had increased its capacity to 140 beds by using corridors and examination rooms as makeshift wards. If the hospital closed, hundreds would die without access to medical care.

He tried to reassure himself that all sides had agreed to respect the hospital's neutrality, but he worried about a stray rocket or that US military might mistake the hospital for a Taliban position. He had learned that the US military had received mixed messages about the hospital. The aid group's office in New York had just received an inquiry from the Pentagon asking whether there were Taliban inside. He had tried not to panic, but it was deeply disturbing news.

Guilhem's point of contact with the US military was a civil affairs officer at Bagram Airfield. The officer, who was part of Col. Johnston's staff, advised Guilhem to put a flag on the hospital roof as an added precaution. He had also successfully coordinated with the civil affairs officer to allow an ambulance to deliver critical medical supplies to the hospital, and asked if the US military would be able to help them evacuate staff in an emergency. The officer had promised to look into it, but he hadn't come back with an answer.

At Bagram Airfield, the SOTF was working on a plan to evacuate hospital staff if needed. It hadn't shared with Guilhem the reports that it had on enemy activity inside the hospital. The US military officials suspected that the insurgents were using it as a command center. They had tracked the Taliban carrying heavy weapons into the hospital grounds and observed the Taliban using ambulances to carry supplies out to fighters in the city.*

At sunrise on the morning of October 1, 2015, the Green Berets hunkering down inside Kunduz police headquarters worked to get their bearings. The building was painted a pale orange, and every room had been looted. The compound was only a couple of stories high, but the guard towers around the perimeter offered a good line of defense. Hutch had the teams check the offices for supplies, particularly hoping to find a map of the city. Their one map, which lacked grids, was spread out on the hood of a truck for everyone to share. The teams came back to report no luck.

Around seven a.m., Hutch was told that visitors were at the gates.

---

* The US military has never commented on allegations that the Taliban took heavy weapons into the hospital or used the grounds as a command center. US military officers interviewed for this book say they have retained evidence that has not been made public. MSF has always denied that any weapons were brought into the hospital in violation of the policy that required visitors and patients to leave all weapons outside.

"Great," he said, scrambling to meet them. He was disappointed to learn that they weren't the reinforcements promised by the Afghan army's 209th Corps.

It was the Kunduz police chief, Mohammad Jangalbagh, and the acting governor, Hamdullah Danishi. The original governor had disappeared, which fueled rumors of a deal with the Taliban to hand the city over. Hutch tried to look on the bright side: the battle for the city must be finished if it was safe enough for VIPs to show up. He left his body armor in a corner and went to greet them. The stress and lack of sleep showed in his face.

The police chief had arrived with a small entourage but without a force to hold the cleared building.

"When are you guys going to come and reoccupy the headquarters?" Hutch asked the two.

"Just as soon as we can get it cleaned up," the police chief promised.

The police chief posed for photos with the acting governor, took a tour, and again promised that reinforcements were on their way. They were gone in less than an hour. Hutch was dismayed to see them leave.

Moments later, bullets started to zip into the compound, sending everyone into high alert. The shots were quickly followed by the crash of a mortar that slammed into a building next to them.

"Incoming! Incoming!" someone shouted over the sound of the explosion.

They were under attack. The first mortar was followed by others, which landed on the compound walls.

The sniper teams scouted the streets to see where the firing was coming from. The Taliban were approaching them in groups from all sides and had reached positions just thirty meters away. Many of the insurgents wore military fatigues. Some were on foot, and others headed toward them in pickup trucks mounted with heavy machine guns. The teams, unsure who was who, shouted at their translators to clarify the situation with the Ktah Khas, who were still on the corners, guarding the perimeter. In the confusion, the

Taliban continued to fire at the compound, and the explosions sent up clouds of dust, adding to the general chaos.

Hutch asked for a show of force to discourage the attack. A pair of F-16s appeared overhead. The jet fighters traveled faster than the speed of sound, and their six-barrel Gatling guns could fire six thousand rounds per minute. The strategy to scare off the enemy below was often effective, but not this time. The Taliban knew that the Americans wouldn't bomb a heavily populated city without being able to see a clear target. The F-16s roared across the sky without effect. Hutch couldn't rely on Apache helicopters either, which were less widely destructive because they risked getting shot down in an urban battle.

An hour later, the police headquarters was still under attack from all sides. Hutch approached the western perimeter, which was taking heavy fire, for an update. The Bagram team captain, Pat Harrigan, briefed him. He was tall and wiry and loved the outdoors. He had a reputation for being outspoken. The Taliban were charging up the main streets, he told Hutch, ducking into doorways and alleys between sprints. His snipers were shooting as many insurgents as they could before they reached the next covered position, but the survivors were now barely twenty meters away.

"Some of our guys have already killed twenty men each," Pat concluded. "If you can believe it."

Hutch realized that early assessments about the number of Taliban fighters in the city may not have been that exaggerated after all. Rockets continued to strike the perimeter walls and land close to the Ktah Khas trucks. He worried they were going to get overrun. Two more low passes from the F-16s failed to stop the shooting. Hutch requested a strafing run, which was less damaging than an airstrike. That move temporarily halted the attack on the western perimeter.

The teams turned to deal with the assaults continuing from the north and the southwest. One of the Bravos, a weapons sergeant, leapt over the wall with a shoulder-fired antitank weapon and shot it into a platoon-sized assault force of Taliban approaching from the north. A sniper team pinned down another group of insurgents on the southwest, forcing them to take cover in a building about a hundred meters away. Air support was critical. The F-16s returned to carry out two more strafing runs close to the perimeter. Two armed drones identified by call signs and controlled by operators hundreds of miles away at Bagram Airfield also joined the battle, hunting for fighters through the city.

One of the drones, call sign Gunmetal, spotted a large group of men who appeared to be armed and heading for the northwestern perimeter and fired a missile at the group. The explosion hit hard, halting the attack. A fresh assault began on the opposite perimeter, but it was halted after the soldiers killed at least a dozen of the men advancing and the F-16s returned to carry out two strafing runs. Things got quiet for a moment.

In the lull, a convoy of about sixty Afghan police officers sent from Kunduz Airfield to reinforce the teams and commandos arrived at the compound. The police, who had evidently been forced to assist the US and Afghan soldiers against their will, immediately stated they did not plan to join in. The entire unit went indoors and refused to come out. It was nearly five p.m. The US and Afghan commandos had been engaged in almost nonstop combat since the morning, and this was their second day in battle.

Hutch was unimpressed. He went to check on the teams guarding the northern and western walls. Adrenaline was keeping them going, but tempers were growing short. They were all running low on ammunition, water, and food. They had prepared to stay for up to forty-eight hours but had shared their supplies with the Afghans. The batteries powering their equipment would soon run out as well, which would create fresh problems with coordinating the various teams and forces. Hutch called the captains to a meeting.

"How about we leave the Afghans here, go back to the base, resupply, and come back out," Hutch said, as the crack of gunfire and rockets continued sporadically around the police headquarters. "If we do it when it's dark, we can probably pull it off."

There was too much gunfire for a helicopter to land with a drop of supplies, and the postage-sized compound was too small to make an accurate drop from the air. The captains thought the Afghan commandos, who were just as exhausted, might abandon the compound if the Green Berets left. The teams all wanted to stay with the commandos. If they failed to retake Kunduz, it could undermine the entire mission in Afghanistan. The Ktah Khas, who planned to rotate teams from the airfield once a day, could bring them ammunition.

Hutch called the battalion with an update on their situation. Col. Johnston had been following the mission moment by moment from the operations center. He was doing everything he could to support them with assets from across the country. He was frustrated with the amount of time it took to get clearance to fire on targets in the city. It had taken him seven hours to obtain permission to destroy one of the Russian tanks that the Taliban had captured and were driving around in celebratory figure eights and ramming into checkpoints.

Hutch concluded that the intelligence on the Taliban numbers may have been accurate after all. He worried that the slightest mistake or miscalculation could end in disaster. In the back of his mind were scenes from the Battle of Mogadishu in 1993. American soldiers in the city had been overrun and killed by Somali militiamen, and some of their bodies had been dragged through the streets. His teams had been lucky so far, but their chances of survival decreased the longer they stayed there.

He wanted to know how much risk the United States was prepared to take to save Kunduz. Would it be worse to lose the province or to lose thirty American soldiers and have their bodies dragged through the city?

"This is like nothing I've even seen before," Hutch told the battalion commander. "What's our level of commitment here?"

Col. Johnston trusted Hutch to make the right decision. He had plenty of battlefield experience, kept a level head, and was well placed to evaluate, from the ground, the best course of action. Gen. Campbell's orders had been, simply, "Go save Kunduz." There hadn't been any further guidance from the top since the night the city had fallen. If Hutch decided it was too dangerous and the teams had to withdraw, then the Special Forces would find another way to save the city.

"How far do you want to go?" Col. Johnston asked him.

The Bagram team leader, Pat, who was listening in on the call, felt dismayed. The Special Forces battalion received its orders from the SOJTF, which in turn reported up to Resolute Support headquarters, under Gen. Campbell's command. Someone in the chain of command should be able to give them clear guidance in the midst of a pitched battle, he thought. The Green Berets were risking their lives to hold the city, and it was unfair to put the decision on them.

Hutch understood the battalion's position. Col. Johnston had put him there to make difficult decisions, and this was the moment. How long they could survive was best assessed from the ground. He didn't want to withdraw. Yet deciding to stay was a big responsibility to shoulder. There were nearly thirty Green Berets under his command, and they could all die if he made the wrong call. *We might be able to punch back to the base, but if we stay here, we could all die*, he thought. *You're going to have Black Hawk Down times two dragged through the streets. The narrative is that we're not in combat, but there will be no denying it if that happens.*

Still, abandoning Kunduz could have a high price. A province falling was a major strategic loss. If the Taliban had a chance to dig in, a drawn-out battle to push them out could level the city. *Many more people could die.*

"We'll stay another twenty-four hours," he finally responded.

CHAPTER 9

"I'm Sorry, Mom"
DR. CUA

WHILE HUTCH WAS MAKING the life-or-death decision to stay in Kunduz and hold position for another twenty-four hours, Tina was packing again. It was fall break in Southern Pines, and the kids were filled with the kind of excitement and sense of endless possibility that comes with having a week off from school. She was getting ready to drive them all to New Jersey to see her mother and sisters and to go apple picking. Hutch hadn't called in a few days, which was starting to nag at her. In the old days, he would go off the radar for a long time, but this time he had mostly been in Kabul, and he kept in regular contact. She finished loading the car and decided she couldn't face an eight-hour drive with two kids in the back and uncertainty clawing away at her.

She went to her computer and began searching for various combinations of "Afghanistan" and "Special Forces." The search produced countless stories about the fall of Kunduz, the first major Afghan city to fall to the Taliban since 2001, where US Special Forces had been spotted on the ground. The news had leaked because residents had spotted the Green Berets at the police headquarters. The US military spokesman in Kabul denied any US role in the combat. But Tina felt worried.

"Afghan Security Forces have full responsibility for their operations in Kunduz," Colonel Brian Tribus said in a statement to media.

"Resolute Support service members, to include Special Forces, are involved in Kunduz in an advise and assist capacity, as Resolute Support is a non-combat mission."

The statement suggested that American soldiers were far away from the fighting. Tina suspected that wasn't true and wondered if Hutch was in trouble. Scouring the news for more information, she came across an AP photo. She froze. It showed two men in conversation at the police headquarters in Kunduz. One was Kunduz's chief of police. The other was Hutch. The photo caught him midsentence, looking pale and tired.

Okay, she thought, trying to reassure herself. *At least he's alive.*

She went to the car feeling uneasy. Get the kids, drive to her mother's house, and wait to hear from him. *You've done this before*, she reminded herself.

Tina had close relationships with her family and found it comforting to be with them. That night, Hutch called from a satellite phone. Usually his calls came through showing a Virginia number. This time a long line of digits appeared on the screen. He couldn't speak for long, but he told her all was well. She felt relieved, but it wasn't enough. She needed him to be in Kabul, back to their routine check-ins, so she didn't have to worry.

Later, Tina was in the kitchen making coffee when she heard a cry from the living room.

"Oh my god, that's my papa!" their youngest daughter exclaimed, standing in front of the TV.

Tina dropped everything and rushed to where her daughter stood. Appearing on the screen was the photo of Hutch that she'd seen online before leaving North Carolina. The news story recounted how American forces, stationed inside Kunduz, had exchanged fire with the Taliban, contradicting the Obama administration's claim that the US role in combat was over. The US military said the shots were fired in self-defense. Even Tina's sister looked shocked. Tina took a deep breath and tried to get everyone to calm down, explaining that she had talked to Hutch, and everything was going to be all right.

As the sun rose in Kunduz on October 2, Josh, the senior Delta who had helped rescue the interpreter's family in the city, realized he was starting to feel the effects of a lack of sleep. As the team's medical sergeant, he had prepared for mass casualties and couldn't believe they hadn't lost anyone yet. Only adrenaline was keeping him going at this point. They had barely slept in the sixty hours since the city had fallen and the airfield had been attacked.

His nerves were wearing thin, and team members were showing signs of stress. They snapped at each other over nothing. The sight of the Afghan police staying indoors, refusing to help them fight, made Josh angry. It was also his son's sixth birthday. He picked up the satellite phone and placed the call. He only had a few minutes.

"Happy birthday!" Josh said brightly. "What have you been doing today?"

Josh's son was used to long-distance calls from his parents. His mother was in Special Operations too. Part of the first year of his life had been spent with his grandparents because both parents had been deployed at the same time. The boy chatted away, and soon Josh had to interrupt him.

"I'm sorry, son, I gotta go," he said. "I'll call you soon!"

"Daddy, why can't you talk to me?"

"I'm sorry, I just gotta go." Josh felt crushed.

What if that was their last conversation? Josh thought back to the first time he'd met his son. He had just returned from a tough deployment to Kandahar's Arghandab valley, where he'd lost friends. His son was ten months old and living with his grandparents. Overnight, Josh became a single dad. At first, his son cried anytime Josh came near him. But by the time his wife got home from her deployment, Josh and his son were best buds. He figured that his responsibility as sole caretaker was the reason he'd escaped some of the post-traumatic stress that had stalked his friends after that deployment.

A few weeks ago, his wife had called with a surprise. She was pregnant again, and this one was totally unplanned. They had two kids, ages three and six, had just sold all their baby stuff, and had moved into a new house. "So, thanks for that!" she said with a laugh.

They had been excited about the new baby. Now it seemed uncertain whether he'd ever return home. The fight for Kunduz city had been insane. This was nothing like his previous deployments. Not even Kandahar's Arghandab valley, where he'd spent time when he was with the infantry, matched up. They had faced an invisible enemy there and were picked off by roadside bombs and ambushes while on patrol. In Kunduz, the Taliban were bold.

He couldn't believe the Taliban's determination in face of American airpower and after suffering a huge number of casualties. He was told that the US and Afghan teams had killed as many as 150 Taliban fighters since the night of the attack on the airfield. The early reports of one thousand Taliban fighters didn't seem so farfetched now. It was as if the insurgents recognized that the battle was a test of the US plan to withdraw from Afghanistan.

Kunduz was quiet that morning. The Afghan police emerged from hiding indoors and joined the Afghan commandos on a mission to the bazaar to buy food. They returned an hour or so later, triumphant, with bags of rice and a Taliban flag they'd stolen from the red-and-white roundabout. The Afghans truly had no regard for their personal safety, Hutch thought. He realized there were some things about this country that he would never understand. Still, he gratefully accepted a plate of hot rice.

After the meal, the Afghan police were pushed out into the streets, to secure checkpoints on the main road.

THE QUIET DIDN'T LAST LONG. The police headquarters came under attack in the early afternoon from the northern and eastern walls. The Afghan police abandoned their posts and returned to the airfield, ceding control of the main road once again. Three Afghan commandos with the Ktah Khas were shot inside the compound. One of the Deltas took over triage and care.

The Ktah Khas commander wanted to send an ambulance to collect the injured commandos immediately, but Hutch managed to talk him out of it since the attack on the compound was ongoing.

"It's too risky to drive in daylight," he insisted. "Let's wait until night. My guys can look after them."

Josh slipped out of the compound with his team and took up a position on the roof of a two-story building nearby to try to stop the shooting. He bounded into the street with a teammate in the direction of fire and pinpointed the group of Taliban that were responsible. The two were in a good position and hadn't been spotted when they opened fire. US military drone footage showed that eighteen insurgents were killed.

Soon after, rockets smacked into the walls from another direction. Pat, the Bagram team captain, was knocked several yards to the ground while climbing a guard tower.

Hutch again called for air support. Within minutes, an F-16 arrived and dropped a five-hundred-pound precision-guided bomb. It struck the target at danger close range, posing a risk to friendly troops down below. The blast caused everyone's insides to rattle, but it didn't stop the rocket-propelled grenades. Hutch cleared the jet fighter for a second drop, which landed on the partially destroyed building, sending a storm of dust and debris into the air. The attack stopped.

Hutch gathered the captains to discuss what to do. The teams wanted to stay; they worried that the Afghans, if left by themselves, might abandon the police headquarters.

Hutch updated Col. Johnston with their decision. The battalion agreed to organize a helicopter drop of supplies that night, including ammunition, batteries, and fuel. The combat controllers were down to one radio, to preserve the last of their batteries. The teams started a rest plan; some were running on practically no sleep since the morning the city had fallen, four days earlier.

Dr. Cua had taken to sleeping on a bench in the dressing room after four days of back-to-back surgeries. She had barely enough energy to change out of her scrubs before collapsing in an exhausted heap around midnight. She was one of three surgeons left at the hospital, and the Afghan staff woke her up to deal with complicated cases. The hospital received over a hundred patients a day, and it was impossible to keep up. On several frightening occasions, she'd been interrupted in the operating theatre to be told that Médecins Sans Frontières was evacuating all eight of the expatriate staff. Both times the departure had been called off and she'd been able to continue surgery. She never knew whether or not to feel relieved. She had barely slept in days and felt guilty for the worry her family back in the Philippines must be experiencing. But she was less scared than she had been. She had grown numb to the sound of gunfire. And so far, the warring sides had respected the impartiality of the hospital.

Rumors were spreading among patients and staff that American forces were in the city and leading a major operation to take it back. Some of the patients with the opposition, including a couple that were apparently senior members of the insurgency, had been discharged against medical advice. In the evening of October 2, there was an unusual lull. Staff were able to step outside to get some fresh air without worrying about being hit by a stray bullet. When Dr. Cua finally went outside and breathed in, the city felt changed. It was colored by the horror of the past few days.

Dr. Nasim, who knew that fighting never stopped for long, took the opportunity to rally the hospital employees. He promised to pay salaries as soon as security improved. They were working day and night without a break and without pay. He addressed the cleaners and caretakers and told them how much the group valued their help.

"Do you know what is the result of your work?" he said. No one replied. "It's not a clean floor. It's not opening the gates. You're saving lives. Do you think the surgeon can operate without you here? You are a critical part of the team, and your work is saving lives."

The doctors decided to take advantage of the quiet moment to schedule follow-up surgeries that had been postponed as nonurgent.

Dr. Cua felt a bit brighter. She had just finished an operation and was writing up the report while her assistant sutured the patient's skin and cracked jokes. It was after two a.m., and several more surgeries were planned for the night.

HUTCH WOKE UP around twelve a.m. on October 3. He had two operations to manage that night: the helicopter drop of supplies and an Afghan commando raid to be led by the Ktah Khas that might require US air support. As the ground force commander (GFC), he was in charge of all ground troops and had the authority to direct the aircraft to fire if lives were in danger. Ben Vontz, an Echo, one of the communications sergeants, was on duty and responsible for keeping in touch with the AC-130.

Ben was certified to work as a combat controller and at twenty-five was one of the youngest Green Berets on the mission. He was in contact with the AC-130 gunship that was circling overhead and ready to support the Afghan operation. The commandos had provided the GPS coordinates for two different targets they planned to raid that night. Ben had the coordinates written down on a luminescent board. The first target was a Taliban-controlled NDS prison. He was unaware that the gunship was having trouble finding it because of a series of problems aboard the aircraft that caused the GPS coordinates to plot to an empty field.

It was one of those nights where nothing seemed to go as planned. The AC-130 had departed from Bagram Airfield more than an hour early to respond to a report of US soldiers under fire and had run into a catalog of problems. Because of the early departure, the gunship's aircrew hadn't received a mission brief or any of the information packages they usually received. Nor had there been time to load the CONOP and the no-strike list into the system. An officer back at Bagram tried to send the packages by email, including the no-strike list, but the messages never arrived because the gunship's communication platform was malfunctioning. The crew repeatedly tried to troubleshoot the system without success.

Then, disaster almost struck: a Soviet-era surface-to-air missile narrowly missed the gunship. They were unaware the Taliban even had those weapons in their arsenal. It was the first one fired in the country in years, and it forced the aircrew to rethink operating procedures. They decided to divert course and fly higher than usual for security. This made their navigation system less accurate.

The TV operator, who was on his third mission over the city since it had fallen, scanned the ground to look for the first target the Afghan commandos were supposed to hit; he spotted a T-shaped building about three hundred meters away from the empty field located by the GPS system. They couldn't see any markings on the roof.

"Unless the grids are off, this is the only large complex in the area," he told the crew.

The crew discussed the matter. They had made contact with the ground troops below, but communication channels were slow. Ground troops usually carried video receivers that could be used to watch the gunship's video feed on a screen, but in this case the ground troops had run out of batteries. They had to make do with voice reports, which were a lot less reliable when the troops couldn't see their screens. In the end, the aircrew decided that the T-shaped building had to be the target, even though it didn't match the GPS coordinates provided.

"TV, I'm just going to update that off you, since that's most likely what it is, so if you can just track there," the fire control officer said, and updated the system with the new coordinates.

But the building they had identified wasn't the NDS prison. It was the Médecins Sans Frontières hospital.

Ben told Hutch that the gunship had locked on to the target to observe the pattern of life and had counted nine people at the site. Hutch told Ben to tell the aircrew the nine people were hostile, as the NDS prison was Taliban-controlled. Without the video receivers, Ben and Hutch couldn't see what the aircrew was watching, and the crew hadn't told them that the original GPS coordinates plotted to an empty field. They were unaware that the crew had identified the target by sight and had locked on the Médecins Sans Frontières hospital.

"Compound is currently under the control of TB [Taliban], so those nine PAX [people] are hostile," Ben told the aircrew.

Aboard the gunship, the TV operator began to feel doubtful. Once they moved closer to the ground, he reentered the GPS grids into the navigation system. This time, the coordinates plotted to a different, hexagonal-shaped building in the same area that looked more like a prison.

"If you look in the TV's screen, you can see this hardened structure that looks very large, could also be more like a county prison with cells," he said to the rest of the crew. "So, I just want to verify that, before we started declaring people hostile, that we are 100 percent sure this is the correct compound."

It was the NDS prison the commandos planned to raid that night.

"Copy," the navigator responded.

The aircrew asked the ground troops for more information about the target they were supposed to be watching.

The Afghan commandos had given the Special Forces a description of the target: a compound with multiple buildings inside and an arch-shaped gate. Ben shared it with the aircrew. The description matched the Médecins Sans Frontières hospital, not the NDS prison. The AC-130 remained locked on the first target, even though it didn't match the coordinates.

It was never clear why the Afghan commandos passed on that physical description, unless their second target for the night was the hospital. The Afghan commandos hated the hospital for treating the Taliban, and they had raided it in the summer while looking for a Taliban commander (who was not there). Perhaps they had planned to raid it again without telling their American partners, who would surely have objected.

A couple of hours into the shift, Hutch heard gunfire from the direction of the prison the Afghan commandos planned to raid that night. He asked Ben to call them to find out what was going on. The interpreter couldn't reach their cell phones. Hutch worried they might be in trouble. After a few minutes, the interpreter said he had managed to get through; the Afghan commandos were under fire and had requested air support.

Hutch ordered the gunship to fire. Ben relayed the order to the gunship, telling them to soften the target. The crew found the language confusing.

"So he wants us to shoot?" the fire control officer said on the crew's internal radio.

The crew asked Ben to clarify what he wanted them to do.

"GFC's intent is to destroy targets of all opportunity that may impede partner forces' success," Ben responded over the radio.

The aircrew was still doubtful. The people inside the compound didn't appear to be carrying weapons, which was one of the criteria used to determine whether an individual was an enemy combatant. But they hadn't explained this to Ben, and they discussed the matter among themselves instead.

"You guys don't see anyone carrying anything that you can tell?" the fire control officer asked, meaning a weapon.

"Not that we can tell," the TV operator said.

They selected the weapons to use on the building and asked whether the GFC had cleared them to shoot people fleeing after the strike started. Ben cleared the crew to fire on both the building and anyone inside and gave Hutch's initials for the strike.

The crew made one last round of checks with Ben to confirm that it was the T-shaped building they intended to hit, and that the gunship was clear to strike the structure and the people inside.

"Affirm," Ben said.

The Lockheed AC-130 gunship opened fire at 2:08 a.m.

"Rounds away, rounds away," the navigator said.

THE FIRST ROUNDS struck the emergency room at the Médecins Sans Frontières trauma hospital. The operating theatre shook and the windows rattled. Dr. Cua looked up from her operative report and exchanged glances with the assistant surgeon, who had finished suturing the patient's wound. They laughed uneasily. It was probably just another clash in the city.

The second blast struck the building with terrifying force. Dr. Cua threw herself to the side of the room for cover with her assistant, still hoping it was a stray rocket. Fear consumed her entire body. Were they under attack? A third, even louder explosion shook the building. She leapt up with her assistant and fled down the hallway into the room at the other end, leaving her anesthetized patient on the operating table. The hospital had three operating theatres, all of which were in use at the time the strike started.

The other surgeons and nurses joined them in the room across the hall, dragging the tables together to provide cover from shrapnel and debris. The explosions continued, filling the room with acrid smoke and the smell of disinfectant.

The first call to Guilhem Molinie, the Médecins Sans Frontières director in Kabul, came from his deputy, Heman Nagarathnam, in Kunduz, reporting that a rocket had landed in the hospital courtyard. A few minutes later, the deputy called back: it was an airstrike. Guilhem was horrified, realizing there had been a screwup. He could only imagine the destructive power of a US airstrike on a hospital full of wounded patients. He immediately dialed the civil affairs officer at Bagram Airfield, praying for a quick response. He felt sick to his stomach.

"The trauma center is under attack," Guilhem told him. "You're bombing the hospital!"

He hung up and scrambled to assemble a team. They started making calls to the US embassy, the Afghan government, and everyone else in the NATO coalition.

THE US CIVIL OFFICER that took his call at Bagram Airfield ran to the joint operations center and pulled the battle captain aside.

"I just got a call from Doctors Without Borders, and they're saying that their hospital in Kunduz is being hit," he whispered.

Col. Johnston was in the next row. He leapt up and asked the officer to repeat himself. It was 2:19 a.m. None of them were aware that an airstrike was under way. They immediately got on the radio and tried to make contact with Hutch.

Aboard the gunship, the crew reported over the radio that the building had caught fire and that around forty or fifty people were fleeing into the yard. Hutch cleared the gunship to shoot them as well. The crew selected the Gatling gun for the strafing run; it was perfect for mowing down individuals fleeing on foot.

Dr. Cua was back in the operating theatre after it had become hard to breathe in the hall. Flames licked at the windows and filled the room with smoke. Some of the nurses escaped through the windows, but she was afraid of getting shot outside. Even through her surgical mask, it was becoming hard to breathe. She watched her colleagues run into the yard and didn't move. Was this an airstrike? Why?

A deafening blast shook the building, and the ceiling came crashing down, plunging her into darkness. She saw her patient's heart monitor flatline. He was a Taliban fighter, about age twenty-eight. He had major wounds to his stomach and other organs, and this was the first follow-up surgery. It had been a success. She tried to get up, but she was trapped in a mesh of wires and cables that had collapsed on top of her.

Her assistant surgeon, who was still at her side, yanked her arm and pulled her free. They crouched against the wall in another room, listening to the hum of an aircraft overhead. The next blast brought more of the ceiling down on them. She felt something wet and sticky on her operating gown, which was covered in shards of glass. She checked herself for life-threatening wounds but found only a gash in her knee. She followed her colleague in the darkness, looking for a way to reach the safe room in the basement.

A slant in the ground appeared in front of them and both slid down, realizing too late that it was actually a drainage well, about six feet deep. The smoke caused Dr. Cua's eyes to stream with tears, and the fire engulfing the building made the walls hot. She felt a deep sense of regret.

"I'm sorry, Mom," she thought silently. She imagined her remains being delivered to her parents in an urn. Or worse still, what if her body was never found?

She felt a terrible sense of guilt for the heartache she was going to cause them. Her mother would feel betrayed because Dr. Cua had told her that going to Afghanistan was safe. Why had she come here? She tried to focus on the lives she had saved in Kunduz, but all she could think of was her parents.

"I'm sorry," she repeated to herself, as her colleague prayed softly.

"Pray with me," he told her. "Allah... la ilaha illa allah."

The ground shook again.

At the joint operations center at Bagram Airfield, the officers had been unable to reach the team in Kunduz because communications were patchy. They were watching an NDS building they believed was that night's target, but the Afghan intelligence agency had multiple locations in the city, and it would turn out to be the wrong NDS compound. One of them called the duty electronic warfare officer to ask for the grids of the target, explaining that Médecins Sans Frontières had just called to report an attack from a US aircraft. As the officers continued urgently trying to reach Hutch without success, they pulled back the video feed of the city. They could see a plume of smoke rising from the center of town and determined that it was likely the site of the airstrike. They pulled the grids from the video feed.

The liaison officer called Guilhem to check the numbers. The grids matched those of the hospital. He returned to the operations center a few minutes later.

"You're hitting the trauma center!" he said.

DR. CUA WATCHED her colleague scramble up the burning walls of the well and climb out. He motioned at her to follow and disappeared. She wasn't strong enough to climb out and kept slipping back down. Tears of frustration and anger stung her eyes. *Calm down*, she told herself, feeling the walls for a foothold. Her hand touched steel. It was burning hot, but she grabbed it anyway, kicked her feet, and hoisted herself into the yard. She saw her assistant waiting under a cluster of roses. He gave her a massive grin.

"Get down!!" he yelled as she ran toward him and threw herself into the grass.

Another Afghan man appeared in the yard as they crawled away from the main hospital. Dr. Cua froze with fear. Was it the Taliban?

"Follow me, there's a safe place here," he said, and led them to a building that was untouched by the strike.

In Kabul, Guilhem made another appeal to the civil affairs officer.

"Please make sure the airstrikes stop. We sustained heavy casualties," he texted.

"I will do my best. Praying for you all," the officer responded.

CHAPTER 10

They're Calling It a War Crime

HUTCH

HUTCH CALLED the battalion as requested.

"We are getting reports that a Doctors Without Borders hospital just got hit," Col. Johnston told him.

"No way," he said. "That's not possible."

He disconnected the call and stopped to process the message. He replayed the past hour in his mind and didn't see how it could have happened. But the gunship was still circling overhead, reloading its guns to start shooting again. He told Ben to tell the aircraft to keep monitoring the target but to hold fire. He didn't tell Ben why. He didn't want to freak him out. It was the last thing any of the guys needed to hear. He heard another round go off and turned to Ben.

"They need to stop shooting, *period*," he said.

This time he explained why. The color drained from Ben's face. It turned out the AC-130 had been clearing a round from one of its guns and had fired into an empty field. Ben seemed to be in shock. Hutch continued to review the night's events. He knew of one hospital in the city, the provincial hospital, and it was a mile and a half in the other direction. There had to be some sort of confusion.

The gunship stopped shooting at 2:38 a.m., after it had fired 211 rounds.

At Kunduz police headquarters, Hutch pushed the incident out of his mind and turned his attention to the resupply mission involving the helicopter. When the Afghan commandos returned, he asked about the strike. The patrol leader said they'd never called for air support and had captured the NDS prison without a problem.

"Hey, so what did we hit?" Hutch asked.

"We think you hit a hospital," the patrol leader said.

Hutch didn't mention the reports of the strike on the Médecins Sans Frontières facility to anyone else. As hardened as some of the guys were, the possibility that they might have destroyed a hospital full of patients would deliver a terrible blow to morale, adding to the stress of the ongoing battle. He tried to suppress the thought and told himself there had been a mistake.

Dr. Nasim, who had managed to reach the safe room, peered out and scoured the yard for people to rescue. He heard screams and saw a figure emerge from the wreckage in the darkness. It was the ER nurse, Zabihullah. He appeared to have been shot by the aircraft and was missing a hand and an eye; blood gushed from a wound that had partially severed an arm. Dr. Nasim hauled him to safety, where they could apply tourniquets to stop the bleeding, and continued the search for survivors.

Dr. Cua cowered in the dark for a long time after the firing stopped. Her phone was buried in the operating theatre. What if everyone else had already been rescued? What happened if the Taliban came next and found a foreigner here among the Afghans? As the sun rose, she heard someone calling her name. It was the hospital logistics coordinator, Benoit. She gratefully scrambled after him to an office building, where the other expats were alive and treating the wounded in a meeting room.

Some of them had assumed she was dead. She scrubbed her hands and helped dress the wounds of a number of children that had been staying at the hospital with their parents. She recognized Zabihullah, who was lying on a table and missing a hand. The ER had been damaged the worst. Dr. Nasim came back carrying one of the ER doctors, Dr. Aminullah Bajawri, whom he'd found in a kitchen.

Dr. Bajawri had escaped the ER after the first rounds hit, but he was shot by the aircraft in the yard. He had managed to call his brother, who had located him and tried to stop his bleeding. Both of his legs had been partly severed, and he was pale. Dr. Cua and a colleague set to work to stop the loss of blood, performing the surgery without anesthesia. All they had was morphine. He died in their hands. He was thirty-two and had dreamed of being a neurosurgeon, a virtually nonexistent specialization in the war-ravaged country. Detached and deep in shock, she mechanically moved on to the next patient. Dr. Nasim tried to reassure the staff.

"Now isn't the time to cry," he kept repeating. "Let's be strong and save those we can save. We can cry later."

They lost the pharmacist next. He would have survived in the pharmacy, but he ran for cover in the main building, where he was fatally wounded. Dr. Nasim felt responsible; the pharmacist was supposed to have taken the week off, but he'd come back one night earlier than scheduled because the team was under pressure.

The hospital smoldered in the first morning light. An initial head count indicated that fourteen Médecins Sans Frontières staff members had died in the strike, but the number was set to rise as remains were identified.* Personnel from the Afghan Red Crescent were shuttling the wounded to the provincial hospital. Two Afghan army trucks arrived at the compound; the occupants were looking for Taliban survivors.

Their commander recognized Dr. Nasim and jumped out. They came from the same town in Takhar.

"Dr. Nasim, what are you doing here?" he asked.

"I've been stuck here for twenty days," Dr. Nasim said.

The commander wanted him to ride in the truck for safety, but Dr. Nasim refused to touch the Afghan army vehicle. One of the

---

* As detailed later in the book, the final count was forty-two hospital staff and patients killed in the strike.

Médecins Sans Frontières Land Cruisers had survived the bombing. He told the commander they had eight expats to evacuate, and if he wanted to be helpful, he could escort them to the airport instead. The commander agreed.

Dr. Cua climbed aboard, feeling like a zombie. In her mind, she replayed the surgery she'd performed on Dr. Bajawri, who had died on the kitchen table. She thought about her earlier patient, who had burned to death in the operating room. All this time, she had worried about Taliban. It was the Americans she should have feared. She seethed with anger at all of them for prolonging the stupid war, and for causing so much unnecessary bloodshed and suffering.

THE CITY WAS QUIET THAT DAY. The Green Berets and coalition personnel relocated to the governor's compound, which contained the residence, headquarters, and a soccer field that made a much better helicopter landing zone. They stayed another night. Apart from the occasional burst of gunfire, there were no further efforts to breach the walls of the compound. The following day, a rocket sailed over the walls and narrowly missed a group of guys in the yard. No one was hurt. At night, everyone swapped out. A fresh team, ODA 3134, and the other half of ODA 3135 took their places at the compound. There were still pockets of insurgents in the city, and it would take days for some degree of normality to return.

The Afghan police and soldiers who were guarding checkpoints on the main highway to Kunduz Airfield cheered as the American convoy drove past. The Green Berets felt like heroes in a movie. They had saved a city from ruin against the odds, which gave them a deep sense of connection to the population. Hutch was elated. It was what he'd secretly dreamed of since childhood, participating in a battle for survival with a small band of brothers. It was what every Green Beret signed up for, but few had a chance to do.

It had been a bloody battle for the Taliban. US drone footage and team reports showed that at least 350 insurgents had been killed in the battle. The Afghan government would receive a boost for appearing to have regained control on its own. Hutch felt a rush of pride for the men serving with him. Some of the soldiers had never been in combat before, and each had performed bravely. Every emotion he'd suppressed during the four-day battle hit him at once. They had made history. His men were high with the feeling of being alive. They weren't prepared for the news.

When they turned on the TV back at the camp, the international media was indeed focused on the battle for Kunduz—but not on the Taliban's defeat. Every major outlet was covering an American bombing of a Médecins Sans Frontières hospital that had led to the deaths of dozens of doctors and patients. There was barely any mention of the significance of the victory in Kunduz. It seemed the entire world had spent the last two days discussing whether the airstrike was a war crime.

The aid organization had provided a detailed accounting of its effort to share its GPS coordinates with the US military as recently as four days before the strike. It also said it had placed two flags bearing the group's red-lettered logo on the roof of the hospital. The death toll included at least thirty people, among them staff and children sheltering at the facility. The tally was expected to rise as more bodies were identified; many of the remains had been burned beyond recognition.

"The main hospital building, where medical personnel were caring for patients, was repeatedly and very precisely hit during each aerial raid, while the rest of the compound was left mostly untouched. We condemn this attack, which constitutes a grave violation of International Humanitarian Law," said Médecins Sans Frontières' general director, Christopher Stokes, in a statement to the media. He called the act a war crime.

An investigation team led by Army Brigadier General Richard Kim had already reached Kunduz; they wanted to see Hutch immediately. The phrase "war crime" had sent a rattle of fear through everyone at the camp. Hutch finished briefing the Afghan generals at the 209th Corps headquarters and went straight to Brig. Gen. Kim's office. An Afghan commander passed him on the way.

"What's our story?" the commander asked.

"What do you mean, what's our story?" Hutch said. "We're just going to tell them what happened."

Hutch was still wearing the same dust-covered, sweat-soaked uniform he'd worn in battle when he entered the room where Brig. Gen. Kim was waiting. He was sure the matter could be easily cleared up once he had a chance to explain. Everyone knew that the teams had been caught in an intense firefight for four days without respite. No one could question whether their decisions had been made in good faith. He pulled up a chair and sat down to face the investigators. The looks on their faces said otherwise.

They stared at him uncomfortably. The media was describing Hutch as a potential war criminal. A Médecins Sans Frontières hospital had just been bombed because of him. He refused to flinch during the questioning and assured them that he wanted to help with the investigation. He was as upset as anyone about the strike, but he believed they'd done the right thing by going into the city. If they hadn't, the Taliban would be entrenched by now, and a door-to-door battle to drive them out would have yielded an even higher human cost. Everyone had done their best in a situation they should never have been put in in the first place.

It had been ten years since Hutch's first tour in Iraq. A decade was a long time to learn how to process the horrors of war. It was clear the bombing was a mistake caused by equipment failure, exhaustion, and human error. He tried to console Ben, the Echo who had been talking to the aircrew on the night of the strike. Ben was in a state of shock.

"I called it," Hutch kept repeating. "I called it."

The facts didn't seem to register with Ben. He blamed himself for the mistake. He tried to avoid reading the news, but he couldn't help it. There was nothing Hutch could say to console him. Ben thought about the people inside the hospital and revisited his decisions over and over again.

At Camp Pamir, the other Green Berets were also coming down from their highs. Many of them felt angry and bitter. Everyone seemed to have forgotten that the soldiers had put their lives on the line for the United States' most important battle in Afghanistan. They hadn't known about the Médecins Sans Frontières hospital in the city. They thought the aid organization should have closed it down during the battle, instead of putting the lives of its staff and patients on the line. War is hell. Their view was that the airstrike was a tragedy, but as soon as politicians sent soldiers to war, bad things happened. The only way it could have been avoided was to not be at war in the first place.

Hutch tried to reason with them. There was nothing that justified the mistake, he told them. And the army's decision to investigate was the right thing to do. But the others didn't agree. Some felt that Hutch was being made a scapegoat for the poor decisions of their leaders, who had allowed them to lose a city to the Taliban.

At Bagram Airfield, an officer gathered the evidence the military had collected of Taliban activity on the hospital grounds and filed it away. If the intelligence became public, it would only cause the US position to look worse by making it seem possible that the hospital had been bombed on purpose.

Hutch called home.

"Is everything okay?" Tina asked. "Because they're calling it a war crime."

PART TWO

REVERSAL

CHAPTER 11

Damage Control in Washington

AT THE TIME OF THE STRIKE, Gen. Campbell, the top commander of US and NATO forces in Afghanistan, was headed to Washington to attend the National Security Council meeting with President Obama and testify on progress. When he landed at Andrews Air Force Base in Maryland, he was told that the deputy chief of staff for operations was waiting on the line from Kabul.

"Sir," Major General Jeffrey Buchanan said. "We bombed a hospital."

Médecins Sans Frontières was reporting that the strike had killed at least twenty-two people, including twelve staff members and ten patients, of which three were children. The number was set to rise as more remains were identified.

It was Saturday morning in Afghanistan, and the story was already spinning out of control in the media. The US military spokesman in Kabul had issued a statement saying that the United States had carried out an airstrike that may have resulted in collateral damage to a nearby hospital. The statement had to be corrected when more details emerged about the bombing, making it seem that the military was deliberately trying to cover up what had happened.

The spokesman provided reporters with a new version of the story in the evening, but it, too, would turn out to be inaccurate, fueling suspicion that the US military had deliberately bombed a protected facility and possibly committed a war crime.

"US forces conducted an airstrike in Kunduz city at 2:15 a.m. (local), October 3, against insurgents who were directly firing upon US service members advising and assisting Afghan Security Forces in the city of Kunduz," Col. Brian Tribus said. "The strike was conducted in the vicinity of a Doctors Without Borders medical facility."

But there were no US forces out in the road at the time of the strike, nor any insurgents firing directly at them. There was not even any evidence that the Afghans had been under threat at the time of the bombing.

The Afghan government, meanwhile, claimed that the hospital had been bombed deliberately because it was sheltering Taliban fighters, which only made the US military look worse. The Afghan army had long hated the hospital for treating the Taliban, and some officials openly defended the bombing. Hamdullah Danishi, the acting governor of Kunduz, went as far as claiming that the Taliban had been shooting on government forces from the hospital.

"The hospital campus was 100 percent used by the Taliban," he told the *Washington Post*. "The hospital has a vast garden, and the Taliban were there. We tolerated their firing for some time."

Other Afghan officials confirmed Danishi's version of events, asserting that the Taliban used the hospital as a base from which to plan attacks against US and Afghan forces.

"There were ten to fifteen terrorists hiding in the hospital last night and they came and attacked," Sediq Sediqqi, the interior ministry spokesman, told reporters on camera. "They are killed, all of the terrorists are killed, but we also lost doctors."

GEN. CAMPBELL was under pressure to explain to reporters in Washington what had happened, but the US military was still gathering all the facts, and it was difficult to get a grasp of the situation. Looking somber, he appeared on Monday morning in the Pentagon briefing room to take questions from the press. It was

October 5, 2015, two days after the strike, and information was still coming in.

"We have now learned that on October 3, Afghan forces advised that they were taking fire from enemy positions and asked for air support from US forces. An airstrike was then called to eliminate the Taliban threat and several civilians were accidentally struck," he said in his opening statement. "This is different from initial reports which indicated that US forces were threatened and that the airstrike was called on their behalf."

He did not say whether the hospital had been the target of the airstrike, nor did he explain why Afghan forces had been able to call in the airstrike when the US military was supposed to have stopped providing air support to local forces. Under the new mission, the United States was meant to operate in a training and advisory role and was allowed to strike only in self-defense or to defend Afghans in extremis. The rules prohibited offensive strikes against the Taliban. The degree to which the US military stretched the interpretation of the rules to carry out strikes in favor of Afghan commandos had not been made public. Reporters now suspected, correctly, that the military had not disclosed the full scope of its operations in Afghanistan.

"Do those rules of engagement allow for the Afghans to call in American airstrikes? And what kind of fallback or fail-safe system is there in that process?" NBC reporter Jim Miklaszewski asked.

Gen. Campbell declined to answer.

"I don't want to go into those great details yet until we get the— the investigation," he said. "And I don't want to cover the rules of engagement in this format at this point in time."

Reporters continued to ask how the strike could have been authorized, and about details provided by Médecins Sans Frontières, including the fact that the organization had repeatedly shared the hospital's GPS coordinates with the US military. To each question, Gen. Campbell replied that it was too early to say, and the investigation would determine the answers.

"I just wanted to make it crystal clear. There were no US JTACs [combat controllers] under fire at the tactical level when this airstrike was called in?" another reporter asked.

Gen. Campbell repeated his opening statement. "What I said was that the Afghans asked for air support from a Special Forces team that we have on the ground providing train, advise, and assist in Kunduz," he said. He clarified that early versions of events provided by the US military in Kabul had been wrong. "The initial statement that went out was that US forces were under direct fire contact. What I'm doing is correcting that statement here," he said.

The briefing only raised more questions about what the US military was doing in Afghanistan. The strike had revealed that the full scope of its operations there had not been made public. A day after facing reporters at the Pentagon, Gen. Campbell went to Capitol Hill to testify about US operations in Afghanistan in front of the Senate Armed Services Committee. The focus of the conversation changed. Whereas the media was interested in an explanation for the hospital bombing, senators were mostly focused on the imminent US drawdown in Afghanistan.

Gen. Campbell was explicit about his opposition to going to zero troops by 2016. The plan, he told senators, neglected to take into account the rise in violence in Afghanistan and risked compromising the success of the mission there. He described the fall of Kunduz and other territorial losses as a setback but credited the Afghan forces for rallying and regaining control of most of the city.

He did not acknowledge the critical role that SOF had played in the battle for the city, and the senators did not ask for details about their involvement.

"I've offered my chain of command several options for a future laydown in 2016 and beyond," Gen. Campbell said, stating that much had changed in Afghanistan since the United States had decided to withdraw all its troops within a two-year time frame.

He declined to discuss the options in detail but insisted that the Afghan forces were worth the investment and that removing US assistance too early would be a mistake. He added that the emergence of a local Islamic State branch was a factor for consideration, along with the Taliban's resurgence and the escalation in attacks. He was careful not to exaggerate the Islamic State threat. The reporting was still unclear, and he was concerned that a warning might not go down well with senior Obama officials, who were already reluctant to support a delay in the planned withdrawal of troops.

He found a sympathetic audience in the committee. The chairman, Republican senator John McCain of Arizona, expressed regret for the Kunduz airstrike but did not press him on the circumstances or why US Special Forces were in the city. He, like the other committee members, was more concerned with the Obama administration's plan to fully withdraw from Afghanistan the following year.

"I just don't understand why this administration does not understand that if we do what is presently planned beginning three months from now, that we will see the Iraq movie again," McCain told the committee, referring to the plan to continue to draw down forces. "There is no doubt in anybody's mind about that."

CHAPTER 12

Obama Changes the Plan

THE SITUATION ROOM at the White House was packed the following day for the National Security Council meeting to strategize about the way forward in Afghanistan. All the main government departments and agencies were due to brief President Obama ahead of the decision on whether to keep troop numbers stable or continue with the plan to draw down. Peter Lavoy, the NSC's senior director for South Asia, pulled Gen. Campbell aside before the meeting started.

The national security adviser, Susan Rice, had eventually consented to an interagency review of military force options, and Pentagon officials had the impression that the argument for extending the US troop presence had gained favor. They hoped she would support their recommendation to keep Kandahar Airfield running in the south, where Helmand was at risk of falling. But Rice remained deeply skeptical of any path that did not lead to an embassy-only presence in Kabul by the time President Obama left office.

"They want to go a different route," Lavoy told Gen. Campbell.

"What? I thought we had agreed on this," Campbell said.

President Obama walked in, and the meeting started. Rice laid out the agenda for the session, and then each agency provided an update.

Gen. Campbell offered an update on the situation in Kunduz and asserted that it demonstrated that Afghan forces had been able to rally against the Taliban to regain the city. He shared the latest information available on the hospital bombing and the ensuing investigation. The CIA and the State Department broadly supported the military's case for staying in Afghanistan, but Lavoy's warning proved correct. Rice recommended proceeding with the closure of Kandahar Airfield and the plan to draw down to fifty-five hundred troops that year.

President Obama turned to General Joseph Dunford, chairman of the Joint Chiefs of Staff and the nation's highest-ranking military officer.

"Joe, what do you think?" he asked.

The gray-haired former Marine commandant with watery blue eyes had served as the top US general in Afghanistan until 2014. He looked over at his replacement.

"Sir, you need to talk to Gen. Campbell," Gen. Dunford responded.

President Obama turned to Gen. Campbell.

"J.C., what's your recommendation?"

Gen. Campbell told him that the United States needed to keep a more robust presence in Afghanistan than originally planned. The Taliban's gains, along with the emergence of the local Islamic State branch, threatened the achievements the United States had made over the past decade and a half and risked allowing a resurgence of al Qaeda. Furthermore, Afghanistan's collapse threatened stability in the whole region. He recommended keeping troops in the country beyond 2016.

President Obama found himself between two unappealing options. He didn't want a permanent war, but nor did he want to leave his successor with no means to blunt the threat of another terrorist attack. He agreed to a change in the plan.

"I don't like handing this perpetual war in Afghanistan to my successor," he said. "I also don't feel that it would be responsible to hand to my successor a growing or just constant and steady terrorist threat, where we remove the best means we have to deal with that threat."

Two days later, President Obama summoned journalists to the Roosevelt Room in the White House. He stepped to the podium and announced that the United States would keep force levels steady that year and would retain a presence of at least fifty-five hundred troops at the start of 2017. It was a major concession. After President Obama had campaigned on a pledge to end forever wars, the conflicts in both Afghanistan and Iraq would still be going after his last term in office.

He framed the decision as a continuation of support for the Afghan government rather than an extension of a war he had promised to end. He talked up Afghanistan's leaders, President Ashraf Ghani and Chief Executive Officer Abdullah Abdullah, sidestepping the issue of the shaky, divided government that had been formed at the behest of Secretary of State John Kerry after a disputed presidential election a year earlier had almost tipped the country into civil war.

"First, I've decided to maintain our current posture of ninety-eight hundred troops in Afghanistan through most of next year, 2016. Their mission will not change. Our troops will continue to pursue those two narrow tasks that I outlined earlier, training Afghan forces, and going after al Qaeda," he told reporters. "Maintaining our current posture through most of next year, rather than a more rapid drawdown, will allow us to sustain our efforts to train and assist Afghan forces as they grow stronger."

President Obama did not acknowledge the critical role that US Special Forces had played in recapturing the city of Kunduz, nor how dependent the Afghan government was likely to remain on US military support for years to come.

"Today, American forces no longer patrol Afghan villages or valleys. Our troops are not engaged in major ground combat against the Taliban. Those missions now belong to Afghans, who are fully responsible for securing their country," he said.

"Mr. President, can you tell us how disappointing this decision is for you? Is this—can you tell us how disappointing this decision is for you?" a reporter asked.

"This decision is not disappointing. Continually, my goal has been to make sure that we give every opportunity for Afghanistan to succeed while we're still making sure that we're meeting our core missions," President Obama said.

Contrary to his assertions, the United States was about to have a much bigger role in combat going forward. The decision to keep Kandahar Airfield allowed the US military to take a more aggressive approach to beating back the Taliban's gains in the south.

The first order of business was to intervene in Helmand, where the insurgency's rapid gains over the summer had left the government in the province's capital all but surrounded. There were real and immediate concerns that the province could fall soon, delivering another humiliating defeat to the Afghan government just weeks after the loss of Kunduz. Things were about to change dramatically for the Green Berets already stationed in Afghanistan at a time when US capabilities and resources, from intelligence assets to surveillance to logistical support, were limited and drawing down.

Furthermore, President Obama's staff would soon sign off on a tranche of new authorities that would give SOF greater freedom to operate in Afghanistan. The rules would allow a more flexible use of airpower and increase the military's ability to dispatch ODAs on missions with the Afghan commandos. In effect, the decision to call off the US withdrawal would extend the SOF's role in the Afghan war indefinitely, and their contribution was set to grow as the Taliban made gains against the government.

CHAPTER 13

The Taliban Must Shoot First

HELMAND

US Special Forces ramped up quickly in Helmand after the White House agreed to keep operations running in the south. The first order of business was to prevent the fall of the province and a repeat of the disaster in Kunduz. The Taliban had captured a suburb on the outskirts of the provincial capital, and the Special Forces were tasked with working with the Afghans to win it back.

Captain Jeff McDonald had served in the Marines before September 11 and first deployed to Afghanistan with Special Forces in 2003. His team was chosen for the mission to save Helmand province's capital, Lashkar Gah. He had more experience than most detachment commanders, having spent years as a communications sergeant. His team, ODA 9114, was always the company's first choice for a difficult mission. Babaji, as the suburb was known, had been the epicenter of Operation Panchai Palang, or Panther's Claw, in 2009—the British army's largest air assault of the war.

Now that Babaji had fallen again, the helicopter pilots refused to drop Jeff's team any closer than ten kilometers off target because it was too dangerous, so they had to drive. Even so, the mission turned out to be a huge success. Jeff's team ran into a gathering of Taliban on the outskirts of the city and stirred up what commanders described as a "hornet's nest." Aided by an AC-130 gunship above, they killed some forty-five Taliban who were fleeing a safe house, US records showed. Even though they didn't make it to Babaji, word of their success spread up the ranks, and the generals were excited.

In the northern region of Helmand, where Caleb's team was based, a crisis was unfolding at the site of USAID's unfinished flagship reconstruction project to add a third turbine at Kajaki Dam. The Taliban had reached the last checkpoint before the installation, and capturing the dam would be a big win. Once the reconstruction project was complete, the hydroelectric dam was supposed to deliver power to almost two million people across Afghanistan's impoverished south, winning hearts and minds in the Taliban's former heartland. Planned for completion in 2005, it remained unfinished a decade later. As was the case with many of the best-intentioned projects designed in Washington, corruption, insecurity, and other problems had caused the cost to balloon, from $20 million to over $300 million.

Caleb's team, which had been assigned to work with the Afghan commandos to prevent the dam from falling, was ordered to deploy to Kajaki as soon as possible. But the team resisted the order, arguing that they were unequipped to carry out a multiday operation in such a remote area. Maj. Gabriel, the company commander, was troubled by the team's reluctance to agree to the mission. He didn't know them well, because they belonged to Bravo Company in Utah, but teams were expected to eagerly comply now that restrictions on missions appeared to be lifting.

Maj. Gabriel knew Caleb from the Special Forces Qualification Course and leaned on him for information. Either ODAs worked as a tight-knit unit or things ended badly in the field, and Maj. Gabriel was concerned that this team was heading for the latter. But Caleb felt uncomfortable, torn between loyalty to the team and duty as a soldier, and tried to stay out of it. The truth was, the acrimony between the team and its leadership that had started before the deployment had evolved into all-out confrontation.

About a month into the mission, Chris Clary, the Bravo who had driven the casualties to the helicopter after the insider attack, had read aloud a letter on behalf of the team; it listed all their concerns about how the captain and team sergeant were running things. Team members wanted leadership to address the chronic logistical problems like shortages of food, water, and ammunition. Their trucks still needed crucial repairs. The biggest dispute was over the procedures at the Tactical Operations Center (TOC), which the team saw as a violation of operational security.

The TOC contained classified computers, the countrywide communications satellite (SATCOM) radio, and classified surveillance feeds, which the Afghans weren't allowed to view, and yet the room always seemed to be full of 215th Corps soldiers. Chris rebelled and built a new operations center for the Afghans to use, with cleared maps and feeds, which upset the captain but solved the problem.

The team's relationship with the Afghan commandos was at rock bottom after the insider attack and difficult to repair due to unresolved legacy issues. The 7th Group team had damaged the commandos' sewage system by blowing up the camp's swimming pool, and it was still in need of work. The 7th Group team had done it apparently to get rid of debris caused by an unexplained fire in the camp. They had also dumped trash on the commandos' camp because they didn't have the means to dispose of it. That didn't help the relationship with the Afghans either.

IN THE END, the Kajaki mission went ahead. Caleb compiled intelligence briefs and gave the guys good news: the forecast said clear and sunny all week. Cloud cover blocked the view of surveillance aircraft like drones, thereby limiting air support. He called home to tell Ashley he'd be offline for a few days, but not to worry. At night, the team loaded the gear onto Chinooks and flew north under the cover of darkness.

The flat, desertlike terrain gave way to mountains and a silvery river that meandered into a lake. The Kajaki Dam appeared on the horizon. They landed at the contractor's base before sunrise and set up in a dilapidated concrete building that had empty frames for windows and gaping holes in the ceiling. The attached infantry squad started a guard rotation while the rest of the soldiers finished unloading. In addition to ammunition, mortars, radio equipment, and food, they had brought their surgical team because there were no medical facilities located within a distance that could be reached in the "golden hour"—the first hour after a traumatic injury, considered the most critical for a soldier's survival.

The Green Berets learned the next morning that the Taliban and the government had a tacit agreement not to fight during the day. There was a daily cease-fire between ten a.m. and four p.m. to give farmers time to tend their crops. No one was in any rush to fight the war. The US team found it surreal. The team's leadership set to work on a plan with the Afghan commandos while Caleb gathered intelligence. Chris and a few others left to set up a firing position on the mountain.

The Afghan army had built a small base overlooking the lower checkpoint in the valley before the entrance to the dam. They hauled boxes of supplies up the steep and winding path, which seemed to cut through a Soviet-era minefield marked with piles of rocks painted white.

"Just stay between the rocks," one of the Afghans said, waving away their concerns as they lugged the mortars up the mountain.

Chris didn't ask what to do in case of an ambush. They'd probably just dive into the minefields and hope for the best. The battalion had selected him for the tour from a different team and considered him one of the most promising weapons sergeants in the company. He noticed climbing equipment affixed to the rocks that dated back to the Cold War. American aid workers with USAID had built the Kajaki Dam in the 1950s as a hedge against Soviet influence. In the 1970s, the US agency added a powerhouse and made plans to expand the dam's capacity, but the project was abandoned before the Soviets invaded. It was now 2015, and the third turbine had yet to be installed.

The Afghan army base at the top of the mountain was built out of mortar cans filled with rocks and corrugated tin. Chris and Ben White, the other weapons sergeant, got to work setting up the mortar system and a camp, with camouflage netting for shade during the day and sleeping bags for the nights under the stars. Caleb headed up to the camp to see how it was going. He'd become close friends with Chris and with Ben. The view was spectacular. The turquoise river ran south out of the reservoir and flowed around the soaring mountains that rose and fell into the horizon.

Chris and Ben were tasked with partnering with an Afghan mortar team during the operation. The team of three Afghan commandos were enthusiastic about learning to refine their technique on the mortars. They spent the day identifying targets for the mission, setting up quick mortar references on the Taliban's positions. The fortified mud-brick compounds were booby-trapped with homemade bombs or appeared to have machine guns positioned at the slits in the walls.

The mission launched that night. Two assault forces of US Special Forces and Afghan commandos drove down toward the valley to attack a fortified line of Taliban positions from the south and west. They aimed to push back the Taliban and recapture some of the lost Afghan army checkpoints. As the assault forces turned into the valley, the US and Afghan mortar teams at the top of the mountain began to fire at the targets they'd scoped out during the day.

They were interrupted by a call on the radio. Maj. Gabriel demanded to know why they had started shooting. According to their rules of engagement, the Taliban had to be the first to fire. He ordered them to stop firing immediately or get pulled out. Chris exchanged glances with Ben.

"They want us to wait for the Taliban to shoot first?" he asked.

Ben stared at him and shrugged. This was apparently an offensive operation, and it hadn't occurred to them that the restriction on strikes would apply in these circumstances. Chris thought it was dangerous to wait until their teammates came under fire in the

Taliban-controlled valley, where the insurgents had had months to settle into heavily fortified compounds that could not be penetrated by gunfire. But they stopped immediately, waiting until the team members called in the "troops in contact" message (which meant they were under fire) before starting on the mortars again.

Lieutenant Colonel Zabihullah Mohmand, the grizzled, heavy-set commander of the 7th Special Operations Kandak, which was responsible for Helmand, stopped the commandos at the last covered position. He wanted the Americans to carry out an airstrike on the Taliban's defensive line of fortified positions in the valley; it was too dangerous to send the commandos over open ground to attack the fortified positions, and the mortars were ineffective.

He could hear the AC-130 buzzing overhead and was furious when the request for air support was denied. It was hard for the Green Berets, who were supposedly their partners in this, to explain that an American life had to be in danger to justify the strike. Lt. Col. Mohmand couldn't understand why the Americans, having finally sent a US Special Forces team all the way to Kajaki, were now withholding critical assets. He was outraged at the request to send his men to the fortified Taliban positions, straight into the line of fire from the heavy machine guns positioned inside. He told the captain that he wouldn't send the commandos to the Taliban's defensive line unless the United States dropped on them first.

The captain tried to relay the situation over the SATCOM radio to Maj. Gabriel, who was observing the operation over video feed from Kandahar, along with the rest of the US military in the country.

"Tell them they have to move forward," Maj. Gabriel said, aware the whole world was watching.

"I can't force him to clear the compounds," the captain replied.

The back-and-forth continued. In the end, Lt. Col. Mohmand, losing patience, ordered his men to retreat before daylight. They failed to capture the Taliban's positions or push them back into the valley and away from the Kajaki Dam. Chris viewed the episode as further evidence of how poorly their leadership understood the operational environment. The commandos weren't cannon fodder. The US military's reluctance to engage was sure to further undermine their relationship with the Afghan soldiers.

Chris thought back to his two previous deployments and how things had been different. In Uruzgan a couple of years earlier, on his second tour in Afghanistan, he had been tasked with raising a militia out of former Taliban fighters. His team shared meals with them and lived in the same village, which built the trust that was essential in a firefight. When he had stepped on a pressure plate bomb and narrowly avoided detonating it, he had felt that the mission was worth it, even after seeing the giant cloud of dust it threw into the air when the soldiers blew it up from a distance. Now, he wasn't sure what they were achieving, except convincing the commandos that America didn't think their lives were important enough to merit an airstrike.

The Taliban ambushed the Afghan checkpoint the following day, taking advantage of bad weather. There was a running joke in the team that Caleb always got the weather wrong. Chris and the other Bravos helped the commandos repel the attack from the mountain using the mortars. They stayed a few more days, drank tea with the Afghans, and helped them set up a new checkpoint in the valley. When they returned to Camp Antonik, the frontline was little changed.

In the capital of Helmand, Lashkar Gah, the early success produced by Jeff's team proved difficult to repeat. Roadside bombs and ambushes bogged down follow-up missions to the surburb of Babaji. Several Afghan soldiers were killed, which made them reluctant to sustain a high pace of operations. After a fortnight, Jeff's team swapped out, starting a rotation with another Kandahar team. While they didn't advance much farther for the remainder of the tour, Lashkar Gah remained in government hands.

The fundamental dynamics of the war continued to undermine the mission: the local government was corrupt, and its security forces were overused, exploited, and poorly led.

CHAPTER 14

Mission to Save Marjah
CALEB

AFTER CALEB's team returned from Kajaki, the US Special Forces battalion wanted them to continue to aggressively push back against the Taliban's gains in northern Helmand, to prevent a string of districts from falling under insurgent control. The captain and the team sergeant remained on poor terms with the team and could not get them on board. Team members argued that Helmand was too isolated for a high-risk mission at a time when air support was so limited.

Maj. Gabriel, the company commander, eventually told them he would be forced to swap them out with another team unless they began to operate in their area. He didn't want to fire the team, but the battalion had noticed their lack of aggressiveness, and there was a perception that northern Helmand was eroding around ODA 9123. Another team based at Camp Morehead in Kabul was edging to run missions and had built a strong reputation with the battalion. Crucially, some of its team members had already rotated to Helmand to assist other ODAs during large-scale operations and had performed well.

Caleb urged everyone to agree on a plan and make the best of the situation. He stood in front of a map of Helmand and dramatically swept a hand over the province.

"Take your pick," he said. "Let's make it a big one. Let's make it worth it."

They were in the middle of planning a ground mission when Maj. Gabriel interrupted them with orders from Gen. Swindell to deploy urgently to Marjah. The town was falling, he told them, and the orders came from the top.

Marjah, a cluster of mud huts and farms irrigated by the Helmand River, had never really been under government control. Operation Moshtarak, which took place there in 2010 and was the largest US-Afghan operation of the war, aimed to deliver the district a "government in a box" and win over hearts and minds. Instead, dozens of US Marines died in the slow-burning battle that followed.

Caleb was skeptical. There was no one at Marjah to hold ground, and the town was sure to fall back into Taliban hands after they left. Still, the team scrambled to prepare and set off at night. They ran into several ambushes along the way, and those, along with the battalion's refusal to allow airstrikes and a broken remote weapon system in one of the trucks, made the trip seem interminable.

In Marjah, they found a desperate scene inside the governor's compound the following morning. A group of Afghan commandos was stranded there without reinforcements. There were ladders on the walls, which the insurgents had apparently climbed, allowing them to fire into the compound. For once, the commandos seemed happy to see the Americans. They told them that a Red Unit, one of the Taliban's company-sized groups of "special forces," was in the area and armed with sniper rifles and night vision goggles.

The team set up a command center in the headquarters, and their attached infantry soldiers established a guard force on the perimeter walls. They found some of the guard towers empty, or Afghan army soldiers inside but smoking hashish or asleep. That night, they heard mortar fire. The Afghans told them it was outgoing fire from an artillery section, but in the morning, as the firing continued and mortars landed close to the compound, they realized it had been incoming after all. An assault force left to clear the area while Chris and the other Bravo stayed behind to set up a mortar tube to fire explosive rounds back at the Taliban mortar team and try to take them out. Ben, known for his dark sense of humor, called it "adult tag" as the stakes were high.

Kalashnikov rounds occasionally pinged into the mortar pit where Ben and Chris set up the mortar system. For a while, the Taliban mortar team seemed to fall quiet.

"I thought you killed those guys," the team sergeant said when another mortar thudded close to the governor's compound.

"We're going to try again," Chris said.

Ben hovered in the doorway, calibrating the compass watch used to aim the rounds, which involved walking in circles around the mortar pit and adjusting the watch at regular intervals. He was returning to the pit when a Taliban mortar landed right in the middle of it. A huge explosion threw him back several feet. He was inside the textbook kill zone, the area in which a mortar round could potentially be lethal. Chris and one of the medics ran outside and rushed to Ben's side. They swept their hands over his clothes to check for bleeds, but the shrapnel had missed him and he didn't have a scratch.

They spent the day in firefights with the Taliban, trying to clear an area around the governor's compound. The insurgents fired nearly two dozen rockets at one of their trucks, but the battalion would not provide air support because of the risk of civilian casualties. The Afghan commandos' weapons kept jamming in the heat, and mortars continued to land in the vicinity of the compound. It was grueling, and the team was frustrated that the Apaches providing air cover could not fire. Any new areas cleared were returned to the Afghan police, who were supposed to man the checkpoints to avoid ceding ground again.

The team was disappointed to learn that no GPS-guided parachutes, which would have accurately guided supplies into the governor's compound, were left in the country because the US military was no longer supposed to be in combat. Instead, they had to secure a wide zone for a nighttime drop of supplies that were pushed out of a C-130 Hercules, the US Air Force's main cargo transport plane. It was an inaccurate method of resupply because the drop could land hundreds of yards off target, exposing the soldiers to attack while they sought to recover it. After the team drove out, located the supplies, and loaded the boxes onto the vehicles, one of the trucks rolled off the narrow dirt track into a canal on the way back.

It was the truck with the broken remote weapon system, and the gunner, Josh, was riding open turret with his night vision goggles on when it tipped off the road. He plunged headfirst into water with the twenty-two-ton truck on top of him. The rest of the team watched in horror and leapt to pull the crew out of the truck, which was filling with water. Many soldiers had drowned in their vehicles in Afghanistan because the huge armored trucks were ill suited to navigate dirt tracks designed for donkeys and goats. Inside, their teammates were unhurt. Josh had survived, but was in shock. It was his second brush with death—the first was when Matthew had volunteered to drive the bus in his place and the insider attack had occurred.

Later in the week, another mortar hit the base. This time it landed at night in the middle of a group of Afghan commandos. Many were seriously wounded. The medics dealt with the worst of the injuries, plastering one man's back with chest seals in a creative effort to stop the blood loss. The medevac helicopters that were called in landed under fire, performing an incredible maneuver inside the compound. It was a testament to their specialized training and reassuring to the soldiers left on the ground as the helicopters took off.

"Well," Caleb said to the others, "at least someone will come and get us if things get bad."

Jeff's team arrived to pull their truck out of the canal and joined them on a mission to clear a route out of Marjah and conduct a raid on a bazaar.

The goal was to clear a route that would allow the Afghan army to send reinforcements by road, but they had to give up on the mission after advancing just a few miles toward the bazaar. The road was heavily mined, and the commandos refused to occupy the cleared ground. The commandos probably figured they'd end up stranded on the road.

The teams had a meeting, and they all decided to leave Marjah the next morning. The police chief was furious after he found out that both US Special Forces teams were heading off; he threatened to take them to court. The police at the newly erected checkpoints around the city shot at their trucks on the way out.

Caleb estimated that there were between three and six roadside bombs buried in the tarmac, and they didn't have the right equipment to clear them. The team had also taken two members of the Afghan bomb-disposal units into custody after they had apparently threatened to kill their American supervisor for treating them with disrespect. After spending a day at the Lashkar Gah base, the team returned to Camp Antonik.

Maj. Gabriel was waiting at the base. He told the team leaders to eat first, but they wanted to meet straightaway, so they headed to the team room. He told them the team was fired. The team had requested and received air assets and supplies for the mission but had called it off without telling the battalion in advance. Those resources could have been put to use elsewhere. Now another ODA would have to pick up the mission where they had left off. The whole battalion had seen the failure, and the team had lost their last chance to prove themselves.

The captain tried to counter that the commandos had refused to cooperate, but it was too late for explanations. The meeting quickly descended into a shouting match as the rest of the team listened outside. They felt as though Maj. Gabriel was accusing them of cowardice, and the words stung.

Outside, he told them it was their last mission in Helmand. It wasn't conceivable to just swap out their leadership. The team would sit out the rest of the tour at Camp Morehead, the training school for the Afghan commandos in Kabul. The British called it Sandhurst in the Sand after the British officer training academy. Among

Green Berets, it was widely viewed as the dullest assignment in Afghanistan because it didn't involve combat operations. The new team was already on its way to Helmand to swap out.

Caleb felt betrayed. Offensive operations were supposed to be prohibited, and there were no resources to hold cleared ground. No one in the chain of command had articulated a change in rules or tactical guidance, or what they were meant to accomplish. Their presence seemed to be a stopgap solution to prevent Helmand from making the news until the US election in 2016. They all could have died in Marjah. This was the final straw.

"We don't know what our goals are because they keep changing all the time," he exploded. "You don't know what we're supposed to be doing, and yet you keep sending us on crazy missions where we could all die for no reason!"

"That's a cop-out," Maj. Gabriel said, trying to contain his anger. "None of you understand the operational environment."

"Well, whose responsibility is that?" Caleb shot back.

Maj. Gabriel watched him storm out of the room.

CALEB and a couple of other teammates were told to stay in Helmand to help the new team settle in. He had mixed feelings about it. It was hard to watch everyone else leave. As difficult as things had been on the team, they were still going back to Utah together. But he also thought he owed it to the new team, ODA 9115, to assist them. They had little time to prepare for Helmand, and he could help them stay safe. Originally from Washington, they were reputed to be a strong group with good leadership. The leader, Andrew MacNeil, was young but capable, and the sergeant, Dan Gholston, had spent years in 5th Group and had served multiple times in Iraq.

The news of the team's firing spread through the battalion, along with rumors about the team refusing to go on missions. It was exceedingly rare for a team to be fired.

The relief in place mission, in which the incoming and outgoing teams run an operation together, went without a glitch. The teams raided the bazaar in Marjah that they'd been unable to reach by road; intelligence gathered earlier indicated that a stash of weapons was housed there. Caleb thought the evidence of a weapons cache was weak, and he was right. The two teams infilled by helicopter and hiked a couple of miles on foot. In the bazaar, they found only fertilizer and no trace of weapons. He viewed the failure to turn up anything more as confirmation of the lack of leadership at this stage of the war. They could have died for nothing on the road seeded with improvised bombs. *What a shock, fertilizer in a bazaar*, he thought.

But life in the camp underwent a rapid transformation under the new team's leadership. They cleared up the mess caused by the fire and fixed the logistics and supply issues, which meant there was enough food and water to go around. An unpopular army colonel, who had been dispatched there to work with the 215th Corps and treated the Green Berets like his personal staff, was evicted from the Special Forces camp. It was still the place where high-ranking officers and other visitors came to "see the war," but the new team established a schedule for visitors' mealtimes, which gave the resident team a chance to eat first, before hot meals ran out. Caleb began to feel more positive about the deployment for the first time since the insider attack. Everyone got on well, which was a nice change, and pranks became a form of entertainment.

The main instigator was Matthew McClintock, a Charlie, one of the engineer sergeants. He was new to the team, and everyone called him Mick. His primary target was the combat controller, Ryan Rynkowski, or Ski. Mick was qualified as a joint terminal attack controller, which meant he, too, could direct combat aircraft, and he drove Ski crazy by taking over his desk and using the phone that connected to the air supervisor, code-named DOOM01. The supervisor was a woman, and Ski had a crush on her. Mick would occupy Ski's chair and keep DOOM01 on the phone talking about air issues for as long as possible after Ski walked in, to make him jealous.

For some time, Caleb had been thinking about switching to active duty to have a steadier income and schedule, and Mick encouraged him to try. It was a complicated process decided by a board, but Mick told Caleb that his qualifications made him a good candidate. Mick also had a young family and was trying to figure out how to juggle his new commitments with army life. He had served with 1st Group and quit after losing a close friend in Afghanistan in 2013. He blamed the army for the friend's death, but he had missed the camaraderie and lobbied to join the tour with the National Guard that year.

Mick's wife, Alexandra, who lived in Seattle, had just given birth to their first son. She had thick, wavy red hair and tattoos, and they had been married for a year. Mick was given leave to return home for the birth and proudly showed everyone photos when he came back. Alexandra had developed severe postpartum depression but insisted that Mick return to complete the tour. The army would have let him stay in Seattle, but she didn't want to keep him from doing the job he loved. He had gone to great lengths to get on the team and deploy back to Afghanistan. She was devoted to him and felt strong enough to recover on her own.

Caleb predicted that the new team would come under the same pressure to go out on operations, and he was proved right. Their goal for the remainder of the deployment, apparently, was to keep the 215th Corps in Helmand from collapse. The team conducted about one operation a week, and between planning, rehearsals, execution, and refit, the tour started to move at an intense pace. Caleb was relieved to have a busy schedule, but he was unconvinced that the army's leadership had any long-term vision of what they wanted to achieve in Afghanistan, except to avoid a catastrophic loss before the upcoming US election.

CHAPTER 15

Internally Inconsistent, Implausible

HUTCH

HUTCH had been sitting at Bagram Airfield for weeks, waiting for the results of the preliminary investigation into the airstrike on the trauma hospital in Kunduz. It was his first experience with living on one of the army's megabases in Afghanistan. Bagram Airfield, a base first used by the Soviets and then split between rival Afghan warlords, was the heart of US military operations in the country and a major transit hub for cargo, passengers, and troops. Even at this late stage of the war, it was still the size of a small town. Soldiers and contractors ate at fast-food restaurants and shopped at base exchanges; few actually saw the Afghanistan outside the base.

Few seemed aware of the life-or-death battles the Special Forces were fighting in Kunduz or down in Helmand. Hutch tried to keep his spirits up and created a routine to fill the time. He ate, worked out, called home, and repeated. He couldn't tell Tina much over the phone, but he tried to reassure her that everything would be fine once the investigation had run its course. Everyone in his chain of command had reassured him the investigation would find that the strike was a terrible mistake that had occurred in the fog of war, and not a deliberate decision to bomb an international hospital.

Tina tried to put on a brave face as well. She texted Hutch memes and jokes to cheer him up and was careful to keep things light with him. She knew others might be reading any communication that passed between them. She longed to see him and talk face-to-face. The truth was, she was terrified of losing him. On the news, analysts still discussed whether the strike fit the criteria of a war crime, and whether those responsible should be sent to jail. The incident had risen to the attention of President Obama, who had publicly expressed his condolences to the victims.

Tina also feared a revenge attack by the victims' relatives. It was a common concern among special operators and their families and one reason their full names were closely guarded overseas. She reasoned that it wouldn't be hard to find their address, and she would be helpless if someone showed up while she was unloading the groceries or collecting the kids from school. She was on her own, just a mom, who was sick, pregnant, and vulnerable. Hutch felt impotent while talking with her, and he was grateful that she was coping. Other partners might not handle things as well as Tina. "I'm not going to jail," he promised her.

Tina knew that asking questions was futile, but she was scared about what was going to happen to them. The images from the hospital were etched on her mind. She couldn't help but read the terrible stories about the staff and patients who had survived, even if in her heart she knew that Hutch had done his best. There were two sides to every story, and she knew better than anyone that the news rarely reflected what actually happened on the ground. Meanwhile, life continued apace. She planned a high school reunion, Christmas, and New Year's, after which her husband would be home. He could tell her everything then.

Hutch really did believe that everything would be fine—at first. A steady stream of visitors who passed through Bagram Airfield offered him moral support, including two former teammates from previous tours in Paktika. They all seemed to feel sorry for him, and some seemed concerned about his fate. But he had to believe that the investigating officers would realize the soldiers had done their best and the strike was an unfortunate mistake made in the heat of battle. He planned to bravely accept whatever punishment the military saw fit to administer and move on. When a chaplain visited from Kabul, he was shocked to find Hutch in good spirits. He was assessed to be a suicide risk. "I'm fine," Hutch told him, trying to sound upbeat.

Hutch tried to believe it himself, even though his early optimism was fading. The mission had succeeded in driving the Taliban out of Kunduz, sparing its residents a long, costly battle that would have destroyed the city and killed more people than those who died in the hospital. The strike was a terrible mistake, and it should never have happened. But, Hutch reasoned, it would have been worse not to go into the city and take it back decisively.

He began to hear that some in the army's headquarters believed he had violated the rules of engagement and wanted him to stand trial for murder. He tried to fight off the depression and negative thoughts nagging at his brain, keeping to his gym routine and assuring everyone he was fine. He was called in for questioning over and over. He felt that people would understand if they heard firsthand how the mistake had occurred. The US military's repeated change of story, followed by the secrecy surrounding the investigation, fueled the public's worst suspicions. Hutch asked to be allowed to explain publicly what had happened. The battalion told him it wasn't a good idea.

Toward the end of the investigation, Brig. Gen. Kim approached Hutch. He didn't believe Hutch's version of events.

"Would you like to change your story?" he asked.

Hutch was outraged.

"No, I don't want to change my story, sir," he said.

Hutch couldn't believe that anyone would question his integrity. He had sacrificed so much for the army. The terrible patrols in Ramadi at the height of the Iraq war. The back-to-back tours in the mountains in Paktika, spent in isolation in service of the Village

Stability Operations. He couldn't count how many times he'd put his life on the line. It finally sunk in how bad this situation could turn out to be. Reluctantly, he stopped cooperating with the investigation and asked for time to consult with his defense counsel, and he asked for written questions in advance.

The biggest question seemed to challenge his assertion that the Afghan commandos planning the raid on the NDS prison had been near the target and under fire at the time of the strike. A picture from a drone feed appeared to show that the Afghan convoy was parked near Kunduz Airfield, about nine kilometers away from the Taliban-controlled intelligence-agency compound. It seemed to show that Hutch had called a preemptive strike on the building, before the commandos had even set off, a violation of the rules of engagement that prohibited offensive strikes against the Taliban.

He was confused. He had been following the Afghan commando convoy's movements on a GPS tracker and remembered seeing the blue pentagram, indicating friendly forces near the NDS prison at the time of the strike. He started to doubt himself for the first time. Perhaps the gunshots he'd heard had nothing to do with the commandos' mission.

Oh my god, he thought. *How could I have gotten all this stuff wrong?*

On October 28, 2015, Hutch went for his final interview. There were two general officers investigating the strike and several subject matter experts. It seemed clear that the investigators didn't believe his answers. He had been through the same line of questioning repeatedly. When they got to the airstrike, the lead investigator, US Army major general William Hickman, again asked how he had determined that the individuals at the site were hostile, since they weren't carrying weapons. He also seemed skeptical of the decision to call for air support for the commandos on the mission to retake the Taliban-controlled NDS prison.

"Okay, you kind of said two different things here," Gen. Hickman said, trying to pin down where Hutch believed the commandos were at the time of the strike. "They're at the intersection taking—you believe—taking fire, and I am trying to understand how you identified where the fire was coming from, and decided where to fire the AC-130 at."

"Yes, sir, it made the most sense that they would be receiving fire from down off the long east-west roads and since that's where I expected them to go," Hutch said, frustrated, referring to their target, the NDS prison.

It was difficult to convey the life-or-death decisions that had to be made in the heat of the battle with only limited communications and equipment.

"Okay, but you authorized fire to be fired into a building on the NDS facility?" he said.

"Yes, I did," Hutch said.

There was silence.

"Okay, that's all I got," the general said, wrapping up.

It would be months before Hutch would find out that the image of the convoy near Kunduz Airfield was labeled incorrectly as the 10th Special Operations Kandak. It was a different group of commandos that had been flown in from Kabul to deal with the crisis and was using local vehicles. The national tracking system team had attached a note to the picture explaining that the tracking system hadn't updated codes for the new commandos, but the investigators had missed it. A follow-up investigation months later would catch the memo and find the convoy that Hutch was tracking near the NDS compound after all, where they had come under fire.

The team that had fought with Hutch in Kunduz continued to fume over their treatment and saw him as a scapegoat. In their view, the generals were responsible for sending them to Kunduz in the first place; there were known risks to sending troops into a heavily populated, civilian area. They had recaptured Kunduz as requested and ought to be recognized for their bravery instead of punished for a strike.

The Bagram team captain, Pat Harrigan, was among the many witnesses asked to fill out a sworn statement as part of the investigation. Before turning it in, he approached Col. Johnston, the battalion commander, to read him his answers, which were highly critical of US Army leadership in Afghanistan.

"I want to make sure you understand this isn't leveled at you," Pat said. "I know there's going to be blowback from this. I just want you to know what I'm writing."

"I can't stop you from writing whatever you need to write in your sworn statement," Col. Johnston said. "But yeah, you'll hear about it again," he added, though Pat already knew that.

The battalion commander had his own frustrations with the way the investigation was being handled, but he kept them to himself. Pat was right: his testimony would have repercussions, but he seemed determined to share it. Pat was already talking about leaving the army.

Pat's written response contained a blistering critique of US military leaders, accusing them of moral cowardice and a profound lack of strategy in their handling of the Kunduz crisis. "Inaction or indecision does, however, enable convenient political expedience, where one can reap the rewards of success without facing the responsibility or consequence of failure," he wrote. "A leader can smile for the camera while handing out an award, or sidestep the bailiff when the gavel drops on the Judge's bench."

No military commander should ever let his men leave the wire without a task, purpose, and end state, Pat wrote, quoting a lesson taught in the Special Forces. He described how the battalion had been left without direction by Gen. Swindell at the Special Operations Joint Task Force and Gen. Campbell at Resolute Support headquarters.

He continued:

No fewer than three times did [redacted] call and ask for the level of commitment from SOTF, who called SOJTF, who called COM-RS [Resolute Support]. Sadly, the only sounds audible were the sounds of crickets from the PHQ [police headquarters] center square, though those were hard to hear over the gunfire.... How have we as a force, as a group of officers become so lost? I will tell you how. It is a decrepit state that grows out of the moral cowardice, careerism and compromise devoid of principle, exchanged for cheap personal gain.... Decisive strategy is costly, but would alleviate the recurrence of Kunduz in the future. Unfortunately for the man on the ground and his family back home, decisive strategy must be planned and executed outside the chains of moral cowardice.... If someone must be held accountable, let it not be the man who was ordered to sky-dive without being given a parachute.

As Pat predicted, Kunduz would fall again, almost exactly a year later.

WHEN THE INVESTIGATION was complete, Gen. Hickman gave Hutch a heavily redacted version of the three-thousand-page report, which included interviews with at least sixty-five people, transcripts from the aircraft, and evidence drawn from drone and satellite feeds. The executive summary said that the ground force commander had illegally ordered a devastating airstrike without properly identifying the targets, resulting in the substantial loss of civilian life.

"The GFC's decision to provide pre-assault fires and the aircraft's employment of fires in a deliberate, nondiscriminatory, and offensive manner without positive identification of a threat resulted in substantial civilian casualties, significant collateral damage to the Médecins Sans Frontières Trauma Center, and operational failure," the executive summary said. "[Redacted] willfully violated the ROE [rules of engagement] and tactical guidance by improperly authorizing offensive operations."

The report described Hutch's account of events as implausible, partly based on the misidentified drone photo, which appeared to show that the commandos on the mission to retake the NDS were in the wrong location, near the airport.

"The [redacted] Version of events surrounding his decision to authorize the strike is internally inconsistent, implausible, and contradicted by other available sources of credible information," the report said.

Hutch was shocked. He could accept having made a mistake and that civilians had died as a result. He could accept that it was preventable, and he was prepared for any punishment the military saw fit to administer. But to be accused of trying to cover it up? That was too much. It couldn't be real. Everyone in his chain of command had told him not to worry. Not only did it seem like his career in the army was over—he was lucky not to stand trial for mass murder. It felt like a nightmare that he couldn't wake up from.

The results of the investigation were turned over to the top US commander, Gen. Campbell, for review. A couple of weeks later, Hutch was summoned to Gen. Campbell's office at the US military headquarters in Kabul. It was located in a security bubble nicknamed the Green Zone after the one in Baghdad. The helicopter touched down on the soccer field, which doubled as a landing zone, and Hutch made his way over to the building occupied by the leaders of the war.

Gen. Campbell invited Hutch to sit down in his office and asked him if there was anything he wanted to add. Another officer, Gen. Buchanan, was in the room. Hutch had prepared a small speech: he said he recognized he'd made a terrible mistake, but he still believed that he had acted legally and morally and done his best in a difficult situation. He blamed his errors on fatigue and lack of sleep and pleaded for his job.

"I fully accept responsibility for all this," he told the generals. "I want to keep serving."

Gen. Campbell looked grim. He told Hutch that he had reviewed the report and determined that Hutch had violated his tactical guidance. He was relieving Hutch of command, effectively ending Hutch's career as an officer on the spot. Gen. Campbell handed him a pen and sheet of paper to sign.

Hutch felt the blood drain from his face as he picked up the pen. His hand trembled so badly that he almost couldn't write his own name. He wrote his signature on a dotted line and then realized he'd signed on the date line. He scratched his name out and signed again. He stared at the mess on the page in stunned silence.

Gen. Campbell watched without offering any reassurance or words of encouragement. Gen. Buchanan gave Hutch a pep talk, and advised him to put the experience behind him and move on to a stage of life outside the army. Still in total shock and feeling shaky, Hutch nodded.

His battalion commander, Col. Johnston, was waiting for him outside.

"I've been relieved of command," Hutch told him.

Col. Johnston couldn't believe it. All along, he'd told Hutch not to worry, that the investigation would get to the bottom of what had happened. He viewed Hutch as one of the most promising officers in the battalion. The circumstances of his dismissal didn't merely end his career in the army. They could make it difficult for him to get hired in the civilian world as well.

They went to the Thai restaurant on the base to kill time before the flight back to Bagram Airfield. Hutch stabbed at his food, feeling depression sink in. It was hard to reconcile how his whole life had led him here. He had given everything to his career in the army, and this was how it was going to end?

GEN. CAMPBELL APPEARED at headquarters in Kabul on November 25, 2015, to read a statement to the media summarizing the findings of the investigation into the Kunduz hospital bombing. He called it a tragic and avoidable accident and said some of those involved didn't follow the rules of engagement and had been suspended pending disciplinary review.

He said the investigation concluded that human error, along with technological and system failures, had led the US aircraft to bomb the wrong building. He declined to take questions. Afterward, his spokesman would not say how many US service members had been suspended or address a question about whether responsibility might lie farther up the chain of command.

Médecins Sans Frontières was outraged by Gen. Campbell's remarks and renewed calls for an independent investigation.

"It is shocking that an attack can be carried out when US forces have neither eyes on a target nor access to a no-strike list, and have malfunctioning communications systems," Christopher Stokes, the organization's general director, said in a statement. "The frightening catalogue of errors outlined today illustrates gross negligence on the part of US forces and violations of the rules of war."

Meanwhile, at Bagram, Hutch packed his belongings and focused on getting a flight home before Christmas. At the last minute he succeeded, finding a seat on a plane with a group of Rangers; they landed at Hunter Army Airfield in Savannah, Georgia. He rented a car and drove home to wait for Tina and the kids to get back from her high school reunion. It was strange to be in their empty house. She had unpacked and set up all the furniture while he was gone.

She called to tell him they were less than an hour away. He felt incredibly happy to be home and lay on their bed to rest for a few minutes. Afghanistan seemed so far away, like another life. Hutch closed his eyes. It was as though Kunduz had never happened.

Tina pulled up at the house. She hadn't told the girls that their father was home. It was going to be a big surprise. He was safe. That was all that mattered at the moment. The kids would be so excited to have him back in time for Christmas. She went to the front door and knocked. His car was in the driveway, but no one came to the door.

She spent what felt like an eternity banging on every door and window, fearing the worst, as the girls protested to be let out of the car. Then she heard a click, and a sleepy-looking Hutch appeared sheepishly behind the door. He threw his arms around her, and the girls flew out of the car and ran to hug him. The family enjoyed their evening together, trying to get back to normality. Then the girls went to bed and the house fell silent.

Tina led Hutch to their room and sat him down. She was five months pregnant and showing.

"Tell me everything," she said, urgently. "What's going to happen to you? What's going to happen to us?"

He related the entire series of events, ending with the report that had been sent to the US Army Special Operations Command, who would review the investigation and decide on the appropriate punishment. They would have to wait for answers.

CHAPTER 16

Sangingrad
CALEB

CALEB was the one to help the new team settle into Camp Antonik in Helmand, as Matthew Roland had when Caleb's team first arrived. The swap had happened in days, and the new team hadn't had a chance to do their intelligence preparation, a process that normally took place in the months leading up to a deployment. Caleb immediately became the senior Fox on the team, and they relied on him to help plan a campaign for the remainder of the tour.

Andy MacNeil, the captain of the new team, thought it would be best to focus on a specific area instead of firefighting all over Helmand. It seemed that the previous team had chased the Taliban from one spot to the other, leaving them always a step behind. He submitted a campaign plan that focused on easing pressure on Lashkar Gah, the provincial capital, by systematically clearing the route to Marjah.

Caleb shared what limited intelligence his team had gathered. US intelligence assets in Helmand were severely reduced, and even the computers that stored intelligence had been sent back to the United States, so there was no historical record of attacks in the province—something that would have been helpful.

The team set their sights on destroying a Soviet ZPU-4, a quadruple-barreled antiaircraft gun, that they had spotted on a drone feed. A Taliban commander liked to parade it on a truck while driving through villages, passing out RPGs to rally crowds. In earlier years, the team would have been cleared to take it out with an airstrike, but this wasn't an option due to the restrictions on engagement and concerns about civilian casualties. The team decided to target it in person.

Maj. Gabriel interrupted the planning cycle with orders to leave immediately for Sangin. Sangin district had been known to British troops as the deadliest place in Afghanistan during the four years in which they were responsible for Helmand before handing it over to the Americans. They nicknamed it Sangingrad after the World War II siege by German troops of Stalingrad, where thousands perished during the Nazi invasion of Russia. The team was ordered to prepare for a joint multiday operation with the Afghan commandos, to prevent the district from falling.

They usually operated at night and left the site of the operation by morning, but Gen. Swindell, the top commander of US and NATO Special Operations, wanted them to stay overday, or through a period of daylight. The sudden enthusiasm for multiday operations was apparently linked to a successful 3rd Group operation in the north that had unearthed a huge cache of Taliban weapons. Andy didn't like the idea of staying through the day. The team was isolated, and the strict limitations on air support made them wary of being out during daylight hours in Sangin, when they would lose the element of surprise and the advantage of night vision.

With brown hair and freckles, Andy was one of the youngest captains in the company. He was brand new to the Special Forces and full of enthusiasm, but he wasn't reckless. He was a former infantryman and had previously deployed to Iraq, where backup troops had never been more than ten or twenty minutes away. He tried unsuccessfully to convince his superiors to let the team leave Sangin before sunrise.

THE TEAM LANDED in Sangin district in Chinooks after the usual discussion with the air force over how close they could get to the district capital, also named Sangin. They were dropped in the brown zone, miles away from the town, and had to hike the rest of the way through mud carrying ninety pounds of gear each. The long distance increased their chances of being spotted.

The town was a labyrinth, and it was hard to imagine patrolling there every day like the Marines and British troops had done before them. Once inside, the Afghan commandos cleared a path by arresting a local resident and forcing him to walk in front of them as a "local guide" on the assumption that he would know where the bombs were buried. Andy found the Afghan commandos difficult to work with and questioned some of their moral choices, but in the end it was their country and not worth losing rapport arguing about everything.

To cover more ground, the team split up into three elements: a command element, led by Andy, and two maneuver elements, one led by Dan Gholston, the team sergeant, and the other by the warrant officer from Caleb's old team. Warrant officers worked as assistants to the team captains. They were looking for compounds used by the Taliban to store weapons and explosives, which were easy to spot because they had been marked with piles of rocks, spray paint, or barbed wire, as a warning to other villagers.

The team had been reprimanded earlier in the night for blowing up a building containing one cache of weapons. When the battalion complained that they weren't allowed to demolish structures, based on new rules introduced after the hospital bombing in Kunduz, the team blamed the Afghan commandos for blowing it up. The Afghans didn't have to follow the US rules.

Caleb was assigned to work with his warrant. When they came to a compound marked with white rocks several hours into the operation, Dan sent the bomb disposal unit to help them clear it.

Kevin, the bomb disposal technician, was on his third day in Helmand. A deputy sheriff in Alabama before joining the military, he was rapidly adjusting to the realities of the field. He didn't have a translator, and his Afghan partner with the civilian mine removal group spoke no English. They communicated with hand signals. They liked each other immediately. The Afghan disarmed the first bomb. Kevin had trained for this moment a thousand times, but he was still nervous. He disarmed his first bomb just inside the entrance to the compound, where two were buried in the ground. The explosive ordnance disposal units had a motto: "Initial success or total failure."

The first building inside the compound contained a stash of artillery rounds and pressure plates of all sizes, used to make the bombs that were buried in roads. Kevin heard Caleb call the dog handler over.

"Hey, send that dog down there," Caleb said, pointing to an escape tunnel he'd discovered just outside one of the larger rooms.

"I'm not sending the dog without me," the handler replied.

The warrant handed Caleb his rifle, dropped onto his hands and knees, and crawled inside. Caleb saw his feet disappear into the darkness several yards away. He emerged after a few moments, unscathed, giving the handler a look of contempt.

"Clear," he said.

That guy is extremely ballsy and kind of fucking stupid, Caleb thought. There was a fine line between the two. If an ordnance had gone off, it would have put everyone else in danger, as they'd be left to deal with the warrant's injuries and the medevac.

They still hadn't found any explosives, so they continued to search the compound for the last components of the bomb-making factory. Improvised explosive devices (IEDs) were made of three parts: the explosive charge, the outer casings that contained the explosives and fragmented into shrapnel, and an initiating system that could be made from a range of household devices like radios, switches, and timers.

Just before sunrise they found the stash of explosives in a small shack at the edge of the compound. Caleb sent the handler with the dog to check it out, along with the Afghan bomb disposal team. After the area was clear, he stepped in to survey the contents. The explosives were homemade.

Great, he thought, *we're done here*. He stepped back out of the doorway, placed a foot by the entrance, and heard a tremendous explosion. A powerful force swept through his body and lifted him into the air. He sailed for several feet and landed hard on the ground, unconscious. He woke up as the dust was settling and tried to grasp what had happened. He realized he had triggered a pressure plate bomb near the entrance of the shack. There were screams from the Afghans inside who had been wounded by shrapnel. He was covered in dirt, and his eyes and throat burned. He looked down to check for injuries.

Oh my god, he thought, momentarily horrified. *I'm going to die.*

There was almost nothing left of his right leg. His left foot was gone too, and the rest of the limb up to his knee was a mass of white, shredded bone, tissue, and dust.

I'm going to die, he thought again, reflexively grabbing the tourniquets from his belt to stop the loss of blood.

In the initial aftermath of an explosion, muscle spasms shut off any bleeding, but once the bleeding started, every second counted. Caleb managed to slip the tourniquets over the remains of his legs, but they had to be yanked tight to prevent the flow of blood. He was in shock and his strength was sapping. He battled the feelings of horror and fear, trying to twist the tourniquets tighter.

Within moments, two of his teammates were at his side and grimly tightened both tourniquets as far as they'd go, heaving to shut off the circulation in his thick, muscular thighs. Caleb howled in pain. They dragged him several meters away from the blast site without checking for other bombs buried around them. A medic appeared with an injection of ketamine, and the world went blurry.

"Was that you guys?" Andy called over the radio. Silence.

He tried again. He was hoping they had blown up a second cache and forgotten to warn the others over the radio, but he knew deep down they would never make that mistake.

"Was that you guys?" he said again, with a sinking feeling.

The warrant came on the line.

"It was us," he responded.

Caleb felt the world starting to fade away.

Andy left his element behind and sprinted toward the sound of the explosion, forgetting everything else. When he reached the compound, he saw the explosives technician, Kevin, dazed and covered in dust. On the ground, safe paths were mapped out with chalk, and glow sticks indicated buried bombs. He stopped at the entrance, trying to see through the smoke and dust. There was a metallic smell in the air.

"Kevin!" he shouted. "Where can I walk?"

Kevin seemed concussed. He eventually gestured at a route in the dirt.

Andy followed his directions, turned the corner, and ran straight into a scene of chaos. It was his worst nightmare. The ground was covered in men who were coated in dust and stained with blood, screaming. One of the Afghans was blinded. He found Caleb, pale and unmoving on the ground, and saw his injuries with horror. At first he thought Caleb was dead. A couple of teammates were working on him. The dog handler was losing blood from a wound on his backside. The blast had partially exposed a huge, 155mm artillery round buried outside the shack and a stack of 140mm rockets.

"Need some guys over here right now," Andy yelled into the radio. "One of our guys has lost his legs, and others are badly wounded."

He was appalled. He had trained for a mass casualty in a minefield scenario but had never seen one of this magnitude. He dropped to a knee and started to pack the dog handler's wound. It occurred to him that he was supposed to be running the show, not down in the weeds. He turned the handler's injuries over to one of the others, had Ski, the combat controller, call for medevac, and then went to work on a landing zone for the medevac. About two hundred meters away from the blast site, Dan found an open field that was large enough to land a helicopter. It was going to be extremely tight because of the mass of power lines running along the sides, but it was freshly tilled, which meant it was unlikely to be mined.

The rest of the team secured the perimeter, positioning a sniper on the rooftop and the Carl Gustaf recoilless rifle, an 84mm anti-tank weapon, on one of the corners, meanwhile taking cover from the shots that zinged across the field. They tried to shoot two gunmen who ran across the landing zone, but the runners were too fast. Across the compound, the soldiers working on the casualties found Taliban stretchers, loaded the wounded, and made a dash through the soft, muddy field designated as the landing zone.

Out of nowhere, another man in local civilian clothes and carrying an automatic rifle broke into the field and sprayed a volley of fire in the direction of the American soldiers, somehow missing everyone and then vanishing into a compound. Mick and two other teammates leapt up with several commandos and tore after him into the mud-brick settlement. Inside, there was a courtyard and three rooms, but there was no sign of the shooter, who had evidently fled.

It was hard to see how the helicopter could land under fire in the narrow field without hitting a wall or getting caught in the lines. The sun was already up and the blue sky was streaked with clouds. The Black Hawks came in incredibly fast and low over the surrounding farmland. Andy was impressed by how expertly the pilots maneuvered the aircraft to the ground, kicking up a storm of dust while taking fire. In minutes, they loaded the casualties and the helicopters were gone.

The team sat against the walls of the compound, taking a moment to rest and process what had just happened. Andy wondered if they'd see Caleb alive again.

Col. Johnston told them to call him using Iridium, a private satellite network, to discuss the mission, rather than the countrywide SATCOM. He asked what they wanted to do. Andy consulted with the team sergeant. A couple of the guys urged them to stay and find whoever had done this. They agreed to continue the mission as planned and exfil (extract from enemy territory) at night. It would be bad for morale to cut and run now, Andy thought, and it was safer to leave in the dark anyway.

The next job was to clear up the compound where Caleb had been wounded. Any bandages, blood, or equipment left behind could be used by the insurgents as propaganda. They found all his gear, except for his night vision goggles, which they suspected might be buried inside the shack with the explosives. They called Col. Johnston back to ask him to request an airstrike. Gen. Swindell gave approval to strike the cache on the condition that they clear an area of one hundred meters around the site.

It was impossible; every time the area was clear and the team pulled back, villagers emerged to see what had happened. The aircraft would radio back to say that the area still wasn't clear. Kevin stepped forward with an alternative plan. He carried explosives with him and could blow it up in place instead. Andy was reluctant.

"The risk is too high, and I'm not getting anyone else hurt in that compound," he told Kevin.

Kevin insisted, and got the job done. The blast flattened the shack. An officer from the battalion came on the radio with a complaint from Gen. Swindell, who was still watching the mission from the operations center.

"The general wants to know why you blew up the structure," the officer said.

"What? You just told me I could drop a missile on it, and we decided we could take care of it ourselves, with less risk to civilians," Andy said.

"Well you're not allowed to blow up structures," the officer said. "We're going to have to talk about this later."

Andy was irate, but said nothing. It was a shack that had just injured a group of guys, and it had been half destroyed anyway. *Goddamn political bullshit.* The team huddled with the Afghans and continued the clearing operation until the following night.

At Camp Antonik, surgeons battled to save Caleb. In addition to blood loss and bacterial infections caused by the soil, the explosion had caused a swelling in his brain that could be deadly. The surgeons also tried to preserve what remained of his left leg, to avoid a second amputation.

Once the rest of the team had returned to Camp Antonik and things had quieted down, Andy talked with the team sergeant, Dan, about how the mission had gone down. He was still processing everything that had happened and was glad to have the company. The events replayed in his mind like a scene from a movie. It was sheer luck that they hadn't detonated any other explosives in the effort to evacuate the casualties.

"Be careful on the radio," Dan told him, as they sat outside under the stars.

Dan explained that the graphic description of Caleb's injuries over the radio could have upset the team. In the future, you need to project calm, he told Andy. Not just for the rest of the ODA, but for all the attached specialists and infantry personnel as well.

"You're the captain, Andy," he said. "When shit hits the fan, the team looks to you. They'll key in on even the smallest inflection in your voice. Make sure you always broadcast calm."

Andy would never forget the lesson.

Mick called Alexandra to let her know he was safe. She was starting to recover from her postpartum depression. She liked her therapist and expected to complete her course of treatment by the time he came home. She was hoping to be well enough by the time Mick got back to take baby Declan to New Mexico to meet Mick's family and spend a few weeks with them. She was shocked to hear about Caleb but was determined not to worry about her husband. She knew he was good at his job and would be home soon. She focused on getting better in time for his return.

IT WAS ALMOST MIDNIGHT in Arizona when the first call came in. Ashley, exhausted, was in bed and drifting off when her phone rang. It was a Utah number. She half opened her eyes. It was probably Caleb. She moved to answer it, but felt a crushing tiredness overwhelm her. Caleb would forgive her. She had to be up in a few hours to get the children ready for preschool and day care, and then go to work. She really needed to sleep. The same number rang again. This time, she answered.

"This is Major Sam Campbell, from 19th Special Forces Group," the officer on the line said. "Can I speak with Ashley Brewer?"

"Speaking," she said, dreading what was to come next.

"There's been an accident," he said. "I called to tell you this: Caleb's heart is pumping and he's breathing."

She paused. A million different possible outcomes raced through her mind. She had known Caleb would be different when he came back because it had been a tough deployment. But she hadn't prepared for the possibility that he might not come back.

"What happened?" she asked weakly.

The officer told her that Caleb had stepped on an IED during an operation. At this stage, he'd lost his right leg. It wasn't clear if it was above or below the knee. A team of surgeons was working to save the left one. He promised to call her back with an update as soon as he heard more.

Ashley hung up, in shock. She called her mom, who came immediately. She waited for the officer's follow-up call while falling asleep on the couch, phone in hand.

The surgeons gave up on Caleb's left leg after about sixty blood transfusions. That number was far beyond the recommended, but they had lived with him on the base and didn't want to fail him. The transport plane loaded him for the flight to the Walter Reed National Military Medical Center in Bethesda, Maryland. The medical team on board had an action plan to keep him alive during the long journey. The aircraft would stop in Germany to refuel.

Ashley's phone rang the next morning. It was her mother-in-law, who was beside herself. She was in a panic after having missed a call overnight. When she checked the number on Google, what came up was a Utah National Guard suicide prevention line for veterans. She was in disbelief. Caleb wouldn't commit suicide. She called, and it turned out to be a multiuse number. Eventually someone told her that Caleb had possibly become a double amputee in Afghanistan and was on his way to Germany.

Ashley hadn't heard that Caleb had lost his second leg. She helped calm his mother, who had already suffered more than her share of tragedy after losing one of her three sons to the opioid epidemic. Caleb's mother agreed to make calls while Ashley packed for Walter Reed. Ashley got up from the sofa and operated as though it were a regular day. She took her daughter Evelyn to preschool, where she asked the teacher how to explain what had happened. She had no idea how to break news like this to a five-year-old.

The teacher said to give Evelyn two pieces of information and let her absorb them. "Answer questions if she asks, but don't give her more than that," she explained. "Let her five-year-old brain process the information."

Ashley called her boss, who promised to help in any way she needed. The last step was to figure out where to go: the army had provided conflicting messages about whether Caleb was going to Walter Reed in Maryland or Brooke Army Medical Center in Texas.

After picking up Evelyn from preschool, Ashley told her what had happened. "There's been an accident. Your father has been injured."

Evelyn looked upset.

"Is he going to be okay?"

"Yes."

"How did the accident happen?"

"Well, he stepped on a pressure plate, and it caused an explosion."

"Did someone put the explosives there?"

"Yes."

Evelyn had no more questions after that.

Caleb's kidneys failed on the journey to the United States, and he was unable to breathe on his own because blood clots had formed in his lungs. The medical team kept him alive on a respirator and a dialysis machine. They suspected he had multiple pulmonary embolisms in his lungs—it turned out to be five—likely resulting from the high number of blood transfusions. He had moments of wakefulness in which he was aware of doctors moving him and prodding him. The blurry figures seemed to be part of a dream, or very far away. Caleb was irritated. He just wanted to sleep.

The doctors scrapped the plan to take him all the way to Texas and decided to keep him at Walter Reed until his condition was under control. The infection from bacteria in the dirt was fast becoming the greatest threat to his life after the loss of his legs. One of Caleb's teammates was waiting for Ashley at Dulles International Airport. It was an hour's drive to Walter Reed, and he tried to prepare her for what she would see when they got there.

"He is super swollen," he told her, "and hooked up to a ton of different tubes. He's heavily sedated."

Ashley nodded.

"His legs are both in bandages," he said. "One of his arms is also wrapped up because of a shrapnel wound to his hand."

He paused, waiting for her to process the information.

"But," he said, trying to sound brighter, "he'll know it's you."

They arrived at almost two a.m. He led her to Caleb's room and left them alone. Ashley stood there in shock, absorbing the sight of her husband and what had happened to him. She didn't know what to say. She touched his hair, which was still the same, and took his unbandaged hand in hers. He didn't move. A nurse eventually came in and gave her permission to stay the night. The nurse returned with a warmed blanket. Ashley wrapped herself up and slept next to her husband.

CHAPTER 17

Eagle Down

ANDY

DAN GHOLSTON fit the stereotype of the grizzled team sergeant. He was fair with a ginger beard and a sometimes dark sense of humor. He ran a tight ship but believed respect should be earned regardless of rank. He'd spent almost fifteen years in the military, with three previous tours in Iraq, and had moved to the National Guard from 5th Group. The truth was, seeing Caleb lying in the dirt in Sangin had shaken him.

He was married and had two small children, and it was his first time in combat since they'd been born. His son had been a week old when he'd left. Dan saw himself dying in a godforsaken village in Helmand and imagined his young children growing up with no father, and perhaps no memory of him, and it scared him. As much as he tried to push the image out of his mind, it nagged at him, always lying on the periphery.

He liked working with Andy. Andy was young but pragmatic and a natural problem solver. He listened to his men, and they worked together to fend off the demands of the SOJTF, which seemed intent on using them to firefight all over northern Helmand. Gen. Swindell, the commander, continued to push Special Forces to take advantage of the increased flexibility in the rules and undertake multiday operations. The team resisted, citing the risks of operating for an extended period in a remote location with limited backup. The struggle with air support in Sangin had made them distrustful and aware of the politics at play that could put them at risk.

Soon enough, orders came down the chain to undertake another multiday mission in Sangin. The trigger was a dramatic Facebook post by the district's deputy governor, who claimed that the district center was surrounded by insurgents and everyone was going to die without immediate backup. The team sent their ScanEagle drone over the district center to see what was going on. The drone feed from over the governor's office showed a bored Afghan army soldier throwing rocks into his helmet to pass the time. There was no sign of a siege on the district center, or even an enemy attack. The team eventually tracked insurgents carrying weapons into a safe house and planned a mission to raid it with the commandos. At the site, the target turned out to be a medical clinic as well. One of the men swept up in the raid spoke fluent English and said he worked for an Italian aid group. It was possible. Emergency, an Italian NGO, operated a trauma hospital in Lashkar Gah and maintained a network of clinics and ambulance services in Helmand. Such were the blurred lines in Afghanistan.

Andy and Dan fought off several more multiday missions, convincing the battalion that night missions would be just as effective and staying overday wasn't worth the risk. Then, they received orders to go back to Marjah. There was intelligence that a high-value target might be in the area. Andy and Dan thought the information was bullshit, but their commanders were adamant. The team's best hope, they both believed, was to temporarily disrupt the Taliban's operations in that area and perhaps find a cache of bomb-making equipment to keep the generals happy.

Dan called his wife, Brianne, who was staying with her parents in West Virginia, to let her know they'd be offline for a while. The other soldiers did the same. Mick called Alexandra. Declan was ten weeks old, and Alexandra's spirits were high. In a sign of the progress she'd made overcoming her depression, Alexandra had done all the laundry in one day, which she rarely did in the best of times. She sent Mick photos of the neatly folded clothes as they were being put away and told him that she and Declan were ready for him to come home.

Andy tried to line up all the available air assets for the mission as well as a quick reaction force (QRF), to give them their best hope of getting backup if things went wrong. Several guys were sent from other teams to assist. After waiting a few days for the weather to clear, they took off. The pilots hazed the team on the way in. One joked on Flightnet, the internal flight radio, that the mission seemed to have no clear objective or likely chance of success.

"This is a nut roll," another said.

"Uhh, the ground force commander is plugged into our net," one of the aircrew said, referring to Andy, who was listening, and they fell silent.

They landed west of Marjah and headed east through a muddy network of canals, irrigation ditches, and farmland that made movement extremely difficult. They were knee-deep in bog, soggy and wet by the time they reached the strip where the Taliban cell was supposed to be located. Each home in the area was fortified with tall mud-brick walls, as was Afghan tradition, and coded on a grid. As usual, to cover more ground they split into three elements, two maneuver elements and one command element, each with about twenty-five Afghan commandos. Dan took the lead and cleared the first compound.

After a couple of hours, the silvery moonlight disappeared, and heavy, low-hanging clouds settled over them. The clouds blocked out surveillance aircraft, and medevac went from red to black, meaning it was too dangerous to fly and there would be no air support. Andy paused the mission and told everyone to gather at the designated command-and-control center, which was labeled on the grid as Alpha-64. It was an ordinary Afghan home, with a couple of rooms, a surrounding yard, and tall mud-brick walls. The team chose it as their command center because the residents displayed a normal pattern of life and it was large enough to hold the whole force. Empty compounds could be booby-trapped. The team would wait there until the weather improved and the maneuver elements could push out and continue to search for the high-level target.

The soldiers rounded up the frightened Afghan family living there, separated the men from the women, and ordered them to sit in a side room. It was a much criticized aspect of the long-running war: the use of local homes for shelter or targets in a raid. Both sides continued to do it, an inevitable consequence of fighting an insurgency. The main living area, little more than mud walls with sticks laid across the roof, was empty, save for a stove with a pot for boiling tea. Outside, the yard was ploughed into neat rows, and tiny green sprouts had started to poke out of the earth.

At sunrise, they saw women and children empty out of the village. It was a bad sign. One of the new team guys asked to fly an American flag over the compound, and Dan allowed it. Someone snapped a photo of him climbing the wall with the flag, looking like an astronaut in military uniform on a mud-colored moon.

Jordan Avery, one of the Bravos, began to work on constructing holes in the walls for them to fire through, while others filled sandbags and established defensive positions at the entrance. They set up the 60mm mortar system as well. Each team member had carried one or two rounds on the way in. As soon as the fog began to clear and air support came back, the team split, and the two maneuver elements resumed the clearing operation in the village.

Jordan was back at the compound standing guard when gunfire broke out. It was hard to see where the shots were coming from, but he fired in the direction of the muzzle flashes and tracer rounds. The nearest building lay across an open field. Casey Gursley, an Echo, was next to him and spotted three men in what seemed to be a trench, about three hundred meters away. He fired at them. Behind him, someone screamed. He turned and saw Ski, the combat controller, on the ground clutching his thigh, with blood gushing out.

More shots zinged into the compound. Jordan and Casey rushed to Ski's side and helped fasten a tourniquet on his leg as quickly as possible. Ski was lucky: the bleeding stopped. Shrapnel from the round could travel up to the groin and pierce the femoral artery, which was fed through the iliac arteries that ran straight from the aorta, rendering a tourniquet useless.

"This hurts a lot more than I thought it would," Ski groaned.

Jordan and Casey helped one of the medical sergeants drag him inside, and they quickly cut off his clothing to check for other injuries. The Delta injected Ski with a dose of ketamine to ease the pain. By the time Andy, who had been out leading two of the elements and moving south, rushed back, Ski was moaning incoherently as the ketamine kicked in. The tourniquet had stopped the bleeding, but the medic was worried about the amount of blood Ski had lost and recommended getting him evacuated as soon as possible to save his leg.

Mick, who was at Ski's side trying to calm him down, offered to go outside to direct the medevac helicopter.

CHRIS FLANNERY, an Army Reserve pilot from Kentucky, ran the twenty-four-hour medevac operation for the south. He had been in the country for three months supporting the Green Berets that were operating in Helmand and Kandahar. He had evacuated Caleb from Sangin in December. His flight crew had trained to be wheels-up within six to eight minutes of receiving a call, sometimes even less.

Flannery was stationed at Camp Dwyer for the Marjah mission and happened to be on duty that morning when reports came in that US troops were under fire and someone had been shot. His crew was ready to go in minutes. It was difficult to make out the terrain through the low-hanging clouds, but eventually he spotted the compound that had been occupied by the US and Afghan soldiers.

There were soldiers on all the walls, and Americans were firing an M240 belt-fed machine gun at a Taliban position outside the compound. Medevac helicopters always flew in pairs, and Flannery, who flew the lead Black Hawk into the firefight, approached the field flying low and fast, banking at intervals to avoid the gunfire.

The soldiers waiting with Ski's litter pressed against the building, feeling the volume of fire on the compound triple as the helicopter descended to about fifty feet from the ground.

Mick, trying to guide in the aircraft with smoke grenades, was frustrated to learn that the crew hadn't dialed in their radio frequency, so they couldn't communicate directly. Flannery circled the building and made an approach. He could see the gunfire and that the courtyard was small, but this was a scenario he had prepared for in training. And he had managed to do it in Sangin. His flight medic saw fire from the left, so Flannery tried to land the aircraft right where he spotted smoke rising from the muddy ground.

Mick noticed that the helicopter was landing in the wrong direction, but he hoped for the best. The soldiers waiting with Ski turned their backs to the helicopter to avoid the blast of dust. Flannery landed the aircraft inside the compound and then felt it sink deep into the mud and shake ominously. For a moment, he wondered if they'd been hit. One of the soldiers gestured at him to hit the gas, but he knew it was too late and performed an emergency shutdown. The helicopter might fly with rotor damage, but there was no way it would make it out of the firefight in that condition.

Jordan felt giant clods of mud hit the back of his head. He turned around and his heart dropped. The helicopter had sunk about a foot into the ground, causing the rotor to tilt to the right, smack into the thick mud wall surrounding the compound. The helicopter was their only way to get Ski out, and that thing wasn't going to fly again. He realized grimly that their situation was about to get a lot worse. They were going to be stuck babysitting the helicopter until the recovery crew came in, and a downed Black Hawk would invite attacks from all over the district.

The second medevac helicopter made an approach and attempted to land in an adjacent field to the north, while Mick tried again to mark the position with a smoke grenade. He had to expose himself to the intensifying gunfire each time he bounded into the landing zone. It was no use: the damaged Black Hawk seemed to have drawn the entire town into a swarm around the compound. The second aircraft, hit repeatedly by gunfire, swerved once again and lifted away. The teams watched it disappear on the horizon. It turned out the pilot had been shot in the leg, and her helicopter had been hit twelve or thirteen times.

The compound was taking mortar fire, and tracer rounds landed at the soldiers' feet as gunfire intensified around them. The medic and crew on board the aircraft went inside to tend to Ski, freeing up the team to defend the compound. Flannery felt crushed and responsible for the situation. He apologized to the flight crew and asked the Special Forces team how they could be helpful. Casey and his teammates took the extra ammunition the aircrew had brought. The Afghan commandos were given positions along the walls.

Andy took several guys, including Jordan and a small group of Afghan commandos, to the north to get eyes on the building that was firing at them and to direct the Apaches that had arrived to provide air support. They got pinned down by gunfire after several bounds. They crouched for cover behind a dirt berm that stood a couple of feet high, trying to be as small as possible. Red-hot tracer rounds used to help shooters aim their sights burned out in the mud in front of them. Andy tried to get the Apaches to fire on two buildings farther north, but the pilots refused.

"Look, I'm the GFC," Andy told the crew in the Apaches. "I'm telling you, we're taking fire and we need you to fire on these buildings, now."

As the GFC, he could order the Apaches to provide close air support to aid US troops under fire. But after the Kunduz hospital strike, concerns about civilian casualties were especially high. The crew responded that they weren't allowed to fire at buildings if they couldn't see a hostile target. The Apaches circled, unable to spot anyone to shoot, and fired into the empty fields instead. Andy continued to argue with the pilots, but they refused to fire.

When it became clear the pilots wouldn't shoot, Jordan tried to mark the building with a flare while the team's Fox, who had been a mortar man in the infantry, attempted to hit the target with 60mm mortars, but it didn't work and eventually Andy decided to turn back.

The team was told there would be no more medevacs until they could secure a landing zone. It turned out that a third medevac helicopter had been forced to pull away after a round hit the gunner's window frame and sent an explosion of shrapnel into his face. It was devastating news. One of the mortars had already landed inside the compound and struck the downed Black Hawk. If the insurgents managed to hit the main building or blow through one of its walls, they could be overrun.

Dan took a team out with some of the commandos to try clearing a neighboring compound that was being used to shoot at them. They headed south through an empty canal. Dan could hear bullets zing over their heads. After several bounds, they were pinned down again. Jordan fired back at the muzzle flashes coming from narrow holes carved into the walls of a building about a hundred meters away, to cover for Andy, who was on the radio with the officer monitoring the battle from the tactical operations center at Bagram Airfield. He was still trying to get the two Apaches that were on station to provide air support.

"Tell those pilots to listen to us," Andy told the battle captain on the radio, remembering Dan's advice to broadcast calm, even though it felt like they were running out of options. "We need air support now!"

The battle captain was resolute. The rules of engagement allowed the GFC to call for air support. They couldn't fire on the buildings surrounding the compound unless the pilots could physically see the shooters, because there could be civilians inside. The guidance from Gen. Swindell was to clear civilians from a hundred-meter radius around the target. He denied the request on the spot.

"Fight the fight," he told Andy. "Fight the fight."

Andy couldn't believe it. They'd agreed to the multiday mission in Marjah against their better judgment, and now the army was going to leave them hanging without air support? He felt a huge burden of responsibility toward all the men he'd brought on the mission. Fight the fight? What was that supposed to mean? *Fuck them.*

He ran across the yard to find Dan. They huddled with the guys that had returned from the field to discuss what to do next. The flight crew medic continued to work on Ski, who had been in a tourniquet for more than two hours. He had given him a blood transfusion, but Ski still didn't have a radial pulse, a sign that his blood pressure remained dangerously low. The crew also patched up some of the wounded commandos. The team felt they had to do something or else they would be left sitting there waiting to get hit by mortars and die. There was clearly no help coming from the battalion.

They decided to keep trying to secure a landing zone to get Ski and the flight crew out, to give them more flexibility to maneuver. Andy suggested trying south again. Dan didn't think it was worth another attempt and proposed going east this time. They settled on a plan to move east, clear two buildings to give them supporting fire from different positions, and create a triangle that would allow a helicopter to land in the middle. They all knew it could be bad, but they were out of options to save their friend and teammate.

Jordan had already fired half the magazines he'd brought with him. As a Bravo, he knew that the tempo of the gunfight was not sustainable. Everyone carried a double basic—about fourteen or more magazines—and at that rate, they would burn through the lot of them in hours. He shared a cigarette with Casey, thinking it could be his last.

"Man, we're going to get lit up out there," Jordan said, breaking the silence.

"We have to do it," Mick said without hesitation. "We have to do it for Ski."

Dan led the team out of the compound, taking Jordan, Mick, Casey, and others, including Kevin, the bomb disposal technician. They slipped into an irrigation canal that ran south and moved forward in bounds, running for meters at a time and then dropping down. The canal was filled with water. They kept their heads low to avoid the gunfire that came at the compound from all directions. They were almost waist-deep in muddy water, and it was cold. Jordan thought it was the last thing he should be worrying about.

Jordan was sure that he'd die every time he got up to run. They moved in single file along the ditch; one teammate ran while the others provided covering fire. RPGs and mortars landed on either side of them. He could see the bullets tearing leaves off the trees behind them. On the fifth or sixth bound, he got up and ran again, feeling the bullets crack and whiz around him. When he completed the bound, he dropped onto the ground and turned to provide covering fire for Mick, who was behind him. He didn't appear. Jordan knew immediately what had happened.

"FUCK!" he screamed, and ran back to where Mick was floating facedown in the canal.

Jordan reached him and pulled his head up out of the water. Mick had a bullet entry wound under his helmet and was completely unresponsive.

"Get the fuck down!" Dan shouted.

Jordan yanked Mick over his lap and held his head, but his friend seemed to be dead. He was the first KIA—killed in action—of the day, and Jordan wondered how many more there would be before they got out. He saw another teammate firing over the berm next to him. Each time Casey poked his rifle over the edge, the ground exploded all around them. The Taliban had accurately dialed in their position, and the soldiers were spread out in the canal about a hundred meters away from Alpha-64, a long distance to cover in a water-logged ditch under fire.

"We have a probable KIA, and we're getting chewed up pretty bad," Jordan yelled on the radio. "We're pinned down and completely unable to move."

Dan relayed the situation to Andy and asked for emergency air support. He was pinned down farther ahead with one of the others, who was firing over the berm. Some of the Harris radios they used to communicate had gotten wet and weren't working. A Delta, who was on loan from a Texas team, reached Mick and checked his vitals.

"He's alive," he said over the radio.

Dan corrected the message on the radio to Andy. There was nothing they could do while trapped in the ditch except keep Mick's head above the water and his neck straight.

Jordan saw a mortar land in the berm in front of Kevin, who dived to the ground, screaming, "FUCK!" Another landed behind them. The Taliban mortar team was bracketing them in. Dan repeated the call over the radio.

"We're pinned down. We need air support now," he said again, trying to sound calm.

Dan couldn't see why the Apaches wouldn't fire. Andy had the second combat controller with him, who was on loan from another team. That was fortunate, because Ski and Mick, who was the only team member that was qualified as a combat controller, were both wounded. The combat controller relayed his request for emergency close air support, giving them Andy's initials, which would make Andy responsible for anything that went wrong with the strike. When an F-16 bomber finally flew overhead, it only carried out a strafing run on an empty field as a show of force that did nothing to stop the volume of fire.

Another mortar landed behind them, sinking into the mud. Dan wondered how long they had been in the ditch. It felt like an eternity. He had been in firefights before, but this was the first time he felt fear. It wasn't death that scared him, but the thought of leaving his wife alone and two young children without a father. He was starting to seriously question his decisions. Why had he come to Afghanistan? An image formed in his mind of his wife and their newborn son at home. He thought of his little daughter, who was still a toddler and probably wouldn't remember him if he died. They had no idea that he was here in this ditch, fighting for survival, perhaps in the final moments of his life.

Dan felt angry with himself for putting everyone in this situation. He thought about Mick's wife and their ten-week-old baby.

Mick could have stayed with them in Seattle. He tried to pull himself together and concentrate on getting them out. He roused himself into action.

"I can't stress this enough," he said on the radio, trying to keep his voice measured. "We are unable to move, completely pinned down. We need air support to take out one of these buildings."

"I know, man, we're doing everything we can. Hang in there," Andy responded.

They waited, returning fire during lapses in the shooting, only for the volume to pick up as soon as they poked their rifles over the berm. There was no sign of air support. They were trapped and freezing, and they couldn't move Mick. Dan told Andy to get the Apaches off station so they could try using the mortars. The Fox lobbed some toward the building, but it was hard to direct them while under fire and without a clear view of the shooters. Bullets started to zip through the canal from the far end.

Jordan realized the Taliban had maneuvered into the canal and were shooting directly at them from inside the ditch. It was a situation known as enfilade fire, the worst possible circumstance they could be in. They had to get out pretty fucking fast. Andy came back on the radio and said that he understood the severity of the situation but was unable to get them air support. The Apaches wouldn't fire. He felt terrible. Dan ordered everyone to retreat back to Alpha-64.

Jordan dropped to his hands and knees trying to figure out how to carry Mick, a two-hundred-pound guy carrying sixty pounds of water-soaked gear. He pushed while another teammate pulled, and the medic kept Mick's head above the water. A fourth carried Mick's weapon and kit. They eventually reached the edge of the compound and waited for covering fire. Most of their rifles were clogged with mud, and Dan's radio was the only one still working. They bounded to the compound and dragged Mick inside. They kept him away from Ski. Death was contagious. They called for the flight medic to come outside instead.

The flight medic saw the gunshot wound to the head and knew that Mick was going to die. He was already showing signs of Cushing's triad, the body's response to a terminal head injury and elevated pressure in the brain, involving increased systolic blood pressure and falling heart rate and respiration. Mick's breathing was erratic and his pulse faint, in the forties. He was also freezing cold in his wet clothing. They cut off Mick's uniform and wrapped him in a blanket to prevent hypothermia. One of the Deltas asked to borrow the medic's ventilator. The medic didn't think it was a good idea, because a ventilator could increase the pressure on Mick's brain, worsening his condition.

"You're better off bagging him," he said.

The medic gave Mick fluids and hooked up a cylinder of oxygen to a mask over his face. The system involved using a manual resuscitator to force-feed air into his lungs. Mick's eyes were fixed, dilated, and unresponsive. The medic worried about using limited medical resources on a casualty who was going to die, but he didn't know how to explain that to Mick's teammates without sounding heartless, so he said nothing. He left the pilot, Flannery, and a crew member to handle the bagging and returned to Ski.

The rest of the guys worked to clear the mud out of their weapons. They were running dangerously low on ammunition, even after distributing the flight crew's ammo among the team and commandos. Jordan's weapon was clogged, so he was using Ski's rifle, and he had only three magazines left. Those wouldn't last long.

The battalion wanted to know Mick's status. Dan approached the team's Deltas.

"What is his condition?" Dan asked them.

"What do you think it is?" the junior medical sergeant said angrily. "He has a bullet through his head and no medevac!"

Dan tried to measure his response, knowing they were under stress. He turned to the senior medic. It was about the chain of command. It was their job to provide an assessment.

"The commander needs his condition to send to higher," he said again, looking at the senior Delta.

"Critical to expectant," the senior medic said flatly.

"Thank you," Dan said.

He sent the report over the radio through the second combat controller the team had on loan. He hoped Mick wasn't suffering. Mick was staring at the ceiling, and his breath came in fits and gasps. Dan went back and forth between the perimeter and Mick's side for the next three hours. A terrible weight fell over the team. They felt helpless, with no hope of medevac and no way of securing a landing zone.

It took Mick hours to die. His body eventually went into spasms, clinging to the last moments of life. There was nothing they could do to save him. When he eventually gave up fighting for air and lay still on the ground, Dan asked the flight medic to check on him one last time. Then he went around to the team members who were guarding the walls to let them know Mick had died.

"Eagle down," Andy said over the radio, and read out the last four digits of Mick's social security number, followed by his name.

They covered Mick's body with an American flag and took turns going into the room to say goodbye. The team's mood plummeted. Mick was the first among them to die, but at a certain point everyone's survivability would go to zero. Without air support, they were going to get overrun. Some of the team members were close to running out of ammunition, counting down every time they fired. Andy was in a rage.

He stormed into the room where the Afghan commandos were sitting with their backs turned to the battle outside. Several had been hit by shrapnel and patched up by the medics. They were done fighting. He wasn't entirely confident that the commandos wouldn't switch sides and turn on them.

"What the fuck are you doing, man!" he shouted at the captain.

He grabbed a number of the commandos and dragged them outside to the walls. Then he turned to Flannery.

"Watch them!" he told the pilot. "Don't let them leave their posts."

Andy didn't know what to do to get air support. The Apaches wouldn't shoot. The F-16s wouldn't drop. The quick reaction force made up of a couple of teams from their company had been ordered to turn around. Could anything else go wrong? He crouched against the wall with Dan, and they surveyed the situation. Another 81mm mortar landed nearby, sending mud and shrapnel raining down on them. A fragment hit Dan's helmet.

"Fuck," Dan said. He shook his head, and he and Andy gave a few hoarse chuckles.

Andy pulled out his map and started writing on the back. It was a step-by-step narrative of the day's events that he planned to read to the battalion. He thought if he could use clear legal terms, the military's leadership would at least be liable for the team members' deaths if they turned them down for air support again. They were all going to die if things didn't turn around fast.

"We're pinned down by sniper fire, machine gun fire, and incoming mortar fire from all sides and unable to maneuver," Andy wrote. "We're running out of ammunition. The aircraft won't fire on the buildings because they can't see anyone shooting, because combatants are firing from inside roofed structures through murder holes in the walls. When they move between positions, they are leaving the weapons in place, knowing we will not fire on unarmed combatants. The commandos won't fight. We have one KIA, one WIA [wounded in action], and no quick reaction force coming."

He read his statement over the radio.

The high level of approval required to sign off on airstrikes meant that the message had to travel through the entire chain of command. It was passed from the battalion, where Col. Johnston was in an intensifying state of frustration, to the SOJTF deputy commander, Brig. Gen. Tony D. Bauernfeind, who was waiting for Resolute Support, the US military headquarters in Kabul, to approve the request for air support.

CHAPTER 18

Get Back Out There

ANDY

THE MESSAGE CONVEYING the team's urgency and despair reached Resolute Support, where the deputy chief of staff for operations, Gen. Buchanan, and a team of legal advisers were tasked with signing off in accordance with the rules of engagement. The request for air support was cleared. Brig. Gen. Bauernfeind, the SOJTF deputy commander, came on SATCOM and authorized airstrikes on the surrounding buildings.

Andy was surprised that the ninety-second narrative he'd read aloud had worked. It seemed headquarters finally understood their desperation. An F-16 thundered across the battlefield and dropped a five-hundred-pound bomb. Nothing happened. It was a dud. The aircraft dropped a second bomb, but again nothing happened. The team couldn't believe it. The jet left to refuel and returned, this time striking several buildings.

Things seemed to have gotten quieter. Andy tried to get a drop of supplies, including water and ammunition. That's when he found out, to his consternation, that there were no GPS-guided parachutes. A C-130 transport aircraft offered to push a box of supplies out to them, even though it was still daylight. It wasn't supposed to fly during the day to avoid the risk of getting shot down.

Andy was reluctant. If the drop landed off target, they would have to recover it somehow, but being resupplied on ammunition was vital. The battlefield erupted with gunfire as the plane swooped across. He watched the parachute sail down toward them and divert course at the last moment, settling into the middle of an open field. Now they would have to go fetch it in the dark. It was easier said than done: the loaded pallet was heavy as shit.

An AC-130 gunship finally arrived on station around five p.m., as the sky was darkening. The pilot asked Andy for the top three targets. Andy went outside and tried to direct them to the buildings that seemed to be emanating the heaviest fire. He stayed outside the compound to guide them, barely aware of the possibility of getting shot at the most critical moment of the battle. The AC-130 thundered overhead and began to fire at the first building.

The blasts from the gun were followed by the echo of the round exploding as it hit the target, causing a cloud of dust and debris to billow into the sky.

The airstrike continued for about two minutes. The pilot came back over the radio. "What was the second target again?" he asked. Andy was ecstatic. The AC-130 had finally made sure target number one wasn't going to give them any more trouble.

The SOJTF wanted Andy to keep reading out his narrative. For every strike, over the course of about two hours, Andy had to pull out his map and reread his statement aloud. By now, he had lost all faith in leadership along with the capacity to be dismayed. *What kind of bureaucratic bullshit was this?*

After the gunship hit about eighteen compounds, the surrounding area grew quiet. There were still military-aged men leaving the vicinity, but the firing had stopped and the battalion ordered a pause. The teams hunkered down in the compound, with defensive positions on the wall, to wait for nightfall. Everyone was exhausted, hungry, and dehydrated. They had been fighting for nearly twenty-four hours.

The flight medic remembered that there were four emergency kits in the helicopter containing snack bars and water. He climbed in and found them. Everyone got a bit to drink. The medic was glad to have been able to contribute. He was worried about Ski's leg. It had been in a tourniquet all day, and repeated efforts to convert the tourniquet to avoid an amputation had failed.

After dark, the team went out to recover the resupply pallet that had been pushed out of the C-130 into the field. They were nervous, but the area remained quiet. An officer from the battalion came on the radio again to ask if they could spend another night in Marjah. Andy was outraged.

"What? No! We *cannot* stay another night," he said into the radio. Who *was* this guy? Andy spelled out all the reasons why it wouldn't be a good idea.

"Well, what if we swap you out with another team," the officer said, "and leave the Afghans behind?"

Andy couldn't believe it. If they abandoned the Afghan commandos, it would destroy anything that remained of the relationship between them. In military terms, it was called a catastrophic loss of rapport. The commandos were deadweight at this point, but they were supposed to be partners, and ditching them in Marjah was not part of the plan.

"No way," Andy told the officer. All they had to do was survive another couple of hours. The quick reaction force, made up of two US teams and a company of commandos, was on its way. It had been waiting at Camp Dwyer all day to be cleared to depart. The troops were dropped several miles away, and it would take them hours to reach Alpha-64 on foot, but the air force refused to drop them any closer over concerns about losing another helicopter.

Dan went into one of the rooms to rest and saw the pilot, Flannery, talking to his crew chief. Flannery looked crushed. "Sir, don't beat yourself up; you're a great pilot," Dan heard the crew chief saying. Dan couldn't resist trying to poke some fun at Flannery. In his experience, humor was the best cure in the darkest of times.

"Did you call 'Black Hawk down' when your aircraft crashed today?" Dan asked, referencing the movie. Flannery looked at him mournfully and shook his head.

"Well, you fucked up a once-in-a-lifetime opportunity!" Dan said, trying to cheer him up. Flannery couldn't help but laugh.

Ski was adamant that the flight medic should keep trying to save his leg, which risked being amputated after spending all day in a tourniquet. He howled every time the medic took the tourniquet off and was forced to put it back on to avoid further blood loss. Around midnight, the medic managed to remove the tourniquet without disturbing the blood clot that had formed at the site of the wound. He kept it loosened around Ski's thigh and told him to minimize any movement to avoid ruining the blood clot.

Soon afterward, the sister teams and over a hundred Afghan commandos reached the compound. They were exhausted after hiking for hours through muddy farmland. The Marjah team was delighted to see them.

"Great to see you, brother," Dan said to one of the team sergeants he knew well. "I have a prime piece of Afghan real estate for you."

The teams secured a perimeter around an adjacent field to create a landing zone large enough for the four Chinooks that would evacuate Andy's team, the attached support soldiers, and the Afghan commandos. The two new ODAs were staying behind to wait for the recovery team to collect the downed Black Hawk. Andy divided everyone into groups, or chalks, and assigned a color to each Chinook to speed up the boarding process.

Dan was relieved when they took off and left Marjah behind. Ski lay on a stretcher on the floor, and Jordan held his hand.

"Okay, let's get out of here," Dan said.

It was early morning when they landed at Kandahar Airfield, exhausted, covered in blood, wet, and freezing cold. The pilots told them this was their final stop. Everyone was dismayed. They were expecting to get back to Camp Antonik, where they could shower, change clothes, and call home. They didn't have cell phones or money with them.

Then they discovered that news of the battle had leaked, and reports about a stranded team of Green Berets and a downed helicopter had been playing on cable TV all day.

Dan asked to borrow his old team leader's office so he could call home. He was worried that Brianne, who was still in West Virginia with her parents, might have seen the story, as her father seemed to have Fox News on in the background all day. But she had no idea what had happened. Andy's parents, on the other hand, knowing their son's team was involved, had been glued to their screens and were almost inconsolable.

The hardest call they had to make was to Alexandra, Mick's wife, to tell her the story of what had happened and to offer their condolences.

Jordan was chosen to travel home with Mick. The two had become close friends during the deployment. Jordan didn't have money, documents, or clothes—everything was still at Camp Antonik. He had to borrow clothes and obtain a new military ID card on the base to be able to travel, which he did without shaving his beard. A close friend on another team lent him his green beret, which was an emotional moment.

Hundreds of people lined up on the tarmac at Kandahar Airfield to watch as Mick's teammates carried his casket draped with an American flag onto the waiting C-17 transport plane.

The company held a memorial for him afterward, in front of a battle cross made of a helmet, rifle, and boots. Andy and the chaplain said a few words. The team was bitter. It seemed to Andy that all the generals were congratulating themselves for getting the team out when their failure to provide air support had resulted in the soldiers dragging their friend's body through waist-deep mud and water with a bullet in his head. Gen. Swindell didn't even show up. He sent his sergeant major, who approached Andy with a pep talk after the speech.

"You need to get back out there and avenge McClintock," he said.

Andy didn't even try to be polite. "We'll get back out there as soon as we have the battalion's support," he replied.

Jordan was drained by the time they landed at Bagram Airfield, the first stop on the long journey to Dover Air Force Base. The tour felt unfinished. He wanted revenge for Mick. He felt guilty for being alive and thought about how to explain his friend's death to his wife and family. He replayed in his mind all the ways things could have turned out differently during the mission and how Mick could have still been alive.

Andy and Dan tried to counsel the team members to avoid making poor decisions after Mick's death. Everyone believed it had been avoidable. There was a pervasive feeling that the army thought their lives were expendable. Some of them wanted to go on a rampage to get revenge. Some of them didn't want to do anything else for the rest of the tour. Neither was a good state to be in during the middle of an operation.

When the battalion told Andy that his team had killed fifty insurgents in Marjah, it only made him angrier. He had signed up for Special Forces to help people, to make a difference. It seemed to him that the insurgents were little more than dirt-poor farmers who lacked education and were paid to pick up a gun. And it still seemed that the Green Berets' only job there was to keep Helmand out of the news until the next election.

ALEXANDRA RECEIVED THE FIRST CALL while driving back from therapy with her father on the day Matthew McClintock was killed. Little Declan was asleep in his car seat in the back. Her handbag was on the floor somewhere, stuffed with forms showing that she had completed her course of therapy. She was feeling good and was ready for the trip to New Mexico to stay with Matthew's family. The only sign that something was amiss was a text from a friend. It said they'd seen the news and were thinking of her husband. She rarely watched the news—she didn't need more reasons to worry—and the message quickly slipped her mind.

"Hello, is this Charles?" the officer on the line asked. "This is Sgt. First Class Clarity with 19th Special Forces Group. Are you Alexandra McClintock's father? Do you have her address?"

Thinking the call was about some military function for families, she told her father to say no. But then she remembered the text from earlier. Matthew had been fine when they'd spoken yesterday. Had something happened?

"It's probably not a big deal," her father said. "You sure you're okay on your own? I can stay if you need me."

"No, Dad, it's fine, don't worry. I'm fine," she said. She dropped him off at his home, which was near hers.

Declan was still asleep. Alexandra had silently spiraled into a panic. Frantically, she started to call all the people on her notification list who would have been informed if anything had happened to Matthew. She called his best friend: no reply. She moved down the list until her friend Jessica picked up. Alexandra asked if she'd heard any news.

"Nah, man, I'm on the way to the airport to pick up my brother. Everything's fine," Jessica said.

Alexandra tried to stem her growing fear. "You're right. It's probably nothing," she said.

A military van drove past the house as she pulled into the driveway. *Everything is fine*, she repeated to herself. She picked up Declan and her handbag and went inside. She began tidying up the living room. The dog started barking. Through the window, she saw figures appear at the door. One of them was wearing a green beret and the other a red beret with a chaplain's cross. She opened the door. She remembered that Matthew had been complaining about a foot injury and wondered if that was the reason for the visit. She felt bad for not taking it more seriously.

"Are you Alexandra McClintock?" one of them asked. She let them into the house.

"The president and the secretary of defense send their deepest condolences and regret to inform you that Staff Sergeant Matthew McClintock was killed in action on January 5, 2016," the officer said.

Alexandra stood there in shock for a few moments. She had spoken to Matthew yesterday. And Afghanistan was nearly a day ahead, because of the time difference.

"But that's today! That's not possible," she said. "You're wrong!"

She marched over to the neighbor's house to apologize for the van in the driveway and stopped halfway there, lost. The officers helped her back to her home and stayed until friends and family arrived to take care of her.

Later that night, she spoke with her therapist by phone. "I don't want to feel anything anymore," Alexandra said.

Her therapist wrote her a prescription for that.

WASHINGTON-BASED REPORTERS were summoned to the Pentagon briefing room for an update on the situation in Helmand as soon as Staff Sgt. Matthew McClintock's relatives had been notified of his death. Fox News had reported that a team of Green Berets had gotten trapped in the village, and a Black Hawk sent to evacuate wounded soldiers had been shot down or had crashed. The White House was under pressure to explain why US soldiers were once again at the center of a pitched battle when combat operations were supposed to have ended a year ago. The new Resolute Support mission, as the Pentagon kept repeating, was only to provide training and assistance to local forces.

Peter Cook, the Pentagon's press secretary, took to the podium at two p.m., wearing a crisp dark gray suit with a pink tie. The Pentagon's logo was displayed on the blue curtains hanging behind him. The roomful of reporters waited to hear the White House's explanation for the botched operation. The United States had withdrawn from Helmand with fanfare a year prior, and all US forces were assumed to have left the province. Their very presence in Helmand raised questions about a cover-up and what the military was really doing in Afghanistan.

The first question went to Robert Burns, a national security reporter with the Associated Press. "Could you explain the context of what's going on in Marjah that required a US combat presence, given that the combat mission is over?" Burns asked.

"Bob, I cannot tell you with specificity at this point exactly what they were doing there at this particular time, other than this was an operation that was consistent with that train, advise, and assist mission," Cook said.

Pure White House spin. It was inconceivable that a battalion would drop a team of Green Berets in the middle of Taliban-controlled Helmand to look for an insurgent commander and not expect them to get into a combat situation.

"We are confident that the Afghan national security and defense forces are continuing to develop the capabilities and capacity to secure the country," Cook continued.

Jim Miklaszewski, a Pentagon reporter with NBC, pointed out that less than a month earlier, one of the Pentagon's own reports had warned of a significant and ongoing decline in security in Afghanistan since the withdrawal of US troops in 2014.

"How can the US have confidence in the Afghan security forces?" he asked, citing the findings in the report. "Or was it a mistake to remove Americans from the combat battlefield?"

"They're not at a point yet, Mik, where they are able to operate entirely on their own," Cook said, "which is why US forces [and] other—NATO forces are there, assisting and providing this kind of training and assistance."

Reporters continued to challenge the claim that US combat operations in Afghanistan were over and tried to force Cook to admit the White House's failure to deliver on a pledge to end the war. Cook stuck to the talking points, insisting that the mission the Green Berets had undertaken in Marjah fell into the scope of the Afghan "training mission."

"Peter, we have one dead special operator. How can you not say the combat mission endures in Afghanistan today?" Lucas Tomlinson of Fox News asked.

"These people are in harm's way, Lucas. There's no bones about that. We're not—we're not dismissing the risk to US forces that are there in Afghanistan. But the mission has not changed for the US troops on the ground, to provide training and assistance to those Afghan forces," Cook said, repeating the talking point.

Reporters continued to press him about the ground that Afghan forces had lost over the year, but Cook insisted the strategy was working and the Afghan government would soon be able to take control of the country. He seemed relieved when the discussion moved on to Syria.

CHAPTER 19

This Isn't Afghanistan Anymore
CALEB

CALEB remained unconscious for days as a vicious fever, caused by a bacterial infection from the soil that had blown into his open wounds, wracked his battered body. His eyes were glassy; his skin was gray and glistened with sweat. The doctors tried to keep his fever under control with medication, but the fiery heat kept coming back. Ashley held his good hand or hovered anxiously as he drifted in and out. She watched teams of doctors come and go and hung on their every word.

The doctors conducted evaluations, debated among themselves, and then floated away, leaving behind few clues about her husband's deteriorating condition. She had never seen so many doctors work on a case at once. There were urologists for his failing kidneys, pain-management doctors, infection specialists, orthopedic surgeons, a trauma team, a specialized surgeon for his hand, and so on. Sometimes a representative came from the medical team; sometimes the whole team showed up. She began to realize that things were much worse than she had been told.

Caleb had five pulmonary embolisms that were preventing his body from absorbing the oxygen he needed to fight the infection. As a result, his fever continued to spike dangerously high as the powerful antibiotics being pumped into his bloodstream failed to bring the infection under control. The infection specialists started appearing in his hospital room more and more often.

Okay, Ashley thought, *this is really, really not good*. She had assumed that the main challenge would be for Caleb to recover from the loss of both legs. She hadn't considered that he could actually die. She feared the worst every time the doctors changed his medication.

Caleb's world had shrunk to the size of his hospital bed, the ebb and flow of pain, the drugs administered at regular intervals, tubes snaking in and out of his body, doctors coming and going. Sometimes his room was empty and sometimes full. The ketamine was a powerful sedative, but it often caused him to wake from terrible nightmares in which he was back in Afghanistan and getting captured by the Taliban.

It took a week for the doctors to get the infection under control. After that, Ashley felt certain that Caleb could make it through anything.

The doctors mapped out a plan for his care, which involved transferring him to Texas before Christmas, where he could be closer to his family and be treated at the military's premier rehabilitation center. He remained semiconscious, his awareness suppressed by a cocktail of drugs that regulated his pain. Still, nothing helped ease the agony he suffered when the nurses moved him to change the dressings.

As the world slowly came into focus, Caleb grasped that his goal was to get to Texas, and for that to happen his condition had to improve. It gave him something to focus on. A target. He knew that his legs were gone, but he felt strangely detached from that reality. It seemed a very distant problem when his immediate challenge was coping with the pain and the ketamine-induced nightmares.

He understood it would be hard to get stronger while being fed through a tube. He asked for a slice of pizza, but nearly choked on his feeding tube after taking a bite and being unable to swallow it. The nurse on duty was sympathetic.

"If it was me, I'd just rip it out," the nurse said.

Good idea, he thought. He pulled the feeding tube out as though he were doing a magic trick. The doctors that came to check on him during the next shift were displeased, but he resisted having the tube put back in.

"Okay. But you'll have to eat two thousand calories a day," one of the doctors told him.

Challenge accepted. He started to eat everything in sight. It didn't take long to realize that was a big mistake. His digestive system was slow to respond, and the drugs made him constipated.

Caleb woke up in the Brooke Army Medical Center at Fort Sam Houston in Texas on Christmas Day. Ashley was on her way by car. She had flown back to Tucson, Arizona, where she'd packed up their baby and five-year-old daughter, Evelyn, as fast as possible. He hadn't seen the children for more than six months.

Caleb's mother had flown with him to Texas but had stepped out of the room. Sedated, he was drifting in and out of consciousness to the beep of monitors when an unfamiliar figure appeared at his bedside. It was the hospital commander, a colonel, with his deputy, doing their Christmas rounds. The colonel plopped a plate of cookies on the table as a gift and began talking about army regulations. Caleb didn't hear him say "Merry Christmas."

"Same army, same paycheck...." The words floated through Caleb's semiconsciousness. He grasped that the colonel wanted him to shave his beard and have a haircut. "This isn't Afghanistan anymore; this is the United States, and at this hospital there are no exceptions to rules and regulations."

Caleb realized that he still had the bushy beard that Special Forces were allowed to grow during deployment because their jobs required them to blend into the local population. But he was back to regular army life now. He blankly looked at the colonel, who was still talking.

"Need to maintain the same standards..."

Caleb sank deeper into his bed, surveying the lines feeding in and out of his body, the bandages over the stumps where his legs had been, and felt profoundly sorry for himself. As well as a deep, laser-focused hatred of the colonel. Who was this guy? He decided there and then not to shave his beard.

"You're going to be fine," the colonel concluded and walked out.

A fiery rage solidified in the drug-induced haze in Caleb's brain. It was soon a familiar sentiment. Over the next week, the colonel sent various people to his room to harass him about the beard. He ignored them all. One of them left a pair of clippers behind as a present. He refused to be humiliated. A lieutenant colonel eventually dropped by with news that the sergeant major of the army was going to visit the hospital.

"You won't be able to see him unless you shave," the lieutenant colonel said.

"I guess I'm not seeing him then," Caleb replied. The beard was all that was left of his old life. The sergeant major never visited the hospital; it had been a ruse to get him to shave.

Rocky, the dog that had failed to find the bomb outside the mud shack, was given a Purple Heart for his service and became an overnight media sensation. Journalists interviewed the dog's handler, who was in the same hospital with shrapnel wounds. No one took any notice of Caleb. Instead, photos of the "heroic dog" appeared in the papers, which only made Caleb angrier. The dog had screwed up! It had missed the bomb. No one seemed to remember the other victims, including Caleb, several Afghan commandos, and the interpreter who'd been blinded by shrapnel.

A friend from 19th Group who had come to visit wheeled Caleb into the hospital parking lot to get some fresh air. Ashley was with them. Caleb gratefully breathed in the crisp December air, feeling refreshed after weeks of existence in the stale hospital environment. Being in a wheelchair still didn't seem real, but overall he felt pretty good. Then the nausea hit, and he threw up his iced tea. A long road still lay ahead.

Ashley was pleased with his progress but worried about their future. Caleb was incredibly strong-willed. But how would he live with what had happened to him? She thought of all the things he loved doing: fifty-mile mountain bike rides, rock-climbing, basket-ball. How would he cope? How would they all cope?

A couple of weeks later, in January, a buddy told Caleb what had happened to his friends back in Marjah. He tried to imagine the Black Hawk crashing down in the compound, his teammates sur-rounded by Taliban and counting their last bullets. In pain and a haze of drugs, he lay in bed, thinking of Mick. He remembered their conversations about transitioning to active duty and how ex-cited Mick had been following the birth of his son. Guilt coiled through Caleb's mind.

I planned that mission, he thought, remembering the intelligence on Marjah he'd shared with the team. *It's my fault.*

He tried to remember the details of the intelligence he'd gath-ered during his first mission there, but it was like groping through mud in the dark. He couldn't think clearly. If he had been present to help them plan the mission, he thought, perhaps Mick would still be alive. He had left the team more exposed.

Caleb blamed himself. He blamed the army. Everything they had been told about Afghanistan turned out to be wrong. He gave in and shaved his beard. He'd never felt so defeated in his life.

CALEB WAS DISCHARGED in early January. He became an outpa-tient at the US Army's Warrior Transition Battalion at Fort Sam Houston and was assigned an apartment off base. He learned to wheel himself around while anxiously waiting for the first prosthetic fitting on his right leg. Doctors told him it was best to start the process before the wound had fully healed so the prosthesis could conform to the shape of the socket. The healing of the left leg was far behind after a skin graft had failed. It required more surgery.

He also became an outpatient at the Center for the Intrepid, a state-of-the-art rehabilitation facility set up at Fort Sam Houston in 2007 for the most seriously wounded patients and staffed by military officers. Established with donor money to improve care for a genera-tion of soldiers that had survived the long-running wars in Afghan-istan and Iraq, it was viewed as one of the most advanced centers of its kind in the world. As a result of innovations in battlefield medicine that helped stop catastrophic blood loss after an injury, soldiers now survived wounds that would have previously been mortal. Just a few years earlier, Caleb likely would have died from the damage his body had sustained in the blast. But improved tourniquets, first aid training, and "golden hour" medical care had allowed him to survive.

During rehab, he realized that the scale of his injuries was minor compared to that of other patients. He saw triple, even quadruple, amputees, as well as soldiers that were horrendously disfigured by burns over 90 percent of their bodies. Some were paralyzed and would never leave their wheelchairs. One of the most inspiring patients was a jovial twenty-year-old artilleryman called Muzzy, who'd lost his sight and both legs above the knee when a round exploded in the chamber of his weapon. Not only did he have to learn to walk again; he had to do it blind.

Ashley struggled to keep her job. Even though the Family and Medical Leave Act gave her twenty-six weeks off to care for a combat-wounded relative, her office insisted they were only required to allow her twelve weeks off. Fortunately, she was able to rectify the paperwork before they fired her. She needed the money to keep up with the family's mortgage payments and other bills.

At the end of January, Caleb tried on his first leg. It had no joints and felt heavy and unstable at the end of his stump. But when he grasped the parallel bars in the lab and stood up for the first time in nearly two months, he felt a swell of excitement as blood rushed through his upright body, causing an unfamiliar, tingling sensation.

He hopped to the end of the bars and back. It felt incredible. Then his stump started to throb under the pressure of the prosthetic leg. It was almost like being injured again. He reached his chair and collapsed into it, exhausted and exhilarated.

In early February, Caleb's squad leader at the Warrior Transition Battalion called to say that the three-star general in command at Fort Sam Houston had requested a breakfast with all the wounded warriors, and Caleb had been selected to attend. The date was set for the morning after Mick's funeral service at Arlington.

Caleb didn't want to have breakfast with any general. Even completing the smallest tasks took huge effort. He still struggled every day just to get himself washed and dressed. He requested to be exempt from the breakfast on the basis that he would be tired after attending his teammate's funeral the night before. The request was denied.

The dress code for the breakfast with the general was the army combat uniform. The battalion authorized Caleb to wear his physical fitness uniform, used during exercise, which was more comfortable. He didn't have one, so Ashley had to borrow a set for the event. All his stuff was still in Afghanistan.

On March 7, 2016, two months after Mick's death, Alexandra appeared in front of the country at her husband's burial service. Her long red hair was tied back, and she tearfully clutched her baby in one arm and a folded American flag in the other as she watched the pallbearers lower her husband into the ground. Mick had been posthumously awarded the Silver Star Medal.

Caleb watched from his wheelchair, thinking how easily it could have been him. He felt both responsible and at the same time remote from the ceremony. His emotions weren't as raw as they were supposed to be in those circumstances. *I should be feeling worse than this*, he thought. He needed to get off the drugs.

At breakfast the next day, Caleb was conscious that he was the only one in attendance who was missing both legs. The staff made a big production of hosting the soldiers as servers brought them food and cameras flashed around them. Feeling like a show horse, Caleb was utterly humiliated as he dutifully performed while nodding and smiling. He was expected to show gratitude for the invitation, as though his injury was an inconvenience to everyone else.

When the three-star general asked Purple Heart recipients to comment on their medical care, Caleb didn't hesitate to express his honest opinion. While he was being treated at the privately funded Center for the Intrepid, he was required to continue with appointments at the army's Warrior Training Battalion. As a result, he had two primary care providers, two physical therapists, two occupational therapists, and so on, all of whom provided overlapping care.

He told the general that the duplication of appointments was a waste of resources and a drain on his energy, which he needed to preserve to focus on the challenge of learning to walk again. The general, dismissive, told Caleb that the battalion didn't really take up much time.

"I want to say a few words about uniforms and standards here at the battalion," the general said, beginning a lecture on the importance of regulations. "We will be doing rounds in civilian clothes to check on the battalion."

The lecture seemed to be a personal slight toward Caleb as a soldier. He was the only one at the breakfast wearing shorts and a T-shirt. It was hard to conceive how the general could have nothing more important to do than go around enforcing dress code with the war wounded. After the breakfast, the battalion's leadership formally complained to Caleb's Special Operations advocate about him wearing a physical fitness uniform at the event. They told the advocate that Caleb was supposed to have worn his combat uniform.

PART THREE

RAMP-UP

President Obama Ramps Up the War

Gen. John Campbell, the top US commander in Afghanistan, lobbied for more troops and authorities until his departure in early 2016. He argued that the near losses of Helmand and Kunduz demonstrated at the very least that the current policy was failing and the survival of the Afghan government was at risk; furthermore, the new Islamic State affiliate in the east was an additional cause for concern. The solution was an open-ended and expanded mission to support the Kabul administration until it could survive on its own. Whether anyone believed that would ever happen was unclear. By the time Campbell stepped down, he had convinced the White House the war was moving in the wrong direction.

The Obama administration was simultaneously dealing with the fallout of its disastrous effort to end the war in Iraq, which seemed to be a warning sign for US policy in Afghanistan. In Iraq, the unilateral withdrawal of all US forces in 2011 had created the conditions that led to the rise of the Islamic State of Iraq and the Levant, one of the most successful terrorist groups the world had ever seen. The group's popularity was blamed on flawed US policies in Iraq that had deposed the nation's leader, Saddam Hussein, dismantled the ruling Baathist party, and worsened a sectarian rift before pulling troops out.

At its peak, Islamic State controlled as much as 40 percent of Iraq and a third of Syria, ruling over ten million people in 2014. It also inspired affiliates around the world to pledge allegiance to its leader. One of those affiliate groups was in Afghanistan. Even though the group's presence was mostly limited to a handful of districts along the border with Pakistan, its brutal methods and attacks were seen by some as evidence that Afghanistan could once again become a safe haven for terrorist organizations if the United States pulled out.

On the Hill, influential lawmakers like John McCain of Arizona, the chairman of the Senate Armed Services Committee, issued dire warnings about a repeat of the situation the country had left behind in Iraq. In early 2016, he warned that Afghanistan would go the same way if the United States continued with its plan to withdraw.

"By now, we should have learned from the precipitous withdrawal from Iraq, and the disaster that ensued, that wars do not end because politicians say so," McCain said in his opening statement at the hearing to consider Lieutenant General John W. Nicholson to lead US and coalition forces in Afghanistan. "As the security situation in Afghanistan continues to deteriorate, it makes no strategic or military sense to continue the withdrawal of American forces."

In Washington, it seemed natural to draw parallels between the wars in Afghanistan and Iraq, and the military had often applied a one-size-fits-all approach to the conflicts. In reality, there were important differences, suggesting that comparisons had limited value. Crucially, Afghanistan did not have a history of sectarian war, a factor that contributed to Islamic State's ascent in Iraq, where the new US-backed administration was led by Shi'ites and the ousted government was mostly Sunni.

Another important difference was that the Taliban did not practice the Salafi jihadist ideology espoused by al Qaeda and Islamic State. In Afghanistan, the influence of Sufism, a more mystical interpretation of Islam, was widespread, suggesting that the radical ideology of Islamic State in Iraq and Syria was unlikely to take hold there. In places where Islamic State pockets had taken root in Afghanistan, they often fought against local Taliban groups for recruits and resources. Al Qaeda had been mostly wiped out, but this did not seem to factor into consideration either.

IN AFGHANISTAN, the threat posed by Islamic State had long been a source of debate among local and foreign officials. It started with local media reports describing sightings of mysterious new groups whose members wore black and clashed with the Taliban in remote parts of the country. A typical example of this cycle occurred in western Farah province, where one of the first Islamic State affiliates in the country reportedly set up a training camp for foreign fighters in late 2014.

Farah lay near the border with Iran but hours away from anything, making it difficult to verify the news. It was a desert haven for narcotics traffickers, smugglers, and weapons traders. The buzz and grind of motorbikes was relentless. Women roamed without male chaperones, covering themselves in a single sheet of fabric worn like a cape. News of the training camp made international headlines, but it turned out that the new Islamic State group comprised local Taliban fighters who had quarreled with a commander and set up a rival faction. There was no sign of foreigners at all. But Afghan government officials played up the news in a bid to get US attention, and the stories were picked up and repeated in US-based media, fueling the argument in Washington that terrorist groups were again taking root in Afghanistan.

As a result, while officials in Washington were painting dire warnings about the emergence of Islamic State in Afghanistan, in Kabul, local and foreign officials were divided over the most basic questions. Did Islamic State or Daesh, the Arabic-language acronym commonly used to identify the group in Afghanistan, have any real connection to the larger group in Iraq and Syria, or did it simply reflect disaffection with the main insurgency led by the Taliban?

As the debate continued, over the next year, a more resilient affiliate emerged and laid roots along the border with Pakistan, in the same mountain range where US forces had hunted for Osama bin Laden at the start of the war. The eastern affiliate called itself Islamic State Khorasan Province, and it was to become one of the US military's principal concerns in the years to follow. Its roots could be traced back to a single, prominent cleric: Abdul Rahim Muslim Dost, a native of Kot district, in Nangarhar province.

Dost was among the first to pledge allegiance to Islamic State in Afghanistan and a prime example of the circuitous conflict. A previous Guantánamo detainee, he was arrested in 2001 on charges that included traveling to Afghanistan that summer and previously joining a former anti-Soviet jihadist group*—one of many backed by the United States in the 1980s. He had never been a member of the Taliban or al Qaeda.

At Guantánamo, Dost dealt with a Kafkaesque justice system that sometimes served to further radicalize inmates. The military tribunal refused to share the classified evidence against him, but reassured Dost during his hearing that court officials had come with an "open mind." He was not impressed.

"If you want to decide on the secret documents that I do not have access to, it is unfair," Dost told the tribunal, documents later released showed.

He also protested against the charge of traveling to Afghanistan in August 2001. He explained that he had returned home to check on land and a gem business that belonged to his family.

"I am an Afghan. It's not a crime to travel to my country," Dost told the court.

Dost resumed his activities as a jihadi scholar after being released in 2005 in Pakistan, where he met a stream of visitors who came to hear about his time at Guantánamo. His guests included

---

* Dost had been a member of Jamaat ud Dawa il al Quran al Sunnat (JDQ) but claimed to have withdrawn from the group sixteen years earlier. The United States believed that JDQ operated militant training camps and included a militant wing and an assassination wing.

international journalists, to whom he spoke about writing poetry in jail.* Later, he published a book in Pashto called *Matí Zawlanē*, which roughly translates to "Broken Shackles."

Dost publicly joined Islamic State soon after the group emerged in Iraq and Syria; he pledged allegiance in a short video declaration in Arabic that was uploaded to YouTube in mid-2014. From where he resided near the border with Pakistan, he started recruiting for the organization, preaching a radical interpretation of Islam and planting the seeds of the movement in Afghanistan. Few took much notice at the time.

Support for Islamic State took off in that region after senior members of the Taliban's branch in Pakistan joined in, breaking away from the main Taliban group after a US drone strike killed its leader and prompted a power struggle over succession. In January 2015, Islamic State in Iraq and Syria formally recognized the group led by the former Pakistani Taliban member Hafiz Sayed Khan as a new affiliate in Afghanistan. The affiliate thus was officially born.

In his final year in office in 2016, President Obama took several steps to escalate the US role in the Afghan war, among the first of which was signing off on new authorities that allowed the US military to launch offensive operations against the local Islamic State Khorasan Province. The revised rules were a victory for Gen. Campbell, who was on his way out but had lobbied for months to be granted authority to target Islamic State. The US military immediately began planning a major operation in the eastern part of Afghanistan that would target the group's hideouts along the border.

A few months later, President Obama authorized a second tranche of decisions that expanded US military operations against the Taliban by granting the new commander, Gen. Nicholson, more

---

* "I would fly on the wings of my imagination," he told *The Guardian* reporter Declan Walsh in 2006. "Through my poems I would travel the world, visiting different places. Although I was in a cage, I was really free."

troops and assets to help the government fight the insurgent group. The decision to ramp up the war once again was made public in July 2016, in a speech delivered in front of reporters in the Roosevelt Room of the White House, where the president was flanked by the chairman of the Joint Chiefs of Staff, Gen. Joseph Dunford, and Defense Secretary Ash Carter.

President Obama cancelled the plan to draw down to fifty-five hundred troops and announced that he would keep force levels steady through the end of his term. The troop cap was set at eighty-four hundred, close to what Gen. Campbell had requested. The president said the decision stemmed from the recognition that the security situation in Afghanistan was precarious and local forces would need support for years to come. Once again, he did not spell out the full scope of the authority he had given SOF, which received more troops and air assets to increase their capacity to support Afghan commandos on the battlefield.

Fernando Lujan, the Afghanistan director at the National Security Council, wrote much of the policy in the hope that flexibility would deliver additional support to his former Green Beret colleagues on the ground. The policy gave SOF more freedom to accompany Afghan commandos and allowed the United States to support major Afghan army offensives with airstrikes. It also allowed the United States to carry out multiple operations in the country at once, a necessary response to the Taliban's success in launching coordinated attacks in different regions at the same time.

But there were still limitations on what the US could do, and offensive strikes could only be authorized at a high level. The South Asia director at the National Security Council, Peter Lavoy, said that continued restrictions were intended to force the Afghan government to become more self-reliant. As a result, the new policy delivered some relief to US and Afghan forces on the battlefield, but it was not enough. The Taliban would extend their gains the following year, recapturing Kunduz and threatening half a dozen other major cities in a sign that US support still fell short.

CHAPTER 21

No Good or Bad Men in War
HUTCH

HUTCH waited months to hear what punishment would be handed down after the investigation into the bombing of the trauma hospital was passed on to US Central Command for review. Tina, weeks away from giving birth, was in a spiral of anxiety over the possible consequences for her family. Would it be safe for them to stay in their current house? What would happen if they were on a kill list to avenge those lost in the strike? It was a remote but conceivable threat after all that had happened.

Hutch spent his days at the office, if only to get out of the house and keep up a sense of routine. He exchanged emails with his bosses, assuring everyone that he was fine. The bitterness that had spread among the members of his group was hard to contain. The teams that had participated in the Kunduz operation felt they were being punished for surviving. Other soldiers questioned their version of events. Hutch knew that some people thought he was a monster and deserved to go to jail, and he tried to reconcile himself with that.

He knew that the teams had gone into Kunduz with the best of intentions: to drive the Taliban out of the city and avoid a long, drawn-out battle that would have cost far more civilian lives. In Iraq, cities were getting razed in the battle against Islamic State. That was the problem with wars: they were messy. The moment soldiers were asked to pick up a gun, bad things happened.

He was used to transitioning between Afghanistan and the civilian world, but this time was harder. He didn't feel ashamed of his service, but he knew that some people wanted him to be. He worried about the younger guys. Ben Vontz, the communications sergeant who had been talking to the AC-130 on the night of the strike, was still in shock. The teams thought that Special Forces was throwing Hutch under the bus.

Hutch tried to reconcile himself to the path ahead, and to the idea of leaving Special Forces behind. Tasting death throughout his career in the military had forever altered his perception of life. Nothing matched the adrenaline rush of a firefight, a sentiment betrayed in his eyes, which lit up at the memory of combat. He channeled a lot of energy into managing his emotions. He called it "balancing the books." The calculation involved processing and storing away all the terrible things he had seen and done, along with the good and those he had helped, based on an alchemical accounting he could never quite explain.

What he could say was this: "There are no good or bad men in war."

For some time, Hutch had entertained the idea of working for an aid group after his commitment to the army was over. It was hard to imagine any organization agreeing to work with him. He considered how he must appear to outsiders in the civilian world: the Green Beret who had gone on a rampage in Kunduz, bombed a hospital full of doctors and patients, and got away with it. But it didn't stop him from dreaming. He had to hope there would be another future if the military door closed. And he would always have his family.

On yet another day of doing nothing at the office, Hutch received a call. He was ordered to report to the commanding general at ten a.m. He went to the general's office and sat down in the chair opposite his desk, as instructed.

The commander told him he'd been reinstated. "I have full confidence in you, and I believe you didn't do anything wrong," he said to

Hutch. "I want you to appeal your relief, and I'll give you full access to the investigation."

Hutch was stunned for a moment. The next words passed in a blur.

"We had to be confident that civilians did die. You must cooperate with the lessons-learned investigation and be honest so that we can figure out how to avoid this in future. We owe it to ourselves, and everyone else, to take a long, hard look in the mirror," the officer said.

The investigators reviewing the case had discovered the error on the tracking system and had found the Afghan commandos where Hutch had said they were: under fire near the intelligence-agency prison. Hutch had been thrown a lifeline. He could still salvage his career in the army. If he could successfully appeal the decision to relieve him of command in Afghanistan and it was removed from his file, he could return to his occupation. At a minimum, he would be able to sit it out a few more years until he could collect his retirement. He owed it to Tina, who had given up her career for him. Hutch went home with the news.

In April 2016, General Joseph Votel announced the final results of the investigation into the strike on the hospital in Kunduz. The military found that the strike was not a war crime but the result of a concatenation of human error, technical failures, and other factors. The US military paid $3,000 to each of the injured and $6,000 to the family of each person killed.

Gen. Votel said that twelve of the sixteen personnel involved in the bombing of the hospital had been punished with removal from command, letters of reprimand, formal counseling, and extensive retraining. The list included a general officer, the AC-130 gunship aircrew, and the US Special Forces team on the ground. He did not provide further details. The names of those punished were never released, but Hutch was among the ones to receive a letter of reprimand, as did his battalion commander, Col. Johnston, and others.

The severest punishments were reserved for the aircrew members, who were found to have made serious mistakes and were temporarily stripped of their certification to fly. Gen. Votel explained that the aircrew members would face recertification boards to determine whether they were eligible to be returned to flight status. They had not flown since the incident. The US military approved $5.7 million to reconstruct the hospital.

Médecins Sans Frontières was outraged. The aid group responded that the punishments were too light in view of the destruction of a protected medical facility, and it called for an independent investigation by the International Humanitarian Fact-Finding Commission. It also released a list of ten questions that remained outstanding. The first sought more information about why the physical description of the target for the AC-130 as provided by Afghan forces matched the hospital. That question remains unanswered.

The aid group also asked to know who in the chain of command was ultimately responsible for the forty-two people killed in the hospital that night. That question, along with all the others, was never answered. The military's findings offered scant consolation for the victims and the survivors of the bombing. The investigation report, at over three thousand pages long, was publicly released, but it was heavily redacted, and the full transcripts between the crew and the various forces on the ground were not released. The basic facts surrounding the strike were still unclear. The survivors continued life in a blur.

Dr. Masood Nasim moved his family to Kabul. For the first two months, he found it hard to sleep, eat, or do anything at all. He almost felt like he had died in the strike. Many of the other survivors felt the same. The expatriate staff were evacuated and returned to their homes in faraway countries.

Dr. Evangeline Cua, back in the Philippines, avoided talking with her family about what had happened at the hospital in Kunduz. She didn't want them to worry. At first she stayed home, but finding it impossible to stop reliving the strike, she volunteered to teach at a medical school to keep busy. She had nightmares, and firecrackers set her off.

She began to heal with the support of a friend who worked as a psychiatrist and helped her talk through what had happened. It was difficult at first. She also started writing. She lobbied to return to Afghanistan to see her colleagues again. Six months after the strike, when Médecins Sans Frontières offered her a position in Kabul, she accepted, feeling glad to be back among her friends.

Dr. Cua spent a couple of months there and then went to Helmand. To others, that might have seemed crazy, but to her, it was all part of the healing process.

CHAPTER 22

Lobster and Canapés with the Taliban

DOHA

In EARLY 2016, US diplomats considered conditions to be ripe for another shot at relaunching peace talks in Afghanistan. Ambassador Rick Olson had moved on to a new role as US special representative for Afghanistan and Pakistan, which put him in charge of the effort that had been torpedoed by the news of Mullah Omar's death.

Mullah Mansour, Omar's successor, was dealing with a rift in his ranks* and was generally seen to be open to talks. The Taliban's political office in Doha, Qatar, agreed to meet with US officials; in a surprising development, they consented to the inclusion of a low-level Afghan government delegation. It was seen as a positive

---

* US and Afghan intelligence agencies tried, ultimately unsuccessfully, to harness the splinter groups against Mansour. The CIA-backed NDS sought to provide financial and military support to local Taliban groups that had broken away from the main branch. Grounded in the idea that "the enemy of my enemy is my friend," the strategy was controversial because, technically, the groups were still Taliban and could easily turn against the government. To an extent, efforts to woo insurgents had always existed, such as the $200 million Afghanistan Peace and Reintegration Program, a defunct six-year plan to pay about eleven thousand insurgents to lay down their arms (it eventually ran out of funding), and the Village Stability Operations, which wrapped up with the US withdrawal of troops in 2014.

sign. The group had long insisted on talks with the US first and the Afghan government second.

Preparations were held in the utmost secrecy to avoid leaks that might scuttle the opportunity before it had reached fruition. The Afghan government was unhappy despite the unexpected invitation to take a seat at the table. President Ghani objected to the United States sending high-level representatives, even though the Taliban's political-office chief was expected to lead the delegation on the other side.

The United States deferred to the Afghan president and agreed to send Ambassador Olson's principal deputy, Laurel Miller; another staffer, Tamanna Salikuddin; and the Afghanistan director at the National Security Council, Courtney Cooper. The State Department's plan to send three women was met with opposition—not by the Afghans or the Taliban but by US intelligence agencies in Washington, who argued it might offend the Taliban or send the wrong message.

Ambassador Olson's view was that Western women in the region were treated like men anyway, so it didn't matter. The State Department refused to change its delegation, and the dispute rose to the level of Susan Rice, the national security adviser. She decided to keep Cooper on board, and that settled the matter. On February 5, 2016, the three women, accompanied by two Afghan government officials, met the Taliban's political chief, Sher Abbas Stanekzai, at a safe house in Doha. The Qataris provided logistics and security but did not attend.

The somber, spectacled Stanekzai strode into the room and introduced himself to Miller with an outstretched hand, to the delegation's surprise. Conservative Afghans did not shake hands with women. Evidently, he wanted to make a good first impression. Two other Taliban, including Haji Mohammad Zahid Ahmadzai, a former minister and close associate of Mullah Omar, accompanied him. Two more Afghans, Farhad Farhadullah and Akram Khpalwak, both members of the High Peace Council, were there too.

Miller's team had a list of issues to raise at the two-day meeting with the Taliban delegation, including the fate of a number of US hostages. The Taliban's foremost concern was to discuss the withdrawal of US troops. The tone was cordial, and the gathering was seen as an icebreaker—the first chance in years for the three sides to sit down together and map out an agenda. The meeting was kept secret, and hasn't yet been reported.

Ambassador Olson, who missed out on the opportunity to attend the first meeting with the Taliban, found himself at the comparatively boring Quadrilateral Coordination Group in Islamabad, which was scheduled for the same day. The four-country process involving Afghanistan, Pakistan, China,* and the United States aimed to kick-start negotiations with the Taliban by sending a unified message to the group from four major regional players.

The United States hoped that the breakthrough would lead to the start of a formal peace process, but the Taliban refused to agree to another meeting that included the Afghan government. The Taliban continued to insist on starting talks with the United States first, before bringing Kabul into the equation. The Obama administration's long-standing policy was that talks with the Taliban had to include the government to avoid undermining Kabul. Thus, the nascent process quickly ground to a halt.

John Kerry, the secretary of state, skeptical about the chances of successfully reviving a peace process, remained more focused on preserving the shaky unity government in Kabul. The United States

---

* China had taken an increasing interest in Afghanistan since the United States had announced plans to withdraw. It worried about militancy spreading over its shared border with Afghanistan into Xinjiang province, where a violent separatist group driven by Uighur jihadists, known as the East Turkestan Islamic Movement (ETIM), had taken root. Beijing believed that ETIM was trained and financed by militants in Afghanistan. In later years, China took further steps to contain the threat of insurgency in Xinjiang, rounding up the Muslim population and detaining at least a million in secretive reeducation camps.

and the Taliban spoke on a call a month later but were unable to reach a compromise.

Months into the effort without any obvious sign of progress, the CIA stumbled into an opportunity to kill or capture the Taliban's new leader. Mullah Mansour surfaced in Dubai in May 2016, on a shopping trip ahead of his wedding in Quetta and possibly meeting with Gulf-area donors that financed the Taliban. In a dramatic sequence of events, the details of which haven't been previously reported, the United States asked the United Arab Emirates to stop the Taliban leader from leaving the country and to arrest him.

The South Asia director at the National Security Council, Peter Lavoy, supported the idea of dispatching Ambassador Olson to talk to Mullah Mansour in jail to pressure him to support the peace process once the UAE had arrested him. But the UAE failed to stop the Taliban leader; supposedly its agents chased after him just as his plane left the gate and was moving down the runway, like a scene from the movie *Argo*.

Some in the US administration suspected that the UAE had missed the opportunity on purpose. Mullah Mansour landed in Iran, and the government continued to debate the right course of action over the weekend.

The CIA prepared a Hellfire missile on the Pakistani side of the border, waiting for Mullah Mansour to cross into Baluchistan to go to his wedding. The area was supposed to be off limits to US strikes, but the opportunity was too good to pass up. When the Taliban leader entered Pakistan, the CIA fired, incinerating the Corolla he occupied and killing all its occupants. His passports were found in the wreckage, with stamps showing that he had traveled widely throughout the Gulf states, either with their leaders' tacit permission or under their noses.

The Obama administration claimed that the reason for the strike was that Mullah Mansour was an impediment to peace, but this wasn't the whole story. The strike was a rare opportunity to kill the Taliban leader, who had been steadfast in his refusal to start talks

with Kabul. With little sign of progress toward a formal peace process, the State Department could not argue against the strike. It
wasn't the first time the United States had conducted a kill operation
inside Pakistan without warning the government. In 2011, US Navy
Seals killed al Qaeda leader Osama bin Laden at his safe house in
Abbottabad.

Pakistani leaders were irate. Interior Minister Chaudhry Nisar
Ali Khan warned that the strike would have "serious implications"
for relations and accused the US of violating international law. But
some in the administration thought the strike in Pakistan had created a new strategic opportunity to raise the costs for Islamabad to
continue to shelter the Taliban's leadership in Pakistan.

The initial play was to encourage Pakistan to push the Taliban's
leadership back into Afghanistan. If Pakistan proved uncooperative,
Lavoy thought that further strikes against other Taliban leaders
would step up pressure on Islamabad to stop sheltering the Taliban
and support a political process to end the war. As long as the Taliban's leaders felt safe and happy in Pakistan, he believed, they could
wait out the contest indefinitely. He mused about a *Godfather*-like
movie scenario in which the CIA took out the Taliban's leaders one
by one, calculating that even a single additional strike could have the
desired effect.

"It was a watershed event. Everyone in the region freaked the shit
out," Lavoy said afterward. "I mean, we had maximum pressure and
influence. And ultimately, we were not able to utilize that for the
effects we wanted to achieve."

At the National Security Council, others put forward strong arguments against a confrontation with Pakistan and raised legal questions
about the idea. It was an election year, and ultimately the administration did not have the appetite to start a fight with Islamabad.

"They didn't want to rock the boat so much. They weren't willing
to be as bold," Lavoy said. "The one-off ultimately didn't have strategic effects. Multiple strikes would have had that effect and I think
entirely changed the equation."

The Taliban announced a successor just four days after the strike: an obscure figure named Mullah Haibatullah Akhunzada. He was a religious scholar from Panjwayi district in Kandahar, the same district that the Taliban's founder, Mullah Omar, was from. Little was known about his past. He had risen through the Taliban's ranks to become the chief of the military court in Kabul, where his task was to strictly enforce sharia law. A rare photograph showed him to be a stern, thin-lipped man with high cheekbones, a white turban, and a long, grizzled beard.

Insiders viewed him as an obvious choice to mend the rifts that had broken out within the group. Mullah Omar's eldest son, Mullah Yaqub, still in his twenties, was too young to take over. Mullah Haibatullah had a reputation for austerity, leading the type of ascetic life favored by Mullah Omar. He would never have been seen shopping in Dubai. A year later, the Taliban would report that his twenty-three-year-old son died while carrying out a suicide attack in Helmand, a sacrifice that resonated with the rank and file.

Mullah Omar's family supported Haibatullah, and Mullah Yaqub assumed the role of second deputy. Thus, the assassination ironically helped unify the Taliban after the split, and the insurgency quickly regrouped. Siraj Haqqani, the leader of the deadly Haqqani network, became the top military commander and launched an effective campaign across the country.

The Taliban's political office in Doha swiftly moved on as well. A second, secret meeting was held between US and Taliban officials in Doha a month later, in June 2016. This time, the top US envoy, Ambassador Olson, led the delegation. The killing of Mullah Mansour was barely mentioned. It was business as usual. The Taliban's demands were unchanged: the United States had to agree to withdraw before they would enter into talks with the Afghan government.

It took several months, until September 2016, for the groups to meet again. Critics of the process viewed the delay as evidence that the Taliban were stalling until President Obama left office. But the US negotiators were also slowed down by the need to coordinate closely with President Ghani, who, as part of the administration's policy, had to be in lockstep all the way. The killing of Mullah Mansour appeared to have convinced the Afghan leader that US outreach would be helpful, on the basis that the Taliban's position was weakened after the strike.

A month later, the United States and Taliban met once more, in one of several conferences that were part of a secret process that took place in the final months of President Obama's second term and has not been previously reported. The Qataris, true to Gulf style, served the delegates a luxurious selection of food that was typical of the five-star hotels and expensive restaurants in the region. Ambassador Olson observed that the Taliban had adapted to the menu, which included items like stuffed lobster and canapés.

Although Kabul was not given a seat at the table, the Taliban did agree to meet with a senior Afghan government representative on the sidelines. On the same day as the US meeting in Doha, the Taliban's political-office chief, Sher Abbas Stanekzai, met Afghanistan's acting intelligence-agency chief, Masoom Stanekzai (no relation), who served as President Ghani's point person for talks. It seemed to be a good sign.

The initially stiff relationship between the Americans and the Taliban relaxed as discussions progressed; they even traded jokes now and then. Ambassador Olson was hopeful the process might lead somewhere and asked his principal deputy, Miller, to work with a technical team to hammer out a roadmap. By the end of a three-day round of talks, the two sides had agreed on a process to formally reopen the Taliban's political office, but they failed to agree on the sequencing of events.

The United States wanted the Taliban to announce the simultaneous start of talks with the United States and Kabul. The Taliban were consistent in their position, and had been for years: they would only agree to starting a peace process with the United States first, and afterward they would agree to talks with Kabul as well. As an alternative, the Taliban floated the idea of a buffer: announcing official talks with the United States first, and then launching a parallel, bilateral process with Kabul later on. But the Americans would not agree. They didn't trust the Taliban to start talks with Kabul once the political office was formally opened in Doha for talks with the United States.

The Obama administration's policy was centered on the view that bilateral talks with the Taliban would undermine the Afghan government and weaken its position at the table. For the equal and opposite reason, the Taliban did not want to concede to talks with the Afghan government until the United States had publicly agreed to discuss the withdrawal of troops. Despite the gridlock over sequencing, the US delegation returned to Washington hopeful that their approach had shown enough progress to be rubber-stamped by the incoming administration and would be allowed to continue—and everyone expected Hillary Clinton to win the presidency.

CHAPTER 23

Thank You for Your Service

CALEB

CALEB used his walker to hop up and down their apartment block, ignoring the pain shooting up his right stump at every step. He was impatiently waiting for the skin graft on his left leg to heal. He couldn't get a prosthetic fitted until that happened, and bearing all his weight on one leg was excruciating. He blamed the slow progress on Coumadin, an anticoagulant that prevented blood clots. When his surfer-blonde hair fell out in the shower, a common side effect of the drug, he secretly stopped taking it.

A condition known as heterotopic ossification was also complicating his recovery. A bony growth at the end of his severed femur protruded into the thin layer of skin covering the bone, causing great pain when pressure was applied to the stump. The bone kept growing because the body mistook the injury for a fracture and sent bone tissue out of the severed end to repair the break. It was a significant complication for soldiers recovering from traumatic amputations. His doctors repeatedly modified the socket to try to ease the discomfort and prescribed strong drugs for the nerve pain. He began to hop laps of the apartment building, building strength. Ashley felt proud of her husband's resilience. It wasn't going to be easy, but things were already looking up.

At the end of March 2016, Caleb went back to the Center for the Intrepid, the privately funded rehab facility, for his first prosthetic fitting on the second leg. It was thrilling to stand on both legs again for the first time in almost four months. He agreed to speak to a congressman about the rehab facility, understanding that this was part of his duty as a soldier. A day before the meeting, he received notification that his health insurance coverage had expired, all his appointments at the Center for the Intrepid had been cancelled, and he was no longer allowed to receive treatment. He knew it had to be a glitch in the paperwork, but he couldn't help feeling a sense of panic. How long would it take to rectify? Why had the army let this happen?

It turned out that his orders, which were required for him to continue treatment, were generated three months at a time, and the current set had run out. As a National Guard soldier, Caleb had to be on orders for any military-affiliated work, including participating in the recovery program at the rehab facility. The Warrior Training Battalion hadn't told him that his orders would expire every quarter, and he expected to spend at least a year in rehabilitation. No one could tell him how to get new orders generated and restart his medical coverage. He had to wheel himself from office to office, asking questions. Until it was resolved, he was banned from the Center for the Intrepid. When his military ID expired and he wheeled himself down to the office to renew it, the staff at the desk turned him away. It was the beard again. He was shaving every few days, and some blonde stubble had started to show.

"You turn back around," the staff member told him. "We're not giving you an ID card until you've shaved."

At the park with Ashley, Caleb fumed when a slight rise in a grassy hill proved too steep for him to walk. Every rock and slope presented a challenge. One day, he tripped and fell over in the grass and was unable to pick himself up. Ashley was strong, but at five feet one inch she was too small to lift him by herself. They hadn't learned the technique for getting him upright. He tried and tried, but he toppled over on the unstable prosthetics and kept falling back to the ground. Three boys, each about ten years old, saw them struggling on the grass and came over to help.

"Thank you for your service, sir," they said, and tried to give him some money.

Caleb felt moved and desperate at the same time. He didn't want to become a victim or a charity case.

OPERATION SURF, a nonprofit, invited Caleb to join a surfing trip in California for wounded soldiers that spring. He didn't feel ready. The idea of taking a plane alone and swimming in the ocean with no legs was daunting. Barely four months had passed since he'd been injured, and he wasn't used to his new condition. Despite his misgivings, he decided to go. The trip turned out to be a huge confidence boost. Caleb discovered that he could manage at the airport by himself. The waves were healing, and the sea-salty air made him feel like a person rather than a patient for the first time since the injury.

There's nothing I can't do, he told himself for the first time. *I just need to adapt to the new situation.*

Caleb wanted to experience the real, unfiltered world, the way it would be for the rest of his life. For months, he had the growing sensation that things were still too good. People kept asking how he felt. He didn't feel bad enough. He still couldn't grasp the gritty reality of being a double amputee. He had broken his existence down into short-term goals to avoid thinking about the future. Over the course of a week after the surfing trip, he quit all drugs.

The cocktail of medication included opiates and Lyrica to block the nerve pain. The withdrawal symptoms were excruciating, and he begged for a break in his daily routine of physiotherapy and medical appointments. When he woke up to the reality of another day without legs, now that he was off the drugs depression set in. Just getting out of bed required preparation.

At the Center for the Intrepid, the doctors were sympathetic, but they refused to pause the schedule. To Caleb, their attitude seemed borderline callous, but he knew it was because they cared. The doctors set goals for their wounded patients that the amputees could never imagine for themselves. On the days when he didn't have the energy to perform the exercises, fighting the doctors was even worse, so he kept going.

It was one thing to walk around in a lab and exercise while hooked up to machines, but the real world was filled with obstacles, curbs, uneven ground, and slopes that were difficult to navigate. The Warrior Training Battalion continued to harass him about standards and task him with impossible duties. One day he was ordered to appear within the hour to pull weeds from the yard, something that was fine for soldiers recovering from minor sprains, but a huge undertaking for someone learning to walk again. He took it as one more sign that the army didn't care what happened to him.

The battalion also ordered him to start appearing at formations twice a day. Caleb was the only soldier in a wheelchair and lived an hour away from the base. He couldn't understand why the army was not encouraging him to invest his mental and physical energy in his recovery. Angry, he wrote to a friend to ask for help dealing with the repeated expiration of his medical coverage and constant battles with the battalion.

"I do not believe anyone has any idea what this does to soldiers' mental health and their perspective of how the army cares for them," he wrote in a four-page letter. "We have been at war since 2002 and this is still a thing!...Someone in my position needs to be focusing on healing mentally as well as physically, not be made to feel they are being chewed up and spit out by the idiotic paperwork maze that is the army healthcare system." It seemed like everyone else could go home at the end of the day. Caleb had to live with Afghanistan every minute for the rest of his life.

He continued to feel angry despite his progress. When he was sent to see a psychologist as part of his routine treatment, he released his rage.

"Everything is difficult," Caleb told him. "I can't even pick up something that has dropped to the floor. The army keeps losing my orders. I'm getting harassed about my beard. Everything's pissing me off, man! I just feel angry at the world all the time."

The psychologist said this was a typical reaction to the events that had happened to him.

"I don't want to be angry all the time," Caleb insisted. "I don't want to be angry with my family and put them through more stress after everything that has happened. Is there something I can take for my anger?"

"The way you're reacting is normal," the psychologist repeated. "You'll manage it better over time." He promised Caleb one more appointment before he was discharged, potentially at the end of the year.

The session made Caleb feel a bit better. A bit more confident. Perhaps he was processing things well after all. Perhaps he was going to be okay.

The Center for the Intrepid offered every type of training scenario that could be imagined to prepare soldiers to return to normal life and activities. There was a driving simulator to assess readiness to get behind the wheel. There was an "activities of daily living" apartment to relearn everyday jobs like making the bed or changing a diaper in an unadapted space. There was even a fifty-foot swimming pool where soldiers could swim laps or try adaptive kayaking, and a "flow rider" that re-created the feeling of body surfing or paddling in rough water at the beach.

For Ashley, the real turning point came when the nonprofit Task Force Dagger took the family on a scuba-diving trip. When the organizer mentioned it to her in December, she thought he was crazy. But sure enough, when June came around, they flew to Key West and learned to dive at the Special Forces school. Caleb thought it was surreal to be here and not get yelled at like a student. Because neither Caleb nor Ashley had tried diving before, it wasn't an activity that had to be "adapted." They learned together.

In the summer, they planned the last step: Ashley had to go back to Tucson. Their older daughter was due to start first grade, and

Ashley's family leave was about to run out. She owed her job to her boss. She had dealt with her own paperwork problems when her employer's administrative department refused to accept that her husband had been wounded at war, entitling her to an extended period of leave to care for him. When Ashley and the children moved back home, Caleb moved into a smaller apartment in Texas, aiming to be discharged by the end of the year.

He learned to survive on his own. He had to drive to the medical center every day, fill the car with gas, shop for groceries, and navigate hills, curbs, and rocks. Although he missed the family, he found a new sense of self-worth. He had one last big goal: participating in the army ten-miler in the fall. When Caleb's family came to visit him, he took his eldest daughter to the track to practice running. Ashley filmed them racing. Caleb wore special prosthetics for running and bounced along, arms swinging, toward the finish line after the little girl, who slowed down at the end to avoid outrunning her father.

On October 9, 2016, Caleb staggered across the finish line of a ten-mile race with his old teammate Chris at his side. It took him three hours, and he was exhausted, and sweat made everything slippery. The prosthetics flopped around, his body throbbed and ached, but he'd done it. He had run ten miles less than a year after stepping on a bomb in Sangin. He pushed to be released from medical care and allowed to start his new life. He planned to leave the army even though others tried to convince him to stay. He didn't want to be recruited to show others how great it was to be injured and still serve. He resented the battalion for the expired orders, the harassment over his beard, and the disregard for his injury. He just wanted to go home. Almost two years had passed since he'd left to prepare for the Afghanistan tour.

A medical board had to approve Caleb's discharge, and he was released in December 2016, just in time for Christmas. In Tucson, he decided to take on the role of primary caregiver at home, to make up for Ashley having looked after the family all year. She went back to work. Their kids were two and seven. Being a stay-at-home parent was harder than he'd expected. He could go to the store, do laundry, and drive, but parenting two small children was another matter. When the dog peed in the house, the kids were both howling, and the house was a mess, he felt overwhelmed. The old rage would return, Caleb would bottle it up for as long as possible, and then he'd explode. He'd hear himself yell and think, *What am I doing?*

Ashley saw that he was struggling, but she couldn't do anything about it. When she felt angry too, she tried to suppress it. She knew he was resilient and would work his way through these difficult emotions. She had weathered his changing states since they were teenagers. He would find his own way. Caleb felt bad about his rages. He didn't want to completely let loose, because he knew that wasn't good, but sometimes he couldn't help it. He was aware that being angry was illogical, and yet he couldn't control it.

CHAPTER 24

Trump Inherits the Afghan War

> Do not allow our very stupid leaders to sign a deal that keeps us in Afghanistan through 2024—with all costs by USA. MAKE AMERICA GREAT! We have wasted an enormous amount of blood and treasure in Afghanistan. Their government has zero appreciation. Let's get out!
>
> —*Donald Trump, Twitter, November 2013*

A BILLIONAIRE real estate mogul and a vocal critic of the war in Afghanistan, Donald Trump was exploring a presidential bid in the 2016 election. Trump's "America First" campaign advocated for the United States to withdraw from costly overseas conflicts. In typically blunt fashion, he called the war a disaster, a waste of billions of dollars, and a misuse of resources that should have been directed to domestic schools and infrastructure. He even created a short video calling for the United States to withdraw.

Trump came under pressure to explain his position as the race for the Republican nomination progressed and it became clear that President Obama would hand over the Afghan war to a successor. Afghanistan was a quagmire that had cost the United States close to $2 trillion by some calculations.* But the national security establishment, given ample coverage in the US media, warned against

---

* This figure comes from Brown University's Costs of War Project for the period 2001–2019.

a precipitous withdrawal. It was difficult to argue that leaving Afghanistan would *not* cause the country to collapse. Whether remaining there indefinitely would inevitably expose the United States to the risk of another 9/11-style attack was another matter.

"At some point, are they going to be there for the next two hundred years? At some point what's going on? It's going to be a long time," Trump told CNN in October 2015, when asked about his position on Afghanistan. "It's a mess. And at this point, you probably have to because that thing will collapse about two seconds after they leave. Just as I said that Iraq was going to collapse after we leave."

IN OCTOBER 2016, a month before the US election, Heman Nagarathnam, the deputy in charge of the hospital in Kunduz during the Médecins Sans Frontières attack, was back in the city preparing to mark the one-year anniversary of the bombing. The building was still in ruins, its black, skeletal remains a dark reminder of that terrible night. The tent on the hospital grounds was ready for the memorial service.

In the middle of the night, Heman heard gunshots and explosions. Outside, the sky was pitch black. *Am I dreaming?* he wondered. He wasn't. Kunduz was under attack again. And as it had the previous year, it fell within hours.

US Special Forces and Afghan commandos were dispatched once again to save the city. The Afghan commandos had seen the Kunduz movie before, but the American teams were all new. The 10th Group, which was historically oriented toward Europe, was in charge of the Afghanistan mission. The battalion commander had augmented the US Special Forces presence in Kunduz from the start, with two ODAs permanently based there and led by Zachary McLain and Mike Saleck.

The 10th Group teams studied Hutch's CONOP as a model should the city fall again, and they adopted a similar plan of attack. They had been warning their chain of command for weeks that Kunduz was ripe for another assault after sustained Taliban attacks throughout the spring. No one seemed to have taken much notice.

Their requests for additional resources had gone unheeded. They still had just three armored vehicles and the same broken printer that disgorged magenta blobs.

The night after Kunduz fell, US Special Forces and Afghan commandos penetrated the city and established a foothold at the governor's office. There were rumors that provincial officials had emptied the safe at the bank and fled. The teams came under heavy fire for days, and it took them over a week to regain control of the situation. They were upset to learn later that money distributed to local officials to compensate residents for damaged shops and houses had been mostly stolen. It was easy to see why locals turned to the Taliban. Unless the US-backed government addressed the root causes of the conflict, the insurgency would continue to grow.

The Pentagon played down the significance of the collapse and denied a US role in the operation to recapture Kunduz, once again calling it a training mission. In Kabul, Brig. Gen. Charlie Cleveland described it as an Afghan operation.

"Our Afghan partners are responding to the increased Taliban activity within the area, and US forces have multiple assets and enablers in the area to provide support," he said in a statement emailed to reporters.

The language belied the extent to which the US military had been involved. The "enablers" were the US Special Forces, augmented by an array of attached infantrymen, combat controllers, explosive ordnance teams, intelligence analysts, and so forth. "Assets" meant air support from an AC-130 gunship, drones, helicopters, and jet fighters.

In Washington, Pentagon spokesman Captain Jeff Davis also played down the loss of Kunduz. "This is largely something we've seen before," he told reporters. "We see the Taliban go into these city centers, do a Western-movie style shoot-'em-up, do some raiding, do some looting, raise a flag, and just as quickly as they do that, they are beaten."

A few days after Kunduz collapsed, and while the battle was ongoing, the Taliban launched a coordinated assault on Lashkar Gah, the provincial capital of Helmand, firing rockets into the governor's walled compound. Areas of the provinces Baghlan, Farah, and Uruzgan also came under attack, giving the impression of complete chaos just as foreign donors met at an aid conference in Brussels to pledge support to the Kabul government for the next four years.

Averting their eyes from the situation on the battlefield, the United States and its allies pledged more than $15 billion in aid. The goal remained to help the government achieve self-reliance in what was dubbed the upcoming "transformation decade." It was wishful thinking. President Ghani was midway through his first term in office and had already lost the confidence of donors in Kabul after failing to appoint an inclusive cabinet or make any real effort to tackle high-level corruption.

While Afghanistan edged toward collapse, America's longest war was a topic that no one wanted to broach ahead of the US election. In the course of three presidential debates, it wasn't a topic for discussion. Hillary Clinton and Donald Trump spoke about the Syrian war, immigration, taxes, Russian influence, Clinton's emails, but never Afghanistan. The topic didn't even come up at the final debate, which took place on the same day an insider attack killed a US soldier and another American at a military base in Kabul.

ELECTION NIGHT, November 8, 2016. The US embassy in Kabul was holding an election-results-viewing party, to which it had invited the expat community, including journalists. Afghanistan was eight and a half hours ahead of the East Coast of the United States, which meant the results would be announced the next morning. It seemed the entire embassy was expecting Clinton to win, and that US policy in Afghanistan would be business as usual. The final results jolted the room: Donald Trump had been chosen as the forty-fifth president of the United States.

The mood among the diplomats seemed to be one of shock. Ambassador Michael McKinley took to the podium and delivered a short speech thanking the audience for attending. An American official sitting near the front, who worked in commerce, wiped away a tear. In the back of the room, the US Marines in uniform seemed to be celebrating. What the impact would be on Afghanistan wasn't immediately clear.

Like his predecessor, President Trump was torn between his instinct to pull out and dire warnings from the national security establishment about the consequences of a full withdrawal. The low number of US casualties made staying tolerable, and there were other, more pressing domestic concerns: health care, the economy, and more. Unlike the war in Vietnam, this one didn't trigger protests in the streets. Most of America was unaffected by the war. Talk was revived about capitalizing on Afghanistan's vast mineral wealth, which had proven impossible to extract due to the security situation and the weak rule of law. What would President Trump do?

The deciding factor turned out to be the ousting of National Security Adviser Michael T. Flynn, who was forced to resign after it was revealed that he had withheld information about a call with a Russian ambassador. Army lieutenant general H. R. McMaster was chosen as his replacement. Gen. McMaster lacked a previous connection to President Trump, but he had strong Republican backing and clear views on the war in Afghanistan.

Gen. McMaster, who had served from 2010 to 2012 during the surge in Afghanistan as the commander of an anticorruption task force, was credited with having taken difficult and meaningful steps to tackle the high-level graft and criminal networks that were responsible for draining the reconstruction money. Since then, he had argued that the Afghan war could be won and that a counterinsurgency strategy could work—if the military was unleashed and allowed to come out in full force for as long as it took to do the job.

He was lauded in military circles for his application of a counterinsurgency strategy in Iraq that led to a reduction in violence at a time when the United States seemed to be on the verge of losing the war. He believed that the same dedication could turn around the war in Afghanistan. Unlike President Trump, he wasn't skeptical about the reasons for the US presence in the country. He blamed the failure to win the war partly on what he considered the Obama administration's defeatist approach, which limited troops and resources and put the war on a timeline.

In fact, he thought the US failure went back even farther, to the Bush administration, which had become distracted with Iraq and underinvested in the war in Afghanistan. The lack of US commitment had forced Afghanistan's president at the time, Hamid Karzai, to cut deals with corrupt elites and former warlords, hollowing out institutions that were critical for the state's survival.

Gen. McMaster was often recognized for his book *Dereliction of Duty*, which delivered a blistering critique of the Joint Chiefs of Staff during the Vietnam War for their failure to stand up to the president and his administrators. Some found it ironic that he should emerge as the chief advocate of prolonging the war in Afghanistan, a conflict that many compared to Vietnam and that had dragged on even longer. But in his view, the stakes in Afghanistan were still high, and the US presence was the only hedge against the country once again becoming a safe haven for terrorist groups.

He thought, probably accurately, that the Afghan government would quickly collapse without significant US backing, leading to the same chaos that had allowed the Taliban to rise in the 1990s after the Soviet withdrawal. His main concern was the presence of transnational terrorist groups. The evidence of this often-cited reason for staying in Afghanistan, as always, was not made public, but he thought the links between the Taliban and al Qaeda were reemerging.

At the National Security Council, Gen. McMaster was charged with putting together a plan for Afghanistan, which included deciding how to approach the unpredictable President Trump, known for a long history of skepticism and ingrained opposition to the Afghan war. McMaster acknowledged that the president wanted to get out of Afghanistan and all other Bush-era conflicts to focus on other priorities. But to him, sorting out Afghanistan was important for national security, and he planned to bulldoze through the administration.

Gen. McMaster later identified a moral imperative behind his strategy: "I thought there was an ethical dimension to this too, by the way, because soldiers were fighting and dying and there was not really a clear articulation of the strategy that would allow them to understand how the risks that they take, and the sacrifices that they might be called on to make, were contributing to an outcome worthy of those risks and sacrifices."

Gen. McMaster and President Trump did agree on one thing: that micromanaging the war was wrong. President Trump swiftly delegated authorities on troops and targeting to the Pentagon and cut back the number of high-level meetings on Afghanistan. He didn't want to hear about it, and the relevant departments and agencies, including the Pentagon and the State Department, believed that keeping the war out of his sight was the most prudent course of action. Everyone feared that the president might one morning see something on Fox News that he didn't like and dispatch the "Tweet of Damocles" that would end the war in a single post.

Gen. Nicholson, supported by the chairman of the Joint Chiefs of Staff, Dunford, and other senior military officials, stayed on as the top commander of US troops in Afghanistan. He, too, advocated an expanded mission, calling for more resources to turn the tide of the war in favor of the United States. President Trump was barely a month into his presidency when the general called on the new administration to fix capability gaps in airpower and troop numbers and warned that Islamic State remained a threat, especially now that fighters under pressure in Syria and Iraq might flock to shelter in Afghanistan.

At a hearing of the Senate Armed Services Committee, he cautioned that the war was at a "stalemate" and that the emergence of Islamic State had created a new enemy. Implicit in his testimony was his criticism of the Obama administration's fixation with numbers and micromanaging authorities. Gen. Nicholson argued that the mission in Afghanistan was a success overall, measured by the absence of major terrorist attacks on US soil. Without providing further details, he also claimed that the US-backed coalition in Afghanistan had stopped Islamic State from carrying out a high-profile attack. He testified that a series of operations called Green Sword that had been launched against the affiliate known as Islamic State Khorasan Province had killed about a third of the group's fighters, including its leader.

Claims about Islamic State Khorasan Province were difficult to verify. The group's spokesman had been killed in a US drone strike over a year earlier, and a successor had not been appointed. Any communication came from the main Islamic State media branch, and its connections to the group in Afghanistan were unclear. Often, it claimed responsibility for attacks hours after the incident had taken place and with little evidence that it was really involved, suggesting that it might be taking credit for violence perpetrated by the Taliban and other groups.

As usual, the audience was sympathetic to the military's call for more troops, authorities, and resources. Senator John McCain, the committee chairman, gave Gen. Nicholson a platform from which to make his appeal.

"Numbers are just one parameter," McCain said when asking about troops. "But it is an important parameter. How many more do you need to get this stalemate reversed?"

Gen. Nicholson replied that the counterterrorism mission was in good shape, but more troops were required to support the Afghan government. "In my train, advise, assist mission, however, we have a shortfall of a few thousand," he said.

AMONG THE GREEN BERETS heading back to Afghanistan under the new Trump administration was Jordan, the Bravo that had fought in Marjah. He had switched teams to be able to return to the battlefield less than a year after coming home with Mick's body. Casey did the same. Going back afforded an easy escape from the guilt that stalked them after the mission. Dismayed, Jordan's wife watched him make the choice to leave instead of getting reacquainted with his family and getting to know his newborn child.

Jordan and Casey were assigned to different teams, both based at Jalalabad Airfield, Nangarhar, where the focus of their mission was targeting the Islamic State Khorasan Province. It was slow at first. But in the spring of 2017, the soldiers were told that the secretary of defense, Jim Mattis, wanted Islamic State defeated by July, and they were to get busy seeing it through. A long-planned, large-scale operation targeting the terrorist organization finally took off. The first stage of the strategy was to clear Kot district, where the earliest Islamic State members had made their pledges of allegiance. It was a poor, rural area near the mountainous border with Pakistan, made up of rugged hills and grassy fields, with clusters of mud-brick villages scattered throughout the farmland.

For a number of reasons, including a lack of available Afghan commandos and a need to win over the locals, the Green Berets were assigned to work with forces from the villages in the province. These forces were streamlined into a new project known as the People's Uprising Program; it seemed very much like the Afghan Local Police program, which was being wound down.

Jordan's team was the second to arrive in Kot district. In contrast to his previous deployment in Helmand, his team had access to everything they needed for the mission, and the rules were more relaxed. Morale was high. They set up a patrol base and began clearing outward toward the mountains. The villagers knew the ways around thick belts of buried IEDs. There had been a massive exodus from the area after Islamic State fighters began experimenting with brutal enforcement methods like those used in Iraq and Syria. Jordan's team slept in their trucks every night, and in the mornings they pushed out. There was no sign of the government on the road, and villages were mostly abandoned. Mud-brick homes and padlocked shops had been left to the elements.

An additional team sent to augment the effort in Kot from a different part of the district was pulled out immediately when their Fox stepped on a bomb and lost part of a leg. Others were injured in the same blast. Jordan had never seen so many IEDs in a single place, not even in Helmand. But air support came when needed, and they seemed to have access to unlimited amounts of ammunition and other supplies. They stayed in Kot for twenty-three days and then moved on to Achin district. The Islamic State had clustered there in the Mohmand valley, at the foot of the Spin Ghar mountain range, which formed a natural border between Afghanistan and Pakistan and contained some of the tallest peaks in the world.

When the United States first invaded, the snowcapped mountains had been a refuge for fleeing Taliban and al Qaeda fighters, including bin Laden, who was believed to have been holed up in the Tora Bora cave complex, located farther west. Another team in Achin district suffered the first KIA of the deployment when Mark de Alencar was shot in an entrenched battle at the foot of the mountains, where the grassy, fertile plains met the rocky, barren peaks. Mark, also a Bravo, had qualified for the Special Forces only a year earlier. He was thirty-seven and left behind a wife of fifteen years and their five children. The operation was barely covered in the US news. His sister-in-law told reporters that she had thought the war was over.

Less than a week later, however, the next step in the offensive seized world headlines. US and Afghan teams were ordered to pull back a few miles for their safety, to allow for an airstrike. For some time, the US military had been wanting to use a bomb that had never been tested in combat, the GBU-43/B Massive Ordnance Air Blast (MOAB), nicknamed the "Mother of All Bombs." It was dropped on a complex of tunnels and caves in the Mohmand valley on April 13, 2017, setting a new record as the biggest conventional bomb ever deployed on the battlefield.

The United States did not release an assessment of casualties, but the spectacle had instant effect. The US media took the strike as a signal that things were going to be different under the Trump administration. Some outlets even suggested that it was a warning to North Korean dictator Kim Jong-un with whom President Trump was engaged in a verbal standoff over the country's nuclear and missile programs.

In Afghanistan, local media questioned whether the country, in its final humiliation, had become a testing ground for American weapons. Similarly, even some in the US military speculated that the strike was motivated by a desire to make use of the Trump administration's flexibility to try out new equipment. At the US military's headquarters in Kabul, word was that the bomb was dropped to avenge the death of the Green Beret in the valley a week earlier. There was also apparently a second GBU-43/B in the country and talk that the US military was looking for a second target to drop the bomb on.

Though the strike had been meant to break the deadlock at the foot of the mountains and to avert further casualties, Jordan believed that it was also partly motivated by revenge. But the Mother of All Bombs didn't appear to have much impact on the ground. When his team reached the scene, the front lines hadn't changed significantly. They returned to their former positions, more or less, and continued to press forward, slowly clearing ground that was heavily mined and defended by cave complexes.

After several kilometers, they set up a camp that became known as Combat Outpost Blackfish and continued to patrol deeper into the valley, trying to clear more ground and taking fire daily. A rocket hit the post and almost landed on top of them on one of their last days there. On the way out, their convoy was struck by a roadside bomb that killed an interpreter. In later years, Combat Outpost Blackfish became a major post on the frontline against Islamic State.

After the operation was over, Gen. Nicholson told reporters that the US had killed sixteen hundred Islamic State fighters, leaving only a thousand in Afghanistan's east in November 2017. But the number of active Islamic State members would increase over the years, regardless of what the United States did, suggesting that the military lacked a clear picture of the situation, or that Islamic State recruitment rates outpaced its losses. Just a couple of months later, Gen.

Nicholson said that the US military had cut the group's numbers in half, and there were now an estimated fifteen hundred Islamic State fighters left in early 2018—a much higher number than reported the previous year.

From the Islamic State branch in Afghanistan, there was silence.

CHAPTER 25

You Don't Believe in Winning?

GENERAL MCMASTER

WHEN PRESIDENT TRUMP took office in early 2017, responsibility at the State Department for the Afghan peace process had passed to Laurel Miller, who had become the acting special representative for Afghanistan and Pakistan. She hoped to continue the push for peace negotiations under the new administration, as the president was vocally opposed to foreign engagements and might be open to bolder steps to accelerate progress.

Miller drafted a proposal for the new secretary of state, Rex Tillerson, to read as soon as he took his place on the seventh floor. It outlined the main points that had emerged over almost a year of secret talks with the Taliban and offered a framework for moving forward. She waited several months but received no reply. Secretary Tillerson's team lacked key staff and was unprepared to hit the ground running. Worried about missing the opportunity to make an impact on policy, Miller enlisted the undersecretary for political affairs, Tom Shannon, to get a response. The third-ranking officer at the State Department, Shannon oversaw the implementation of regional and bilateral policy.

Soon he came back with a reply: Secretary Tillerson had signed off on the proposal. No questions asked. Miller was taken aback.

She thought the news that the United States had been talking to the Taliban for almost a year would come as a surprise, perhaps even a shock. After all, the United States had been fighting the Taliban without pause for over fifteen years. But apparently the secretary thought that continuing with negotiations was a no-brainer. The message, according to Shannon, was something like: "If you've been doing this for some time, and think it might eventually lead somewhere, have at it." The White House signed off on a trip.

In the first week of April 2017, Miller left for another round of talks with the Taliban in Doha, accompanied by her Pentagon counterpart, Jedidiah Royal, the acting deputy assistant secretary of defense for Afghanistan, Pakistan, and Central Asia. Unlike Secretary Tillerson, the secretary of defense, Mattis, had taken a personal interest in the effort and had given Royal detailed guidance and feedback before their departure. As always, the talks were held in secrecy and have not been previously reported in the media.

The US negotiators, pushing hard for a breakthrough, tried to convince the Taliban that this could be a last opportunity to prove that the process was viable. The new administration might close the door to further talks, they warned. The Taliban didn't buy into the scheme. Their position remained, as always, that official talks needed to begin with the United States before the Kabul government was brought in. The US delegation lacked the authority to put troops on the table or offer any other bargaining chips. The process hit a wall.

At the National Security Council, Gen. McMaster was planning an interagency trip to Afghanistan and the surrounding region to finalize policy options for President Trump. He wanted to get all departments and agencies on board to ensure a cooperative approach. Too often, strategies failed because one agency or another did not really buy in. But executing his plan wasn't so easy. The idea of an interagency trip was met with stiff resistance from both the State Department and the Department of Defense.

Gen. McMaster thought their opposition stemmed from timidity: they were reluctant to confront a difficult problem with bold new ideas. Bureaucrats preferred to maintain the status quo. He asked Fernando Lujan, who was filling the vacated role of acting senior director for South Asia after Peter Lavoy's departure, to work on options for a new South Asia strategy until Lujan's replacement could start.

The national security adviser's focus on Afghanistan caused consternation at the agencies. The Pentagon worried that proposing a new and escalated effort in Afghanistan would invite President Trump's wrath and potentially backfire. President Trump had repeatedly expressed his disapproval of the Afghan war and his intention to end it, not ramp it up. If Gen. McMaster pushed too hard, President Trump might remember that the war was still going on and pull the plug. The State Department, for its part, worried that Gen. McMaster would bulldoze over the talks, which already faced criticism due to the lack of progress made after a year of secret meetings, and put negotiations on hold indefinitely.

By the time Gen. McMaster launched the trip in mid-April 2017, his staff had drafted an early version of the South Asia strategy that was working its way through the interagency process. He planned to stop in Afghanistan first, for two nights, and then travel on to Pakistan for a half day and India for one night. He didn't have his new team in place, and he felt that some of the holdovers from the previous administration were ill-suited to their roles. He was particularly skeptical of the State Department's Laurel Miller and her focus on reconciliation. To his mind, the Obama appointees just didn't have the courage to commit to the war and failed to understand the potentially disastrous consequences of letting Afghanistan slide out of control. He thought there was a real risk that the country could become a training ground for terrorist groups like al Qaeda and Islamic State if it collapsed.

He was pleased that the National Security Council's new South Asia director, Lisa Curtis, was due to join them in Pakistan. Lujan was on the trip, along with Courtney Cooper, who was still the Afghanistan director at the council. Laurel Miller and Jed Royal joined from the State Department and the Pentagon, respectively, having recently returned from their trip to meet the Taliban in Doha. Gen. McMaster summoned them to his office during the flight to Afghanistan to brief him on the progress they'd made so far with the talks.

Miller had prepared a pitch that summarized the takeaways from the past year and what approaches could be taken to advance the process.

"Well, I think we're just wasting our time," Gen. McMaster said as soon as she was finished.

He proceeded to outline his vision for US strategy in Afghanistan. It did not involve peace talks anytime soon. The first step, the national security adviser said, was to turn around the trajectory of the conflict. The United States had to stop the Taliban's advance on the battlefield and force them to agree to concessions in the process. He criticized the Obama administration's botched troop surge, which had been undercut by the tight eighteen-month deadline to start withdrawing. He had served in Afghanistan in 2011, when the US presence was at its peak of one hundred thousand troops, and believed that pulling out early, just as the surge was showing signs of progress, had sabotaged any chance of victory.

He told Miller and the other staff members present that US talks with the Taliban would only succeed when the United States returned to a position of strength on the battlefield and was "winning" against the insurgency. At the mention of winning, the Afghanistan director, Cooper, tried not to roll her eyes. She thought back to all the previous generals that had come and gone in Afghanistan, each of them promising to turn a corner. She didn't think the United States could force the Taliban to make concessions simply by ramping up on the battlefield. Nor was President Trump likely to endorse such a plan.

Gen. McMaster saw her expression out of the corner of his eye. "What? You don't believe in winning?" he asked.

In Afghanistan, the national security adviser was pleased to find that everyone was enthusiastic about his proposed course of action.

The US military had been advocating for additional authorities and troops since the drawdown. The Afghan president, Ghani, along with the rest of the government, was delighted. Senior Afghan officials remembered Gen. McMaster from his tour in Afghanistan and expected him to lift the Obama-era restrictions on US operations that had allowed the Taliban to make gains in the preceding years.

After returning from the trip, Gen. McMaster felt that everyone understood the importance of getting on board with the process and unifying around a new strategy. The next step was to produce a framing document that would present a cohesive appraisal of US interests in the region and the situation in Afghanistan, and a shared view of US goals. He wanted the South Asia strategy to recognize that the policies for each country in the region had to be interlinked to shape the outcome in Afghanistan.

That process proved simple enough, to his surprise. Everyone was ready to put more pressure on Pakistan for sheltering the Taliban, a complaint that Gen. Nicholson had repeatedly testified about in Congress. The trouble began when the time came to refine options for President Trump and decide how to present them. Usually, agencies gave the president options to choose from, with scenarios for each. Gen. McMaster wanted to offer four options, including withdrawal, which the president clearly favored. He encountered resistance from others who countered that President Trump might just pull out if given the choice.

In a sign of how security was ailing in Afghanistan, a huge truck bomb exploded at the gates of the German embassy in the center of Kabul at rush hour on May 31, 2017. The blast left a nearly fifteen-foot crater in the ground, killed over 150 people (the vast majority Afghan civilians), and wounded hundreds of others. No one claimed responsibility. The Taliban rarely took credit for bombings that had a high toll on the civilian population, and Islamic State, which sometimes took credit for attacks hours after they had occurred, didn't emerge either.

The bombing signaled that the Western-backed government was unable to secure even the most heavily fortified part of the capital city, and foreign embassies further scaled down or suspended their operations. US embassy officials and other Western diplomats were severely restricted in their movements. Even before the attack, the US embassy had relied on a contractor to shuttle staff between the embassy and the Kabul airport by helicopter because the mile-long trip by road was considered too dangerous. The flights cost thousands of dollars each way. Things only got worse after the bombing.

The South Asia strategy was supposed to be finalized before Afghanistan came up at a meeting of NATO defense ministers at the end of June, but disaccord at the National Security Council delayed the process. By that stage, reconciliation had effectively dropped off the agenda. Miller's contract at the State Department was set to expire, and there were no plans to keep the office of the special representative for Afghanistan and Pakistan running. On Miller's last day, Alice Wells, who was set to take over the role of acting assistant secretary for South Asia, was asked to take on its responsibilities instead.

When the National Security Council finalized its proposal for President Trump in July, it outlined three options. The first was an increase of up to seven thousand troops and certain adjustments to the US military's authorities; the second was a full withdrawal, which would guarantee chaos and US humiliation; the third was turning the war over to contractors, who would be guided by US Special Forces and the CIA.

There are different accounts of how the process went down. The best is to be found in Michael Wolff's book *Fire and Fury*, which is mostly based on a version of events provided by Steve Bannon, then the chief strategist at the White House. It describes how President Trump lost his temper as soon as the plan was presented, angrily railing against the mess he'd inherited in Afghanistan and threatening to fire almost every general in the chain of command. Again and again, President Trump returned to the same point: we're stuck, we're losing the war, and nobody has a plan to do better than that. "The generals were punting and waffling and desperately trying to save face," Wolff writes. "Talking pure gobbledygook in the situation room."

President Trump compared the interagency process to an episode that had taken place at the 21 Club, one of his favorite New York restaurants. It had closed for a year, during which it had hired an expensive team of consultants to analyze how to make the business more profitable. The advice was to get a bigger kitchen. "Exactly what any waiter would have said!" President Trump shouted, according to Wolff's account.

After a couple more attempts, Gen. McMaster finally succeeded in convincing President Trump, who was also under pressure from lawmakers and the media to make a decision, to sign off on the plan to moderately increase troops. The South Asia strategy, which framed Afghanistan as integral to stability in a volatile and strategic neighborhood, was presented to the public in August 2017. It involved increasing pressure on the Taliban and taking a tougher approach with Pakistan. It lifted restrictions on US action against the Taliban and fully relaunched the US war in Afghanistan with a potentially open-ended commitment.

"The Taliban was not a declared enemy force. It was crazy!" Gen. McMaster said later, in an interview in his office at Stanford University. He said the plan he pushed through marked the first time the United States had had a "sound strategy" in Afghanistan since the beginning. It aimed to be tough on Pakistan by cutting off aid and treating the country as an antagonist for hosting the Taliban and terrorist groups, rather than as an ally.

Following the announcement of the South Asia strategy, a slow-burning bureaucratic battle ensued between Gen. McMaster and government agencies. In our interview, he launched into a denunciation of the Taliban's attacks on Afghan-government and US forces, and complained that getting agencies to implement the strategy had been difficult. The Pentagon slow-walked the directive to increase pressure on Pakistan, he said, and took too long to send more troops to Afghanistan. In the end, he had to write a memo to Secretary of Defense Mattis, urging him to press ahead with the order to ramp up operations.

"I mean, it was extraordinary. There was a lot of friction on that," Gen. McMaster said. "I wrote a memo that said, hey, the president said the Taliban's a declared enemy force. What don't you guys understand about this?"

He also had difficulty controlling the State Department. Despite being advised not to talk to the Taliban, to allow the full force of increased pressure on the group to sink in, they "fell all over themselves" to talk to the Taliban, in his words. Alice Wells traveled to meet with Taliban officials in Doha soon after inheriting the responsibility of the special representative's office, to continue the relationship where it had left off.

Gen. McMaster thought it would never be possible to reach a meaningful settlement with the Taliban without an unending commitment to stay, as outlined in the South Asia strategy. "Thinking that's going to get us anywhere in a negotiation with these people—who have a vision for Afghanistan that is, I think, a modern-day form of barbarism—I mean it was crazy. If it had been up to me, I would have closed the Taliban political office. I think it was a total waste of time," he said.

President Trump supported the idea of naming a new envoy for Afghan peace ahead of the South Asia strategy announcement, but it failed to gain traction during the interagency process for various reasons. Opponents did not want peace to become a distraction, feared losing influence over policy, or were skeptical that talks with the Taliban would lead anywhere, citing the State Department's failure to make progress over a year of meetings.

The new authorities meanwhile led to a massive surge in US operations and airstrikes. The United States dropped 4,361 munitions in Afghanistan in 2017, more than triple the total deployed a year earlier. The escalation helped keep the Taliban out of major cities, but it failed to stop the erosion of government control in rural areas.

In Kabul, Western diplomats remained largely confined to heavily fortified compounds.

For the Special Forces who were heading to Afghanistan in 2018, the outlook was very different than in earlier years. Fewer restrictions on airstrikes and on partnered operations gave them much greater freedom to operate. Air support was limited by the availability of assets, rather than by policy, and strikes could be authorized at a lower level than in the past. All these changes increased the military's flexibility to support troops on the ground. Despite this, the military continued to run into crises when the Taliban renewed efforts to capture a provincial capital, this time turning its focus to western Farah and southeastern Ghazni.

Although President Trump signed off on the South Asia strategy, he did not keep Gen. McMaster around for much longer. He fired the general in 2018, in part over his handling of Afghanistan. Unlike other cabinet-level officials, he was at least spared the humiliation of receiving the news via Twitter. The new national security adviser, John Bolton, favored a continued US presence to fight terrorism but was less preoccupied with the quagmire in Afghanistan and did not believe the war could be won.

President Trump also began a hunt for a new commander to replace Gen. Nicholson, complaining that he wasn't winning the war even after receiving the requested additional authorities and troops. Senior military officials tried to reason that it wasn't possible to turn around the war with still-limited resources in a short period of time, but Gen. Nicholson's public comments about victory being around the corner only added fuel to the fire.

CHAPTER 26

Green Berets Unleashed
JOSH

LIEUTENANT COLONEL JOSH THIEL, the commander of 3rd Battalion, 1st Special Forces Group, was tapped to lead the mission soon after the new South Asia strategy was announced. Based at Joint Base Lewis-McChord in Washington State, he had nine months to prepare for the deployment, which was scheduled for early March 2018. Josh was athletic with short dark hair and a chiseled jaw. He kept a small axe in his bunker-like office, and he sometimes used it as a prop while talking to emphasize a point.

He had served two combat tours in Iraq and one in Afghanistan. From the start, he had a clear picture in his mind about what he wanted to achieve during the deployment and energetically threw himself into planning for the mission. US Special Forces had three advanced operations bases (AOBs), or regional headquarters, made up of eighteen teams in total, which for several years had been firefighting all over the country alongside some eighteen thousand Afghan commandos to prevent major towns and cities from collapse.

Josh had the daunting task of reversing the impression that the country was descending into chaos, and his first goal was to prevent the loss of any provincial capital. It had happened every year in Afghanistan since Kunduz first fell in 2015, giving the Taliban a steady stream of opportunities to make it look like the government was unable to control its territory. He planned to use the floating teams to distract the Taliban and draw them away from major city centers.

Second, Josh resolved to accelerate the US military's operations against the Islamic State affiliate in the east. The group was lodged in the mountains, and he planned to try to push them even farther out, if not erase their presence altogether. Some reports said that Islamic State Khorasan Province, as the military called the affiliate, had established a capital in Deh Bala, and he planned to take it. He thought he could use the defeat as propaganda to slow funding and recruitment.

Josh spoke to his men in plain terms ahead of the tour. "I'm not going to tell you we can win this war, but I am going to make sure that we will damage the enemy more for every risk you take."

The younger Green Berets were excited about the upcoming deployment, but it was sobering to the older soldiers who had lost friends on every trip and had already completed multiple tours in the nearly seventeen-year war in Afghanistan. At almost forty, Josh had shed much of the idealism that had driven him to join the Green Berets after the 9/11 attacks. But he believed that channeling his near-limitless reserve of energy into the tour would do justice to the men whose lives were on the line. As was the case for many Green Berets, his commitment to the force had come at a price: a strained marriage, missed events in the lives of his children, and traumatic stress after multiple overseas tours.

Josh's vigor came naturally. He had been raised in a hardworking family in Indiana. His mother worked as an intensive care nurse and studied nights to get a university degree, while his father owned a small sporting-goods shop and fought a constant existential struggle against superstores and online retailers. His grandfather was a World War II veteran and local celebrity as the longest-serving volunteer firefighter in the nation, having served for sixty years. He often made the local news, and his grandmother collected all the clippings, which Josh looked forward to receiving year after year.

He scraped his way into West Point to escape small-town Indiana and traded his first assignment at Fort Lewis for a prized one in Hawaii with a soldier who wanted to live in Washington State to be near his girlfriend. "Networks of influence are more important than class rank," he said. He had planned to leave the army after five years, but like so many he changed his mind after September 11. He had a new purpose: become a Green Beret and answer the call to serve, like his grandfather had sixty-five years earlier.

Josh made it through the Special Forces Qualification Course and graduated in 2005. It took longer to get to the war. His first overseas tour wasn't to Afghanistan or Iraq, but to the island of Papua New Guinea for a mission to train the local army; he lived there for several months with his team at a small former Australian base surrounded by densely packed forest, volcanoes, and deadly snakes. It was another year before he got to Iraq for his first tour in 2007.

By the time Josh took over the battalion, nearly a decade had passed and the war in Afghanistan was ramping up. He ordered his intelligence unit to read through two hundred years of Afghan history and to take note of key battles, nodes, and events, all in an effort to discover a pattern of attacks that would predict the Taliban's behavior that summer. Josh was interested in war games and strategic analysis.

The intelligence unit spent weeks trawling through books and then entering data for the seven changes of power that had taken place in Afghanistan over two centuries into Palantir software, used to analyze data. Josh had previously used the software in the Philippines to identify two militant leaders. He grew excited when two strategies for taking control of Afghanistan emerged. One began in the south and moved through rural provinces, forming a ring around Kabul until the capital fell—the Taliban's strategy in the 1990s. The second was a Kabul-first approach, popular with foreign invaders, like the Americans had done in 2001.

Josh finalized the troop disposition accordingly, matching up teams to areas and skill sets. He put a number of ODAs in hot spots like Helmand and Kunduz. Breaking with tradition, he decided the rest would float. Teams usually were assigned an area and expected to master the details of its geography, power structures, and networks. Turning them into mobile strike forces was unconventional, but because the teams were constantly firefighting anyway, he decided it was best to maximize flexibility.

In March 2018, the battalion arrived in Afghanistan and took over the war from 10th Group. Josh found there were still too few ODAs to deal with the many crises and a shortage of Afghan commandos available to pair up for missions. Although the Afghan army was churning them out, the commandos were seeing rising attrition rates from casualties and unauthorized absences, and were still being used primarily to guard checkpoints and VIPs or to rush to one crisis or another with little notice. There was virtually no limit on the scope of their operations under the new presidential administration. Resources, rather than authorities, curbed their missions.

Josh started out with a surge of five teams in Helmand and Uruzgan in the south to target Taliban prisons and drug labs to cut off the group's sources of income and drive the insurgents farther north.

In Logar, just south of Kabul, he had a team led by Captain Kyle Harnitchek that worked with the Afghan intelligence agency to push the Taliban away from the capital. Security in the province, which had long been problematic, was worsening. During the team's first week on the ground, Logar's deputy governor and his bodyguards were assassinated in broad daylight after falling into a trap and stopping at a fake checkpoint operated by the Taliban. The Taliban administered government resources, from the subjects that were taught in schools to who got government jobs. Their white Islamic Emirate flags were visible from the main highway. Kyle's team's first big mission aimed to take out the Red Unit, a local team of Taliban "special forces" that had executed the deputy governor, and over several days they hunted down and killed all twenty-two members.

In Nangarhar province, near the border with Pakistan, Captain David Kim led the team, ODA 1331, responsible for laying the groundwork for a major operation planned against Islamic State. David had been born to South Korean immigrants in New Jersey and was raised to believe that "you're not a man until you've served." It was his third tour in Afghanistan, after two with the conventional army.

At the end of April, David's team drove into Deh Bala district, past miles of poppy farms until the fields ran out. The Taliban grew poppy and controlled most of the district. When Islamic State took over an area, they brought in their own families and customs, and banned growing poppy. It was easy to tell where the Taliban's territory ended because the poppy fields disappeared. Using poppy fields as a marker, David's team stopped the convoy and began work to set up a mission support site, named Camp Blackbeard, and an observation post on a ridge overlooking an Islamic State settlement. It was believed to be the group's capital, located in Gurgoray valley, which led to the Spin Gar Mountains. The Battle of Tora Bora had been fought there nearly two decades earlier, and Osama bin Laden was thought to have fled into Pakistan over those same peaks at the start of the war. The team ate military rations, known as meals ready to eat, or MREs, until the kitchen was set up. They were grateful when the Afghans brought food—steaming rice with raisins, carrots, and greasy chunks of meat on the bone—even if someone always got sick afterward.

The team also located a settlement of displaced Afghan villagers who had fled their homes to escape Islamic State brutality, and sent a psyops team to conduct interviews with the locals.

JOSH WORKED ON A PLAN with the AOB-East commander to launch the offensive once the teams were ready. They planned to focus attacks from the observation post to drive Islamic State to build up defenses toward the east. After a month, they would drop in teams behind the Islamic State settlement and attack it from behind. Their goal was to complete the operation before the Brussels Conference in the late summer, during which nations would once again meet to pledge financial aid to Afghanistan.

Josh found that planning a large operation required a certain amount of lobbying for resources. He got to know the commanders in charge of various air assets and organized weekly dinners with them. He also tried to get Brigadier General John W. Brennan Jr., the commander of US and NATO forces in eastern Afghanistan, on board. Gen. Brennan was interested in the plan but skeptical about obtaining a weeklong commitment of air support from the coalition.

"What if we do it on Eid?" Josh said. Eid al-Fitr was a Muslim holiday that marked the end of the holy month of Ramadan, the equivalent to Christmas in Afghanistan.

The US general in charge of air assets agreed to support him. The last question was how to convince the Afghan army to sign off on the plan. President Ghani and the coalition had promised no offensive operations against the Taliban during the holiday period, which meant the commandos would be free—and Islamic State wasn't the Taliban. Josh outlined the plan for Gen. Nicholson, emphasizing the suffering of locals under Islamic State and the potential to go after foreign fighters. The argument that the group was made up of foreign invaders won favor. The plan was approved. Josh ordered the psyops team to brief the Afghan commandos about the interviews with the villagers. Everyone was fired up.

CHAPTER 27

Special Forces to the Rescue

JOSH

Josh's plans to launch the operation against Islamic State were interrupted by his first major crisis of the deployment: a Taliban assault on the capital of Farah, a remote and sand-swept province on the western border with Iran. A vast rural area sparsely populated by poppy farmers, smugglers, and bandits, it was where one of the first Islamic State affiliates had surfaced years earlier.

Farah's capital city, also named Farah, had a population of around fifty thousand. It had come under repeated attacks and swiftly erupted into chaos in May 2018. As always, the skirmish started in the early hours of the morning. The governor fled, but security stayed behind to guard the compound, which by noon appeared to be the only building still under government control. The police chief was killed in the assault. The Taliban claimed to have captured the city within hours and posted pictures and videos of themselves driving around in Afghan army vehicles and celebrating in the main square.

The attack was a blow to Josh's goal to make it through the tour without losing a provincial capital. Military leaders, as they had during the crises in Kunduz and Helmand, turned to the Green Berets and Afghan commandos. Much in the same way that Col.

Johnston had been ordered to save Kunduz years earlier, Josh found himself tasked with regaining control of the city.

"Go now. You have all priority for assets in Afghanistan," Gen. Nicholson told Josh as the reports came in during his visit to the AOB-South headquarters in Kandahar.

Josh tapped the AOB-South commander, John King, to fly into Farah with two teams to work with the commandos to restore order. John, an old Afghan hand, flew in and set up a control center in the city. Farah's layout was a big point in their favor; the airport was located on the outskirts of town and surrounded, conveniently, by an expanse of desert territory. John arrived with a light tactical vehicle equipped with a satellite system that could send and receive information, including surveillance feeds and imagery the US military and the commandos could use once they had driven the Taliban out of the city, to show that the situation was under control.

The first two teams landed within ten hours of the attack, and a third arrived by road in four armored trucks from Herat province, the only way to ensure they would have access to vehicles. The command center operated from the airport, while the teams took turns using the four trucks to go out alongside the commandos.

Josh watched it all from the joint operations center, where his seat in the middle gave him a view of approximately twenty TV screens that transmitted feeds from drones and other aircraft. His staff included a strike cell, a battle captain, and an intelligence unit that reviewed reports as they came in. Within a day, the Taliban were gone.

As usual, US military officials who briefed reporters did not disclose the key role that the Green Berets, backed with close air support, had played in restoring order to Farah city. The Trump administration had loosened the rules, but the spin was the same: it was a training and support mission, and the US role in the war was over. A spokesman acknowledged that the US military had ground attack jets flying over Farah but credited the Afghans alone for recapturing the provincial capital.

"The Afghan security forces are bringing their full capabilities, consisting of army, police, commandos and Air Force, to bear on the situation," the US military said in a statement. "As we have seen over the last couple of days, the Taliban are unable to hold terrain during such isolated attacks."

Despite the relatively quick reversal in the city center, the Taliban continued multipronged attacks in other parts of Farah province and harassed police and army checkpoints at night, sneaking up on isolated posts and killing everyone inside before reinforcements could arrive. The Taliban evaded US surveillance by choosing to attack when skies were cloudy. On night five, the Taliban group miscalculated. An Apache pilot, who volunteered to fly in harsh wind and sandy conditions, caught them off guard and chased down the insurgents, killing most of them as they fled. There were no more ambushes on remote government outposts in Farah after that.

In the east, the team responsible for managing the offensive against Islamic State had set up Camp Blackbeard for the operation and was ready to launch; they were equipped with a surgical team, resupply for ammunition, and food and water. David, the captain, looked forward to rising every morning to a view of the mountains—peaks and ridgelines as far as the eye could see. The Islamic State had built defensive bunkers out of concrete, and for several weeks the team had focused on getting rid of those using mortars.

The operation was named Hamza 003—the third in a series of campaigns that had taken place each year to drive the Islamic State affiliate deeper into the mountains. David was also trying to work with provincial officials in Deh Bala to raise a village-level force that could hold the territory once it was cleared. In late May, six teams deployed to the district and surrounded Gurgoray valley, making it the focal point of American military might in the country.

As an opening move, Josh had the US Air Force drop four two-thousand-pound bombs on the ridge to clear roadside bombs and create a fighting position for the Green Berets. The F-16s usually carried five-hundred-pound bombs; he had specially requested the larger munitions under an authority known as terrain denial fires. It was another example of how things had changed under the new administration; in earlier years, airstrikes had only been allowed as a last resort, in self-defense. Now, no one questioned the tactic as a means to clearing a path for US troops to launch an attack.

The valley was shaped like a teardrop. One team became responsible for strike operations in the north while two others dropped into the west without commandos, attacked the Islamic State settlement from the rear, and began clearing operations. Although they usually operated with commandos, in this instance insertion was complex, and resupplying a large force in that area would have been difficult.

The sudden, large-scale assault surprised the Islamic State affiliate, which had built trench-like defenses on its eastern flank; as Josh had anticipated, the group was unprepared for the attack on the west. On day two or three, Islamic State put out a call for all cells to come and defend the capital of the caliphate. That confirmed to the coalition teams on the ground the true value of taking the valley, which turned out to contain administrative records and documents of foreign fighters who had traveled from as far as Europe to join the group.

The villages they recaptured in Gurgoray valley were mostly in ruins through a combination of neglect and damage caused by the clearing operation that unearthed dozens of IEDs, some charged with seventy or eighty pounds of explosives. Almost immediately, Afghan villagers began trickling back to inspect the remains. Many had been away for nearly three years. Josh used emergency funds* to pay for local police to cover the area, but in the end they still fell short. When US troops and Afghan commandos pulled out at the end of the operation, they were forced to leave a portion of the newly cleared ground unguarded.

There were no US casualties during the operation, but David's team ran into trouble later in the deployment. The combat controller stepped on a roadside bomb and lost a leg; others nearby suffered shrapnel wounds and traumatic brain injury. Another teammate was

---

* Under the Commander's Emergency Response Program.

shot in the face in a separate incident. Luckily for him, the round went through his cheek without striking bone.

In June, during Eid al-Fitr, the Taliban agreed to a three-day cease-fire with the government that gave the world a shocking preview of what life in Afghanistan could look like without the war. Afghan soldiers and police hugged bearded Taliban fighters in tunics and camouflage vests, wept, and ate ice cream in the town centers. It wasn't to last. Once the three days were up, fighting resumed, and repeated US and Afghan-government efforts to produce another cease-fire were in vain.

JOSH RAN INTO THE SECOND major crisis of the deployment weeks later. After building up for months, the Taliban attacked the eastern city of Ghazni in August 2018. Ghazni had over a quarter million residents, and in 2013, the UN had designated it an Asian Capital of Islamic Culture for its rich heritage and its many historical sites that needed to be preserved. It was also strategically important due to its location on the main highway connecting Kabul and Kandahar. The insurgents had been consolidating in the districts surrounding the provincial capital for months, but the ODAs stationed in the province were unable to go out on operations because they couldn't find a partner force. The commandos were dispersed around Ghazni and beyond. The teams watched security deteriorate with little scope to react until the day the city collapsed.

Almost immediately, the Afghan army sent two helicopters to reinforce local troops on the ground, who had retreated to fortified bases on the outskirts. It was a bad idea. Ghazni's airport was in the middle of the city, and both helicopters were shot down. The Afghan government continued to broadcast messages claiming that the situation was under control, but images of the Taliban and other local militias ransacking the city showed otherwise. Once again, the spotlight fell on how the Special Operations Task Force, under Josh's command, was going to regain control of Ghazni.

Josh didn't have any teams in the city, and there was no chance of flying them into the airport without getting shot down. The only solution was to send them by road. He committed three teams from nearby provinces along with the AOB company commander to the mission. They planned to secure footholds inside the city and regain control of the main government buildings by pushing outward.

It was a time-tested playbook, but the CONOP-approval process was slow. By the time the team in Kabul, ODA 1334, was approved to leave, their Afghan partner forces had left, and they were forced to travel alone. Josh tried to use air support to scatter an ambush that targeted the Afghan convoy ahead of them, but they ran into trouble at a different section of the road, twenty miles north of Ghazni. The route was planted with roadside bombs, and insurgents lay waiting with RPGs. The teams came under attack, and Josh had to medevac two team members immediately; a third stayed on with shrapnel wounds to a hand.

As an added frustration, Josh had to wait forty-eight hours to receive strike authority in Ghazni. Until authority was delegated down to him, every strike that wasn't carried out in self-defense had to be approved by high-level commanders at Resolute Support headquarters, and opportunities disappeared by the time approval came down.

A second team, ODA 1333, fared even worse in Ghazni city. They ran into an ambush and got pinned down while driving between government buildings to respond to a call for support from the Afghans. The team was pummeled with rockets, and all four vehicles in the convoy ended up disabled. Josh told them to get to safety and hunker down. They hooked the damaged trucks to others that were still running and limped to the nearest base.

By then, it seemed that every rogue insurgent group or criminal gang had seized on the opportunity to contribute to the mayhem in the city. Shops were looted, and black smoke rose above the buildings. The disorder in Ghazni made headlines around the world. The Taliban turned off cell phone towers, which made it impossible for the US teams to send images to counter the ones that showed the city in chaos. Flying imagery out was too risky, so they were limited until the signals team built an alternate system that was dropped in.

It took Josh's units ten days to fully regain control of the city. The United States estimated that it killed 226 enemy fighters through airstrikes alone, while just 10 US soldiers were wounded and none killed.

After the deployment, Josh was asked to fill out a report that asked him what he would do to control Afghanistan if he were in charge for a day. He offered a controversial solution. Instead of buying bombs for airstrikes, he would spend the money on paying local leaders and strongmen in exchange for peace. Everyone had a price, and the United States could afford to buy off Afghanistan. It was often hard to tell when Josh was joking and when he was serious. But that's what he said in the official report.

"The most foolproof way to get Taliban leaders over to our side is to buy them off," he wrote. "Many of them are just local strongmen that aren't tied to a specific ideology, but will side with whoever enables them to best lead their tribe/village. If we can be that entity then we will secure their support."

PART FOUR

ENDINGS

CHAPTER 28

Back to War, Again
HUTCH

THE TRUMP administration settled on Army General Austin "Scott" Miller to lead the war in Afghanistan. Gen. Miller had spent his life in Special Operations and was in charge of secretive missions at Joint Special Operations Command, including Delta Force and SEAL Team Six. He was short but had a strong, athletic build and looked fitter than many younger soldiers. He had a full head of gray hair and did everything with a sense of purpose. Gen. Miller had enjoyed a legendary career, having served as a Delta Force captain in Somalia during the Battle of Mogadishu, the story of which was told in the book and movie *Black Hawk Down*. He was also known for aggressively stepping up Delta Force operations while in charge of the unit in Iraq. His arrival was expected to mark a similar escalation in US operations in Afghanistan. He started the job in September 2018.

Gen. Miller inspired a cult-like dedication in his team. He was respected at all ranks and viewed as the sort of rare general officer that looked out for his men. He had spent enough time in Afghanistan to know many mid-level Afghan commanders on a personal basis, including some that by then had ascended to senior ranks in the government. With restrictions on US operations lifted, there were anecdotes of Afghan commanders who called Miller personally from the field to request support.

He brought austerity to Resolute Support, the US and NATO headquarters in Kabul. Thirty-nine nations still contributed to the mission. The close quarters, concentrated numbers, and shared alcohol smuggled into RS had caused relationships and dramas to blossom. Gen. Miller insisted on the strict enforcement of rules and did away with recreational activities that he viewed as unsuited to the seriousness of war, like evening salsa-dance classes and the drinking of contraband booze.

He also led intense physical-training sessions on Sunday mornings that aimed to build team spirit among the many branches and nationalities that made up the NATO mission. He invited me to join when I visited Afghanistan in mid-2019 to research this book. Watching Gen. Miller lead the session reminded me a bit of the movie *War Machine*. He was in better shape than anyone his age—in stark contrast to the graying NATO generals who struggled in the dusty, smog-filled air that hung over Kabul in the summer. The youngest, fittest soldiers took it as an opportunity to show off, competing to lift the heaviest weights or perform acrobatic exercises.

Hutch was there too. Gen. Miller had personally requested him for an open-ended assignment, and he had deployed to Kabul in late 2018. Even minus the fun, the sprawling Resolute Support headquarters wasn't a bad place to live. There were still restaurants, a salon, and an Italian supermarket that sold prosciutto and cheese. A bazaar on the base opened daily for shopping. Hutch hadn't expected to set foot in Afghanistan again after the hospital bombing. But institutional memories in Afghanistan are short and turnover is fast. Several other Green Berets had also been given another chance under Gen. Miller after falling from grace for one reason or another.

Gen. Miller chose Hutch for his experience during the Village Stability Operations (VSO) setting up village-level militias. Hutch's new mission was to assist with the creation of a similar nationwide force of local units, known as the Afghan National Army Territorial Force (ANA-TF). The theory made sense: communities were more invested in their own security and more likely to fight for it. The practical application was more complex. To some, it seemed to be a repackaged effort to sell the village militias, known as the Afghan Local Police (ALP), under a new name but with less supervision and fewer resources than before. The strategy raised alarm among human rights groups. Hutch often found it difficult to sell as a new concept. "I spend most of my time explaining how it isn't the ALP," he said.

The design of ANA-TF, sometimes called the territorial army, was supposed to address mistakes that had been made during the VSO. The ANA-TF was meant to break from the past, first by being incorporated into the Ministry of Defense rather than the Ministry of Interior. A review of the program by the Afghanistan Analysts Network, a locally based nonprofit that produced some of the best research on the country, noted that many changes addressed previous pitfalls.

For one, it was to be staffed by soldiers hired from the local population, but crucially, they were to go through the same basic training course as the regular army. Each local force was put under the command of officers drawn from the reserves in different provinces to reduce the risk of capture by local, factional interests. As an added safeguard, each company would be responsible for an entire district rather than a village and its surroundings. Soldiers that had previously served in the local police or other militias weren't allowed to join. The salary was 25 percent lower than the salary paid by the regular army, to reflect the benefit of serving near home, but the soldiers still had to live on the base.

The initial plan was to start a pilot program in ten locations to measure progress and then to adjust the program as needed. The ANA-TF received its first recruits in April 2018. The Afghanistan Analysts Network review found that by the summer, Gen. Nicholson had fast-tracked the expansion and opened fifty-two more locations, initiating phase one before the pilot program was complete. His action confirmed fears that once again the US military would rush into a project only to abandon it halfway through. In this instance, expanding the program without the proper checks in place could create yet more militias that were difficult to control, the last thing Afghanistan needed. That in turn would further alienate the population and add fodder for the insurgency.

When Gen. Miller took over in September 2018, he halted the expansion and tapped Hutch to lead the program. Hutch was remembered for helping to drastically reduce violence in Paktika by setting up a local village force that pacified and secured a Taliban stronghold. He knew Afghan culture well, having spent back-to-back deployments living in villages without electricity or running water; in this sense he was an ideal pick.

Among the many problems that emerged with the territorial army was the shortage of officers in the reserves to command the various units. The Afghanistan Analysts Network quoted a defense ministry official who reported that only eighteen hundred out of eighteen thousand reserve officers on the payroll showed up for duty. The rest were dead, had left the country, or were otherwise missing.

In Afghanistan, Hutch recruited a small group that included one of his former team members from his Viking days in Paktika. Few outside of Special Operations circles knew of Hutch's association with the ill-fated campaign in Kunduz. He was evidence of the short memory caused by the turnover at headquarters, which someone once described as the "annual lobotomy." But more than anyone, Hutch represented the generation of US Special Forces soldiers that had given their adult lives to the war and for a host of reasons were unable to let it go. Afghanistan had made his career, destroyed it, and now presented him with a second chance.

Hutch was in his element in his new role. Green Berets were trained to work with indigenous forces, and it was his job to oversee the local units across the country. He was comfortable navigating all channels, whether it was discussing Paktika tribal politics with rank-and-file Afghan soldiers, talking to generals about policy, or explaining the ANA-TF to skeptical academics. He was among a lucky few. Green Berets in Afghanistan still commonly griped that they were being used to put out fires instead of building ties with foreign armies. Their language and cultural training went to waste. There was no time to build rapport with Afghan commandos, who were either stuck on checkpoints or lived on separate bases due to the risk of insider attacks.

IN LATE JUNE 2019, I was invited to spend the day with Hutch in northern Baghlan province, an impoverished, mostly agricultural area that had long been considered an insurgent stronghold. Baghlan lies between Kabul and the northern province of Kunduz, and its main strategic importance is the highway connecting the capital to the north, a road that was often closed down by fighting or Taliban checkpoints.

Hutch organized the visit to give the Afghan defense ministry a chance to take ownership of the scheme to develop the ANA-TF. The trip started in the VIP waiting area at the RS headquarters, where leather sofas were arranged around glass coffee tables, and refreshments of tea, coffee, and juice were laid out alongside American-style cookies and cereal bars.

One of the first people to arrive was a member of Hutch's new team named Greg, a tall, very fair man in his thirties who was instantly recognizable as one of Hutch's former Viking crowd.

"You know Hutch's history, right?" he asked me. He fished out his phone and showed pictures of his old team, asking if I could identify them. With his white-blonde hair and beard, Greg was the easiest to spot. I recognized Hutch a few moments later, disguised among the others with a thick beard. I had only ever seen him clean-shaven.

Next, Greg scrolled to a picture of the camp on fire, with flames licking out to the sky, a column of soldiers ambling to the rescue. No one looked particularly concerned.

"Rocket," Greg explained.

Reminiscing about the good old days concluded with the arrival of military bureaucrats and protocol. Three paunchy Afghan generals and their staff settled into chairs, followed by various British and Italian military officers, whose purpose there was unclear except for the fact that they were NATO advisers. It was hard to imagine what any of them could contribute at this stage. The entourage was set to expand further, as the German army was sending advisers to Baghlan as well, because the province fell under Train, Advise, and Assist Command–North, the regional headquarters technically led by Germany.

More people arrived, including two young American soldiers from public affairs who were shooting video for internal use and had vague instructions to make sure I didn't wander off or get lost in Baghlan. Last to show up was a female deputy minister who, according to Hutch, had caused a local media scandal on a previous trip by wearing open-toed shoes.

We were divided into groups and dispatched to Baghlan on Chinooks, flying open ramp. A lone airman sat on the edge of our aircraft, attached by a strap, his legs swinging into the abyss. We coasted over the vast settlement of houses that makes up Kabul, climbed to the edges of the Hindu Kush mountains, and flew among its soaring peaks toward the gorge that forms the Salang Pass. The peaks were still capped with snow in the height of summer. Cool, crisp air filled the interior of the Chinooks. Our helicopter fired a flare into one of the valleys, which set off with a whoosh and a bang and left behind a trail of smoke. It was supposedly to scare off anyone attempting to shoot us down, though the mountains looked empty to me.

We landed at the Afghan military base in Baghlan, where the heat was intense and everything was the color of dust. The Afghan soldiers had prepared a salute for the generals, and the German military was waiting as well. Greg and Hutch were unable to fit inside the meeting room with the top brass; instead they took off on a tour of the base to find the territorial army and see "what's really going on." Hutch turned back a handful of infantry soldiers who were following him and Greg around. "Someone has to stay behind and watch our gear," he told them.

The first challenge was to find someone who could work as an interpreter since the only one assigned to the visit was busy in the meeting. Eventually, an Afghan computer technician with broken English became our guide, and Hutch and Greg asked to see the barracks. At the barracks for the commandos, a handful of young, worn-out-looking soldiers emerged from the darkness and shooed me back to the entrance. No women allowed. The stench of sewage was strong even from the doorway, and the tiled floor was dirty and dark.

"*Urdu-e Manteqawi*," Hutch explained, asking to see the barracks for the new territorial army, not the commandos. Hutch spoke only limited Pashto, not Dari, which all the soldiers seemed to find entertaining, especially after he mentioned the fearsome Commander Aziz of Paktika, his former VSO partner, who had been murdered during a picnic a year earlier. Eventually, the officers in charge of the territorial army appeared, men who probably looked about ten years older than their age.

The deputy commander, Islamuddin, was a thuggish-looking fellow with thick, jet-black hair. He had a permanently amused expression on his face, as though the arrival of all these foreigners was privately entertaining. Islamuddin told us he'd come down from Faryab, another area that was perpetually on the brink of collapse, to take command of a force that numbered 79 men, out of a total of 120 slots to fill. It wasn't a bad ratio, for Afghanistan. The officers explained that the new territorial force was being used to guard two checkpoints near the base and was not able to run missions out in the district because it still lacked critical equipment.

We were led to their armory, where everything was annotated with serial numbers and labels. The somber-looking staffer in charge showed us the weapons assigned to each soldier: a DShK or PK machine gun plus some RPGs and ammunition. The main problem, the soldier explained, was that the radios didn't work—which, as Greg pointed out later, could easily have been fixed by getting them antennas and batteries.

Greg and Hutch fired off every possible question that could be covered with our limited translation; even I had been recruited to help with the Dari. Do you have water? Electricity? What about uniforms? How many people at the check posts? How are they re-supplied? What do locals think about the territorial army? (We got stuck on the word for "support," which the Afghans thought meant sport or physical training: "Oh yes, every morning.") Can you go home? (It was too dangerous for them to do so in uniform, so the soldiers went in civilian clothes and vehicles.)

The rest of the time was spent sitting in the shade under trees with rank-and-file Afghan soldiers while waiting for the generals to emerge from their afternoon meetings. The soldiers described the usual problems: maintaining Humvees and getting paychecks. No one had been paid the previous month. Hutch explained that there was a technical, countrywide issue with the new payroll sys-tem. Greg promised to send a team to help them sort through any other issues. The Afghans smoked all Greg's cigarettes, asked about Paktika, and took pictures. Then we boarded the Chinooks and left.

Back in Kabul, we found out that two more American soldiers had been killed that day in Uruzgan province: a 10th Group soldier on his sixth deployment, and an explosives expert whose wife was expecting their first child. A few days later, a second 10th Group soldier died in a noncombat incident in Helmand province. Their deaths brought the total to ten American soldiers killed in the first six months of 2019.*

I had dinner with Hutch before leaving Kabul, at the same Thai restaurant on the base where he'd had his last meal with Col. Johnston after getting fired back in 2015. Not even the menu had changed. Hutch conceded that he needed many more staff to man-age the advisory mission. He said, "I need fifty guys, instead of five, that are free to go to all thirty-four provinces. But that could mean,

---

* The soldiers killed in Uruzgan province were Master Sergeant Micheal B. Riley of 2nd Battalion, 10th Group (A), and Sergeant James G. Johnston of the 79th Ordnance Battalion (Explosive Ordnance Disposal), 71st Ordnance Group, both of whom died in a firefight on June 25, 2019. The soldier who died in Helmand province was Sergeant First Class Elliott J. Robbins, a medical sergeant.

say, losing two guys. The army isn't willing to expose itself to that risk. Thus they [the US Army] have to make do with the limitations and the probably limited outcome."

He talked about the two US soldiers killed in Uruzgan and pondered whether it would be worse to die at the end of a deployment, like they had, or near the start. He said, "I always start a deployment thinking I'm not going to come back. Toward the end, you've made all these concrete plans with your family. I think that would be worse."

"I'm not sure Tina would look at it that way," I said.

He smiled sheepishly. When something consumes you this much, it's hard to imagine it won't consume you altogether, he explained. "I didn't realize how much at a loss I had been when they took all this away from me," he said. "Until they gave it back."

CHAPTER 29

Recovery
CALEB

After I got back from Afghanistan in July 2019, I went to Arizona to spend a weekend with Caleb's family in Tucson. We chatted at the kitchen table, Caleb leaning back in his wheelchair with his hands clasped around his left stump, which had part of a tattoo stretched over it. He spent most of his time in the chair because his prosthetic legs were causing him pain after he'd overexercised the previous week. No matter how long you spend with Caleb, it always comes as a surprise to think of him in a wheelchair or as disabled. It's his spirit.

"We haven't found anything I can't do yet," he said, more than once.

It's true, sort of. I watched his old teammate, Chris, pick up Caleb's four-year-old daughter, Emily, and toss her into the air, making her "fly" around the room. I wondered how that must feel for Caleb, his legs sore because of the bones growing at the end of his stumps that made it painful to wear his legs. When we went to watch the sunset over a nearby valley, Chris was the one to carry Emily to the top of the viewing point while Caleb stayed at the bottom with Ashley and nine-year-old Evelyn, who was afraid of heights.

Emily was as fearless as Evelyn was cautious. I pondered how much the contrast had been caused by the amount of change the elder daughter had experienced in her short life. She had seen her father's and her family's before and after. The younger girl knew nothing different. Caleb ran a ten-mile race less than a year after losing his legs, and then a full-length marathon a year later. He never felt sorry for himself, at least not in public. He did everything with confidence and refused to show signs of frustration or helplessness.

When he struggled to get back to the car after the sunset, he blamed it on the beer—not the lack of legs—and on the fact that it was dark, and thus more difficult to navigate the rocky path. He went into a detailed explanation about a problematic mechanism in the knee that caused it to swing freely and lock, making it harder to walk.

"There's been a lot of time throughout the past three years where the realization of not having legs will catch up to you. You can easily feel sorry for yourself. I think if I had to put it in the ratio, good to bad days, the good days far outweigh the bad days because of my family, my friends, good support network. It's not all rainbows and unicorns, and sometimes it just sucks. I want to go, without doing any prior planning, just go running somewhere. You know what I mean?" he said. "I can go run, but there's a lot of deliberation, putting things together, switching out parts, making sure I'm not in pain. There's days where it definitely sucks, and sometimes I get angry. And now I've realized it's easier to calm down, and filling my life with good things has helped outweigh the bad things."

Caleb found new meaning after getting training certifications through CrossFit and nonprofits supporting adaptive sports in mid-2017. He started training wounded vets and other people with disabilities, which was a turning point. Being required to focus on others made all the anger, selfishness, and self-pity disappear.

"It just turns it completely around," he said. "I found my calling: my passion is helping people in the gym. I've seen direct results of what can happen for people with disabilities or not, anybody—their mental, physical, emotional—and it changed me. I feel good, felt a sense of purpose, felt good about helping people."

One client was a sixty-five-year-old amputee who had lost a leg to diabetes. He started training with Caleb in October 2018 and by the following spring went to his doctor and found out that he wasn't diabetic anymore. Teaching him and other elderly folks how to get up off the ground without assistance, and seeing them cry and hug him, was an amazing feeling for Caleb.

"Really it could be worse. I'm interacting with other folks that don't have the same support networks that I do through the VA [Veterans Affairs]. Seeing them struggle to find the right prosthetic care, the right-fitting socket, insurance won't pay for whatever.... I can show them tips and how to adjust things, and what to look for and stuff. It helps me realize I'm really fortunate in that aspect," he said. "I haven't found anything I can't do yet."

Caleb's next plan was to go to physical therapy school in Texas. "Right now I don't have to work. I could literally sit in this chair, drink beer all day long, get on Facebook, bitch about the VA, how my life sucks, [how it was] back in war. All these snowflakes nowadays," he said. "When I say snowflakes, I mean, like, all the skinny-jean-wearing hipster people, people from Seattle."

"I've never heard that term," said Ashley.

"You guys never heard the term? Where everybody's told you're an individual, special," Caleb said.

"I got Urban Dictionary going," said Ashley, reading from her phone. "Where someone thinks they're unique and special but they're really not. Gained popularity from *Fight Club*. Funny."

Caleb had just returned from a scuba-diving trip to Saipan in which he'd helped search for the remains of missing-in-action US service members from World War II. The group he was with, Task Force Dagger Foundation, performed underwater archeology on planes that had crashed in the harbor and hadn't been recovered. In class before the dive, Caleb had heard that unexploded bombs might still exist on the harbor floor. He started to feel panicky. The anxiety developed into sweats. His heart pounded, his mind shut down. He couldn't listen to any more of the lecture; he was thinking about the bomb in Sangin, flashing back to the explosion over and over.

"I could be digging in the sand, this bomb could have been here for seventy-five years, I could just go boom! And it would explode.

So these things are running through my mind," he said. "I have this fear, which was crazy, but at the same time part of my mind was like, you know it's not going to happen, all explosives are degraded, it's not going to happen."

Caleb also had visions of an American WWII pilot being shot down, plummeting toward the sea. It would have been like his stepping on the bomb in Sangin. He felt a strange connection to the man whose body they were potentially going to recover. He was freaking out. In group settings, he'd stop talking and just replay the scene in his mind.

"He's up in the air, couple of thousand feet, gets shot down, plane's on fire. Just hurtling down to the water at hundreds of miles an hour, a sense of hopelessness. Fear. I'm going to die and there's nothing I can do to control that," he said, imagining the episode. "That's a lot of the feelings I felt after the explosion, like, oh my god, what's going to happen? I felt this weird connection to this guy. To the circumstance. It was just weird. Just processing it through my mind…thinking about why we're there, potentially to recover somebody."

Caleb found that focusing on the task allowed him to control his own fear and face the difficult emotions he still carried with him after stepping on the bomb in Sangin.

"It helped me to develop, to overcome these feelings, to where I was able to be digging around in the sand, knowing there could be bombs. It was the weirdest self-progression I've had in a long time," he said. "My mind is wired. You can plan anything perfectly, [but] bad things can still happen. Logical and illogical as it sounds at the same time."

He continued, "Someone told us the canisters were napalm. Then we learned they were rocket boost assistors for the seaplanes. The booster helps the plane get up, and then nothing, they're inert. I went through all this emotional turmoil over all this stuff, and it turned out to be nothing."

Emily walked into the dining room. "Hi," Caleb said to her, with a tender smile.

CHAPTER 30

Ending (and Trump Gets the Deal)

As Col. Josh Thiel was leaving Afghanistan, President Trump appointed a successor to the post of top US envoy for Afghan talks, which had been vacant for over a year. Zalmay Khalilzad started in September 2018 with a new title but essentially the same role as the one vacated by Laurel Miller. His orders were to get a deal with the Taliban within a year and negotiate the full withdrawal of troops that the president had wanted in the first place.

Khalilzad was an Afghan-born diplomat who had been involved in the Afghan war from the very start. He served as President Bush's special envoy to Afghanistan in 2001 and then was appointed as US ambassador there in 2003. He was closely involved in the drafting of the country's new constitution. He was a controversial figure, but few diplomats matched his experience and understanding of Afghanistan.

To launch talks, Khalilzad needed an authoritative interlocutor. At the request of the United States, Pakistan released Mullah Abdul Ghani Baradar, the cofounder of the Taliban and a senior figure who was seen to be open to negotiations. He had tried to surrender to the US on behalf of the Taliban at the start of the war and made other attempts to negotiate. By the time the US was ready, the Taliban had the upper hand. After just over a year of talks, the United States and the Taliban signed a deal in Doha, on February 29, 2020.

Under the terms of the four-page document, the United States agreed to remove all troops within fourteen months in return for a Taliban pledge to ensure that Afghanistan would never again be used by terrorists as a safe haven from which to plan attacks. The Taliban agreed to start talks with other Afghans, but there was no requirement to reach an agreement or cease-fire in the document. Critics of the deal were swift to point out that the terms were vague. US officials privately said that conditioning the departure of troops on a settlement among Afghans would give the US-backed government reason to draw out the process indefinitely.

Problems began at the outset. The Afghan government, which was not a signatory, was required to free up to five thousand Taliban prisoners for the talks to launch. Unsurprisingly, Kabul balked at the requirement, and preliminary discussions with the Taliban over the prisoner release broke off within weeks.

It didn't help that Afghanistan's leaders were locked in a contest over the outcome of a fraud-marred presidential election and more focused on claiming victory than starting a peace process with the Taliban. Soon after the US deal with the Taliban was signed, President Ghani and his rival, Abdullah Abdullah, held competing presidential inaugurations.

The United States responded with a $1 billion cut in aid to pressure the Afghan government to set rivalries aside. Ghani and Abdullah agreed to share power and completed the prisoner releases in September. Talks between the Taliban, the government, and other parties launched in Doha but had made little progress by the time President Biden commenced his term in January 2021.

After months of deliberations, Biden announced in April that all US troops would leave without preconditions on a date that eventually became August 31. Veterans' groups, congressional officials, and many others called on the US to make good on a promise to shelter those who were at risk for having supported the US during the war, including applicants to the Special Immigrant Visa (SIV) program set up to help Afghans who had served alongside US troops, diplomats, and other government agencies.

The Biden administration eventually caved to pressure to do more and began evacuation flights for families who had completed the most steps in the SIV process. But just over a fortnight after the first planes departed, the Taliban seized Kabul following a lightning offensive in which city after city fell with barely a shot fired.

Afghanistan's collapse prompted a desperate scramble as thousands of Afghans flocked to Kabul airport seeking to escape on US military and charter flights in the remaining two weeks of the war. It seemed the entire world was watching in horror as Afghans clung to planes and fell from the sky, and desperate families hurled tiny babies over the walls where US Marines were guarding the perimeter.

Afghans reached out to their former American colleagues for help, and many, like Michael Hutchinson, worked feverishly through the night to get their friends out. Lists were shared, buses were loaded, and drivers were given elaborate directions for how to make it through secret airport entrances. Ultimately it seemed totally arbitrary who could get through the gates at any given time. Hutch counted 164 people that he was able to save before the airport closed.

Days before the deadline, a suicide bomber ravaged the scene, killing more than two hundred Afghan civilians and thirteen US troops. In the chaos, the United States was unable to extract the people it wanted to save, leaving behind tens of thousands of dual American citizens, permanent residents, and other visa holders and applicants.

The Taliban are establishing rule in Afghanistan, and overnight my colleagues can travel anywhere without worrying about bombs buried in the road or kidnappings or airstrikes. So far, although there are reports of reprisal killings, especially among security forces, fears about widespread killings have not played out. But for women, a curtain is being pulled closed between them and the world. Male government workers have been invited back but not female workers. Most girls' secondary schools are closed, and it is unclear whether they will reopen. Women are allowed to attend university in very limited circumstances. No one knows if they will be allowed to work after graduating, or whether classes will continue for long.

Afghanistan faces a humanitarian and economic crisis on a massive scale, and still no country has recognized the Taliban. Yes, al Qaeda has been decimated, but US intelligence analysts say it could reconstitute in a short span of time. The war seems to have completed a full circle, with little to show for it beyond the shattered dreams of a generation of young Afghans, and the lifelong scars carried by those that fought there.

Army Staff Sgt. Matthew "Mick" McClintock was posthumously awarded a Silver Star for his actions in Marjah in 2016. Alexandra wouldn't let him be buried until the paperwork came through. She didn't trust the army to deliver.

She would spend years looking back, examining all the moments when it would have been possible to set history on a different path. The first was letting Matthew return to Afghanistan after Declan's birth. But there were others. Like their first meeting at the dive bar in Seattle.

"Nice T-shirt," she had said, recognizing the logo of a military charity. He replied with a look that she interpreted as an insult.

"Okay, I guess I'll just go over there and fuck myself then!" she added.

"Well, that will be an interesting sight!" one of his friends piped up, striking up a back-and-forth.

Matthew had come to find her at the end of the night. "I'll try to see you at a fundraiser sometime," she said.

"Do or don't. There is no try," he said.

"Did you just quote Yoda at a metal concert?" she asked.

"Did you just recognize Yoda?" he replied.

What if she hadn't said anything at all? For a long time, she felt that it would have been better if they'd never met and she had been spared the unspeakable pain of losing him. When the United States announced that it was going to negotiate a deal to withdraw from Afghanistan, Alexandra crawled back into bed and stayed there.

"If we're going to withdraw, then my husband died for literally nothing," she said, thinking of all the other widows in her community. "I don't know. I wish I knew the answers. I know that I can't let Matt, James, Mike, and all these people I've gotten to know through their families, I can't be okay with them dying for nothing. And I've met some amazing Afghan people, and I hope we find an actual solution."

She is now studying for a degree in psychology with a minor in politics at the University of Washington and applying to PhD programs. She has submitted a Freedom of Information Act request for the investigation into her husband's death. She lives with Declan in a beautiful home in a great school district, with parks nearby. She is involved in fundraising for the Special Forces community and remains in touch with Matthew's former teammates. Declan was diagnosed with autism, and she has been learning about the condition. He has a busy therapy schedule and is doing very well. On Memorial Day weekend, they spend the day at Matthew's grave in Arlington with a tent, coolers, friends, and family. Recently, she has tried dating again.

"I've tried, I've put myself out there. I've gone on dates. But how do you fill those shoes?" she said. "I'm not lonely. I'm still in love with my husband, today just as much as yesterday. I hope I love him this much or more every day for the rest of my life. When I married him I promised that I would be his wife until the day that I died. He got out of that deal a little early. I intend to hold my promise to him, and I intend to die as his wife."

She went on, "Yeah, maybe I get a second chapter. Maybe I don't. And I'm okay either way. I've got a fantastic kid who takes all of my time and all of my life. If something else comes along, he will have to be really cool. I won't date somebody unless I think Matt would love him."

ANDY AGONIZED over his decisions for a long time after the ill-fated mission in Marjah that led to the downed helicopter and Mick's death in the effort to secure a new landing zone. Perhaps they should have hunkered down at the compound. Perhaps Ski's injuries could have waited until nightfall. Perhaps they could have tried to raid the building from a different direction. He knew one thing for sure: he was proud of the team for finding a way to battle through a terrible situation, and he believed that many more could have died that day if it hadn't been for their bravery. He was disillusioned with military service and felt like a political pawn that was ultimately abandoned. As the captain, he felt responsible for having put so many men in a bad situation without recourse. He needed a fresh start. He went to business school and landed a well-paying job in tech. He has bought a small cabin in the mountains of Lake Tahoe.

Dan also struggled with his decisions in Marjah. Like Andy, he felt incredibly proud of how the team had performed during the deployment, and especially under fire during that mission. He did not return to his civilian job and instead spent time at home with his family. He started the Special Forces Warrant Officer Course in the summer of 2016. When he was taken on a tour of Washington to visit the FBI, the CIA, and the Pentagon, he met the top Special Forces planner and asked him what the strategy was for Afghanistan. The officer stared blankly at him and said, "There is no plan. We keep going there because no commander wants to be the first one to not have a combat rotation." After completing the course, Dan began a new career at the State Department while also leading a Special Forces team in the National Guard. He figured that perhaps helping to advance diplomacy would prevent wars. He plans to move with his family to work at an embassy overseas and has transitioned to the Army Reserves.

Jordan was proud to have been part of a team that displayed courage and competence in the face of chaos, danger, uncertainty, desperation, and sometimes what felt like certain death. Every man felt fear that day, but none showed it, he said. He found closure after the tour fighting Islamic State in Nangarhar, left the army, and lives a quiet life in Montana with his family, where he teaches fly-fishing. He said nothing could match up to being a Bravo on a military team, but he wanted to devote himself to his family and avoid the scars left by repeated deployments that he saw in older soldiers. "Living that life, the longer you do it, the harder it is to adjust," he said. He wanted to find something peaceful and healing. "I was meant to live old," he said.

The team members were all nominated for awards for the Marjah mission, but many were downgraded or denied. Some of the soldiers thought it was because the army didn't want to draw attention to combat operations that occurred at a time when the war was supposed to have been over. Dan and Jordan were each awarded a Bronze Star with Valor for exposing themselves multiple times to enemy fire to aid a wounded teammate. Six other members of Alpha Company were awarded Army Commendation Medals with Valor, but others were turned down for awards that would have recognized their bravery under fire for almost twenty-four hours.

The members of the crew that flew the C-130 transport plane over the battlefield to push the parachute drop of supplies were all awarded Distinguished Flying Crosses.

Flannery, the helicopter pilot who crashed in Marjah, finished the deployment, but after returning to the United States he decided never to fly again, even though becoming a pilot had been his childhood dream. Flying was never the same after the crash. "It's hard to explain," he said. "It's something I once loved and don't care about anymore." He bought a boat instead and takes it out on the lake often. He recently separated from his wife, with whom he has two children, and lives close to them in Kentucky, where he serves as a police officer. He plans to travel the world after retiring in a couple of years.

CHRIS LEFT THE MILITARY. He remained close to Caleb, visiting him and Ben, the senior Bravo on their team, at every opportunity, to hunt or spend time with their families. Civilian life was dull after having experienced the raw emotion that came with a firefight or a patrol, the elation of survival and the darkness that came with loss. When Chris was asked to draw on his experience as a veteran, he found it hard to package the dirty, messy emotions that accompanied war into a shiny conference-room pitch. At home, few had any experience of war, and it seemed many Americans had long forgotten about Afghanistan.

SINCE LEAVING AFGHANISTAN, Dr. Cua has completed missions in Jordan, Syria, the Central African Republic, South Sudan, and Cameroon. She enjoys traveling the world and being able to help those in need and describes herself as happy. She still thinks about Kunduz, but with less bitterness these days.

In early 2020, Dr. Cua returned to the Philippines for a long vacation and to work part-time in a government hospital. She is expecting to deploy soon to Houdaidah, Yemen, and then Bentiu, South Sudan. She has volunteered to go back to Kunduz if Médecins Sans Frontières succeeds in reopening the trauma center.

It took a year for Dr. Nasim to emerge from the trauma and begin to experience any emotion. He talked to a psychologist, started taking medication, and began to exercise. He still exercises to keep the depression at bay. Years later, he remained pessimistic about the future in his country and planned to move his family abroad to give his children better opportunities.

When asked about his hopes for Afghanistan, Dr. Nasim said that war had irrevocably damaged the fabric of society, and it would take hundreds of years to repair. The country's government, constantly feuding internally for power and reputed to be among the most corrupt in the world, offered no way out. When he looked around him, all he saw were wild people fighting for their own survival, with no respect for others, the law, or anything else.

"Afghanistan is worse than the jungle," he said. "Every jungle has a law. Here, there is no law."

Guilhem Molinie, the country director for Médecins Sans Frontières, said the hospital strike changed his perception of how the organization should operate. The fact that the US military was capable of bombing a heavily populated area with barely any information about the target meant that humanitarian workers were exposed to a far greater risk than he had realized. He criticized the US military for heavily redacting the version of the report released to the public and leaving key questions unanswered. He brought up the first question on the organization's list: Why did the US Special Forces team give the aircrew a physical description of the T-shaped hospital instead of the hexagonal NDS prison?

"I think, in my mind, I reached closure when I stopped trying to know more for now. I am waiting for the declassification of the documents. Hopefully I will still be alive or maybe my children will be," he said from his new post as the country director for Médecins Sans Frontières in South Africa.

I stopped when I understood and said to myself, actually, what they tell us is almost as bad as [if we had been] a targeted strike. It tells us they don't really know what they're doing. That a hospital that has been there for fifty years can still be an unknown location, even if it's on all the Afghan maps and it's listed as a hospital. When I realized that, as they said, it was a mistake, that's as bad as if it had been an intentional strike. Honestly. It means they are waging war in a city full of civilians [and] NGOs, not knowing what they're doing.

ACKNOWLEDGMENTS

THIS BOOK would not have been possible without the time and investment of a great many people who believed in the project, took risks to support it, and invested time and energy in its production. I hope to have done their stories some measure of justice and conveyed a sense of the tremendous bravery and sacrifices that make up the invisible costs of the Afghan war.

As someone with no firsthand experience of military service, the patience of the soldiers and their families was critical to understanding the details and nuances of their narratives. Many agreed to relive painful and traumatic experiences, repeatedly and in detail. And for every episode told in this book, there were many, many more that didn't make it into these pages.

In particular, I am grateful to Mike (Hutch) and Tina Hutchinson, Caleb and Ashley Brewer, Alexandra McClintock, Rosemarie Chapman, Andy MacNeil, Dan and Brianne Gholston, Jordan Avery, Casey Gursley, Josh Thiel, and many others that wished to remain anonymous. Chris Clary was an early supporter of this book, made introductions, and acted as a sounding board throughout.

Elias Altman, my agent, gave me the confidence to believe in the project from the start and was my guide throughout the publishing process, from the writing of the proposal to the final draft of the book. Colleen Lawrie, my editor at PublicAffairs, took on this book at a time when the war in Afghanistan had long ago faded from the public's consciousness. Colleen's advice, observations, and edits were always spot-on. I was lucky to benefit from Kelley Blewster's excellent copyediting, Melissa Veronesi's sharp eye for detail, and support from the rest of the team at Hachette Book Group.

The Wall Street Journal granted me an indispensable period of leave to research the book and use of the bureau in Kabul when I traveled to Afghanistan in mid-2019. Over more than five years at the paper, I have worked closely with many inspiring editors and reporters who have made me a better journalist. In particular, Bob Ourlian, the *Journal*'s indefatigable national security editor, and Paul Beckett, the Washington, DC, bureau chief. Also, my editor in Afghanistan, Peter Wonacott, the Middle East North Africa bureau chief.

The experience and generosity of many *Journal* colleagues also helped make this a better book. Michael Phillips, a staff reporter with decades of experience reporting from Afghanistan among other places, undertook a detailed edit of the manuscript and caught small errors that might otherwise have escaped unnoticed. He also introduced me to Lieutenant Colonel Josh Thiel, whose story makes up the final chapters of the book. Yaroslav Trofimov, the chief global correspondent, was an invaluable resource throughout the writing of the book and also provided feedback on an early draft.

At the *New York Times*, I was fortunate to be able to count on T. M. Gibbons-Neff for honest advice and moral support anytime I needed it. He was an early reader of the book and provided important feedback. And when I first moved to DC after more than six years reporting on the wars in Afghanistan and Libya, C. J. Chivers provided counsel on how to recover.

The Office of the Chief of Public Affairs at the Department of the Army approved my request for access to personnel, facilities, records, and photographs. The US-led Resolute Support mission in Afghanistan granted embeds with the troops, and multiple battlefield circulations to Special Forces bases around the country in late 2015. General Austin "Scott" Miller took the time to listen to the scope of the book and supported my trip to Baghlan with Hutch (and, of course, led those Sunday PT sessions) in 2019.

Many former US military and State Department officials also agreed to repeated interviews and helped with fact-checking, which provided critical insight into the political backdrop in Washington, DC, and Resolute Support headquarters in Kabul during the early years covered in this book. Later on, current and former officials provided important details and understanding during US negotiations with the Taliban in Doha, Qatar, until the signing of the deal in February 2020.

The Afghan Ministry of Defense granted me access to personnel, facilities, and records during my time at Reuters and *The Wall Street Journal*, and when I later returned to Afghanistan to research this book in 2019. The Ministry of Interior and National Directorate of Security also provided access to personnel, facilities, and records that shed light on the security situation and efforts to combat the insurgency.

In Doha, the Taliban's political office granted me interviews with their members and access to the site of the talks during the negotiation of the deal with the United States.

At home, my husband, Juan Gamboa, supported me throughout the writing of this book, which took several years of late nights and working weekends. He saw me through the many highs and lows, moments of greatness and of great doubt, and never lost enthusiasm for edits, commentary, and discussion.

AUTHOR'S NOTE

ALL THE MAIN CHARACTERS cooperated for this book, providing repeated follow-up interviews, photographs, and other materials. They also introduced me to their family members, colleagues, and friends, who offered invaluable background and context.

Most of the secondary characters also cooperated, sitting for one or more interviews, checking sections for accuracy, and providing additional context or people to speak with so I could further my research. Some wished to remain anonymous, and for this reason the bibliography does not contain detailed interview notes for each chapter.

Many of the battle sequences were reconstructed based on the recollections of the soldiers involved and are not intended as definitive accounts. The military declined to make radio transcripts, after-action reports, or other forms of documentation available. The one exception was regarding the operation to retake Kunduz. A heavily redacted version of the investigation into the Médecins Sans Frontières hospital bombing was released to the public in 2016.

Much of the reporting for this book was conducted during the four years in which I lived in Afghanistan, first as a correspondent for Reuters and then as *The Wall Street Journal*'s bureau chief in Kabul. During that time, I traveled widely to report firsthand on the way policy changes were impacting the war. On most trips, we stayed at local hotels or embedded with Afghan forces, from village militias to groups of Afghan army commandos.

I made two such trips to Kunduz, before it fell in 2015 and after it fell again in 2016. I also spent time in Helmand in late 2015 to reconstruct the secret US Special Forces mission to push the Taliban out of Babaji and save the provincial capital.

I accompanied US military officials on field visits when possible. In 2015, the US Army in Afghanistan offered me a rare opportunity to accompany Sergeant Major James Napolet, the program manager for the Special Operations Joint Task Force, Afghanistan, on a series of field visits to ODAs stationed throughout the country. It was on one of those trips that I met Chris Clary, Caleb Brewer, and the others on ODA 9123 at Camp Antonik in Helmand, a few days after the insider attack.

I also made multiple trips east to cover the emergence of Islamic State, and I was among the first foreign reporters to reach the scene after the US military dropped the "Mother of All Bombs" in eastern Nangarhar in early 2017, when I was traveling with my *Guardian* colleague Sune Engel Rasmussen and the photographer Andrew Quilty.

None of my reporting would have been possible without *The Wall Street Journal* reporters Habib Khan Totakhil and Ehsanullah Amiri, who patiently explained Afghan history, custom, and practices. Their energy and enthusiasm were always an inspiration, and both often took great personal risks to get to the bottom of a story. I also made many Afghan friends who helped provide perspective, context, and understanding.

I moved to Washington, DC, in 2017, which allowed me to conduct in-person interviews with many of the policymakers that feature in the book. I also had the privilege of spending time with 1st Battalion commander Lt. Col. Josh Thiel at Joint Base Lewis-McChord in Washington State, where I interviewed many of the soldiers who participated in the battles described in the final chapters.

In July 2019, I returned to Afghanistan to further my research for this book. *The Wall Street Journal* supported the trip by granting a request for book leave and access to accommodations at the Kabul bureau. Gen. Austin "Scott" Miller was kind enough to listen to my pitch and gave me an opportunity to travel to Baghlan province with Hutch to see his efforts to assist with the development of the Afghan National Army Territorial Forces.

BIBLIOGRAPHY

PREFACE

Donati, Jessica, and Habib Khan Totakhil. "A New U.S. Front in Afghanistan?" *The Wall Street Journal*, November 18, 2016.

Obama White House Archives. "Remarks by the President at the National Defense University." May 23, 2013. https://obamawhitehouse.archives.gov/the -press-office/2013/05/23/remarks-president-national-defense-university.

Resolute Support, Afghanistan. "Kunduz Casualty Release." November 3, 2016. https://rs.nato.int/news-center/casualty-reports/2016/kunduz-casualty-release .aspx.

CHAPTER 1

Cavendish, Julius. "Afghanistan's Dirty War: Why the Most Feared Man in Bermal District Is a US Ally." *Time*, October 4, 2011.

Connett, Ty, and Bob Cassidy. "Village Stability Operations: More Than Village Defense." *Special Warfare*, July–September 2011. www.soc.mil/SWCS /SWmag/archive/SW2403/SW2403VillageStabilityOperations_MoreThan VillageDefense.html.

Smith, Graeme. *The Future of the Afghan Local Police.* International Crisis Group report, June 4, 2015.

CHAPTER 2

For a complete list of US fatalities in Helmand, see the database https://icasualties .org, an independent website that tracks US and coalition deaths in Afghanistan, in Iraq, and in service of Operation Enduring Freedom (2001–2014). Created by Michael White, a software engineer based in Georgia, it operates as a nonprofit. Accessed July 21, 2020.

Amiri, Rahmatullah. *Helmand (2): The Chain of Chiefdoms Unravels.* Afghanistan Analysts Network report, March 11, 2016. www.afghanistan-analysts.org/en /reports/war-and-peace/helmand-2-the-chain-of-chiefdoms-unravels/.

Obama White House Archives. "Remarks by the President in Address to the Nation on the Way Forward in Afghanistan and Pakistan." December 1, 2009. https://obamawhitehouse.archives.gov/the-press-office/remarks-president -address-nation-way-forward-afghanistan-and-pakistan.

Rose, Megan. "Afghanistan Waste Exhibit A: Kajaki Dam, More Than $300M Spent and Still Not Done." *Propublica*, January 19, 2016. www.propublica.org /article/afghanistan-waste-kajaki-dam-more-than-300-million-spent-still -not-done.

Special Inspector General for Afghanistan Reconstruction, Quarterly Report, July 30, 2016. https://www.sigar.mil/pdf/quarterlyreports/2016-07-30qr.pdf.

Stancati, Margherita. "Last US Marines Leave Afghanistan's Helmand Province." *The Wall Street Journal*, October 27, 2014. www.wsj.com/articles/last-of -u-s-marines-leave-afghanistans-helmand-province-1414410005.

United Nations. "Opium Harvest in Afghanistan Hits New High in 2014." 2014 Afghanistan Opium Survey, November 12, 2014. www.unodc.org/documents /crop-monitoring/Afghanistan/Afghan-opium-survey-2014.pdf.

CHAPTER 3

BBC staff. "Afghan Taliban Splinter Group Names Mullah Rasool as Leader." BBC News, November 4, 2015. www.bbc.com/news/world-asia-34719314.

Borhan, Osman. "The Murree Process: Divisive Peace Talks Further Complicated by Mullah Omar's Death." Afghanistan Analysts Network, August 5, 2015. www.afghanistan-analysts.org/en/reports/war-and-peace/the-murree-process -divisive-peace-talks-further-complicated-by-mullah-omars-death/.

Cicilline, David. "US House Passes Bill to Honor Sergeant P. Andrew McKenna Jr." Press release, website of Congressman Cicilline, March 5, 2018. https://cicilline.house.gov/press-release/us-house-passes-bill-honor-sergeant -p-andrew-mckenna-jr.

Clark, Kate. "The Triple Attack in Kabul: A Message? If So, to Whom?" Afghanistan Analysts Network, August 10, 2015. www.afghanistan-analysts .org/en/reports/war-and-peace/the-triple-attack-in-kabul-a-message-if-so-to -whom/.

Gannon, Kathy. "Taliban Close Qatar Office to Protest Flag Fracas." Associated Press, July 9, 2013. https://apnews.com/c40133b1619b44ebb95bbf7827875322.

Petraeus, David, and Michael O'Hanlon. "The US Needs to Keep Troops in Afghanistan." *Washington Post*, July 7, 2015.

Specia, Megan. "'A Dumb Decision': U.S. Said to Waste $28 Million on Afghan Army Camouflage." *New York Times*, June 21, 2017. www.nytimes.com/2017 /06/21/world/asia/afghanistan-army-uniform-camouflage.html.

Yusufzai, Mushtaq, and Fazul Rahim. "Mullah Omar's Death Leaves Taliban Locked in Leadership Struggle." NBC News, August 3, 2015. www.nbcnews .com/news/world/mullah-omars-death-leaves-taliban-locked-leadership -struggle-n402936.

CHAPTER 4

BBC staff. "Taliban Capture Key Helmand District of Musa Qala." BBC News, August 26, 2015. www.bbc.com/news/world-asia-34062664.

UK Ministry of Defense. "Bye-Bye Bastion." October 27, 2014. www.gov.uk /government/news/bye-bye-bastion.

CHAPTER 5

DPA staff. "Profile Mullah Abdul Salam: The Man Behind the Kunduz Assault." *DPA*, October 1, 2015. www.dpa-international.com/news/asia/profilemullah -abdul-salam-the-man-behind-the-kunduz-assault-a46818569.html.

Filkins, Dexter. "In Blow to Taliban, 2 More Leaders Are Arrested." *New York Times*, February 18, 2010.

Jordans, Frank. "Afghanistan Airstrike Haunts Germany, 10 Years On." AP News, September 4, 2019. www.apnews.com/7a9f9afa839743469aaad9318896 2bf8.

Osman, Borhan, and Kate Clark. "First Wave of IS Attacks? Claim and Denial over the Jalalabad Bombs." Afghanistan Analysts Network, April 22, 2015. www.afghanistan-analysts.org/en/reports/war-and-peace/first-wave-of-is -attacks-claim-and-denial-over-the-jalalabad-bombs/.

Roggio, Bill. "Taliban Mass in Northern Afghanistan to Swear Allegiance to New Emir." *FDD's Long War Journal*, August 27, 2015. www.longwarjournal .org/archives/2015/08/taliban-mass-in-northern-afghanistan-to-swear -allegiance-to-new-emir.php.

Walsh, Declan. "Pakistan Frees Taliban Prisoners, Renewing Hopes for Peace Talks." *New York Times*, November 12, 2012.

CHAPTER 6

Harooni, Mirwais, and Jessica Donati. "Taliban Attack Airport After Seizing Northern Afghan City." Reuters, September 29, 2015. www.reuters.com /article/us-afghanistan-attack/taliban-attack-airport-after-seizing-northern -afghan-city-idUSKCN0RT0JO20150929.

Médecins Sans Frontières. "On 3 October 2015, US Airstrikes Destroyed Our Trauma Hospital in Kunduz, Afghanistan, Killing 42 People." Accessed July 5, 2020. www.msf.org/kunduz-hospital-attack-depth.

CHAPTER 7

US Central Command. *Summary of the Airstrike on the MSF Trauma Center in Kunduz, Afghanistan on October 3, 2015; Investigation and Follow-on Actions.* Released April 28, 2016. Redacted version released to the public: www3.centcom.mil/foia_rr/FOIA_RR.asp?Path=/5%20USC%20552%28a% 29%282%29%28D%29Records&Folder=1.%20Airstrike%20on%20the%

20MSF%20Trauma%20Center%20in%20Kunduz%20Afghanistan%20
%203%20Oct%202015. (Hereafter referred to as *Summary of the Airstrike on the MSF Trauma Center in Kunduz.*)

CHAPTER 8

Aikens, Matthew. "Doctors with Enemies: Did Afghan Forces Target the M.S.F. Hospital?" *New York Times Magazine*, May 17, 2016.

Cua, Evangeline. "Kunduz: This Is My Story." Doctors Without Borders, April 3, 2016. https://msf-seasia.org/blogs/16903.

Schogol, Jeff. "Special Forces Return Fire on Taliban in Kunduz." *Air Force Times*, October 1, 2015 (AP photo of Hutch talking to the Kunduz police chief before the compound comes under fire). www.airforcetimes.com/news/your-air-force/2015/10/01/special-forces-return-fire-on-taliban-in-kunduz/.

US Central Command. *Summary of the Airstrike on the MSF Trauma Center in Kunduz.*

CHAPTER 9

Smith, Josh, and Zubair Babakakhail. "US Special Forces in Firefight with Taliban at Kunduz." *Stars and Stripes*, October 1, 2015.

US Central Command. *Summary of the Airstrike on the MSF Trauma Center in Kunduz.*

CHAPTER 10

Neuman, Scott. "Doctors Without Borders: Kunduz Airstrike Was 'War Crime.'" NPR, October 4, 2015. www.npr.org/sections/thetwo-way/2015/10/04/445773358/doctors-without-borders-kunduz-airstrike-was-war-crime.

US Central Command. *Summary of the Airstrike on the MSF Trauma Center in Kunduz.*

CHAPTER 11

"Afghan Government Confirms Airstrike on Kunduz Hospital—Video." *The Guardian*, October 3, 2015 (AP video). www.theguardian.com/world/video/2015/oct/03/afghan-government-confirms-airstrike-on-kunduz-hospital-video.

C-SPAN. "General John Campbell, Commander of US Forces, Afghanistan, Testified on US Operations in Afghanistan." October 6, 2015. www.c-span.org/video/?328585-1/general-john-campbell-testimony-us-military-operations-afghanistan.

Craig, Tim, and Craig Whitlock. "Afghan Response to Hospital Bombing Is Muted, Even Sympathetic." *Washington Post*, October 4, 2015.

Department of Defense Press Briefing by Gen. Campbell in the Pentagon Briefing Room. Transcript. October 5, 2015. www.defense.gov/Newsroom/Transcripts/Transcript/Article/621848/department-of-defense-press-briefing-by-gen-campbell-in-the-pentagon-briefing-room/.

Gibbons-Neff, Thomas. "From 'Collateral Damage' to 'Deeply Regrets': How the Pentagon Has Shifted on the Afghan Hospital Attack." *Washington Post*, October 6, 2015.

Médecins Sans Frontières. "Afghanistan: Kunduz Trauma Center Bombing." October 7, 2015. www.doctorswithoutborders.org/what-we-do/news-stories /story/afghanistan-kunduz-trauma-center-bombing.

Obama White House Archives. "Statement by the President on Afghanistan." October 15, 2015. https://obamawhitehouse.archives.gov/the-press-office/2015 /10/15/statement-president-afghanistan.

Smith, Josh. "US Air Attack Suspected in Kunduz Hospital Deaths." *Stars and Stripes*, October 3, 2015.

CHAPTER 12

Arjomand, Noah. "Eagle's Summit Revisited: Decision-Making in the Kajaki Dam Refurbishment Project." Afghanistan Analysts Network, January 25, 2013. www.afghanistan-analysts.org/en/special-reports/eagles-summit-revisited-aan -report-about-decision-making-in-the-kajaki-dam-project/.

Background on USAID's Kajaki project: *Special Inspector General for Afghanistan Reconstruction*, July 30, 2016, Quarterly Report to Congress.

Boone, Jon. "Battle of Babaji: A Fight for Hearts and Minds in Afghanistan, but None Are to Be Found." *The Guardian*, June 24, 2009.

Farmer, Ben, and Danielle Moylan. "Taliban Seize British Stronghold in Helmand as Security Unravels." *The Telegraph*, October 20, 2015.

Rasmussen, Sune Engel. "British Engineers Evacuated from Key Afghan Dam as Taliban Approach." *The Guardian*, September 18, 2015.

CHAPTER 14

Department of Defense Press Briefing by General Campbell via teleconference from Afghanistan. Transcript. November 25, 2015. www.defense.gov/News room/Transcripts/Transcript/Article/631359/department-of-defense-press -briefing-by-general-campbell-via-teleconference-fro/.

Shear, Michael D., and Somini Sengupta. "Obama Issues Rare Apology over Bombing of Doctors Without Borders Hospital in Afghanistan." *New York Times*, October 7, 2015.

Stancati, Margherita, and Jessica Donati. "US Troops Suspended After Afghan Hospital Bombing." *The Wall Street Journal*, November 25, 2015.

US Central Command. *Summary of the Airstrike on the MSF Trauma Center in Kunduz*.

CHAPTER 17

Ayling, J. "Managing Head Injuries." *Emergency Medical Services* 31, no. 8 (2002): 42.

Harooni, Mirwais. "Afghan Official Warns Helmand Province May Fall to Taliban." Reuters, December 20, 2015. www.reuters.com/article/us-afghanistan-taliban/afghan-official-warns-helmand-province-may-fall-to-taliban-idUSKBN0U30DB20151220.

ProlongedFieldCare.org. "Video AAR of the Jan 2016 Marjah Firefight and PFC MEDEVAC." Accessed July 21, 2020. https://prolongedfieldcare.org/2016/01/05/video-aar-of-the-jan-2016-marjah-firefight-and-pfc-medevac/.

CHAPTER 18

Department of Defense Press Briefing by Pentagon Press Secretary Peter Cook in the Pentagon Briefing Room. Transcript. January 5, 2016. www.defense.gov/Newsroom/Transcripts/Transcript/Article/639998/department-of-defense-press-briefing-by-pentagon-press-secretary-peter-cook-in/.

Lee, C., K. M. Porter, and T. J. Hodgetts. "Tourniquet Use in the Civilian Prehospital Setting." *Emergency Medicine Journal* 24, no. 8 (2007): 584–587. https://doi.org/10.1136/emj.2007.046359.

CHAPTER 19

US Army. "Survival Rates Improving for Soldiers Wounded in Combat, Says Army Surgeon General." August 24, 2016. www.army.mil/article/173808/survival_rates_improving_for_soldiers_wounded_in_combat_says_army_surgeon_general.

CHAPTER 20

C-SPAN. "Afghanistan Operations Commander Confirmation Hearing." January 28, 2016. www.c-span.org/video/?403828-1/lieutenant-general-john-nicholson-confirmation-hearing.

Johnson, Casey Garret. "The Rise and Stall of the Islamic State in Afghanistan." United States Institute of Peace, November 2016. www.usip.org/sites/default/files/SR395-The-Rise-and-Stall-of-the-Islamic-State-in-Afghanistan.pdf.

Jones, Seth G., et al. *Rolling Back the Islamic State*. RAND Corporation. 2017. www.rand.org/content/dam/rand/pubs/research_reports/RR1900/RR1912/RAND_RR1912.pdf.

Lubold, Gordon. "US Clears Path to Target Islamic State in Afghanistan." *The Wall Street Journal*, January 19, 2016.

New York Times staff. "The Guantanamo Docket." *New York Times*. Accessed July 21, 2020. www.nytimes.com/interactive/projects/guantanamo/detainees/561-abdul-rahim-muslim-dost.

Obama White House Archives. "Statement by the President on Afghanistan." July 6, 2016. https://obamawhitehouse.archives.gov/the-press-office/2016/07/06/statement-president-afghanistan.

Osman, Borhan. "The Islamic State in 'Khorasan': How It Began and Where It Stands Now in Nangarhar." Afghanistan Analysts Network, July 27, 2016. www.afghanistan-analysts.org/en/reports/war-and-peace/the-islamic-state-in-khorasan-how-it-began-and-where-it-stands-now-in-nangarhar/.

Osman, Borhan. "Messages in Chalk: 'Islamic State' Haunting Afghanistan?" Afghanistan Analysts Network, November 17, 2014. www.afghanistan-analysts.org/en/reports/war-and-peace/messages-in-chalk-islamic-state-haunting-afghanistan/.

Walsh, Declan. "Return My Work, Says Guantánamo Poet." *The Guardian*, April 3, 2006.

CHAPTER 21

Department of Defense Press Briefing by Army General Joseph Votel, commander, US Central Command. Transcript. April 29, 2016. www.defense.gov/Newsroom/Transcripts/Transcript/Article/746686/department-of-defense-press-briefing-by-army-general-joseph-votel-commander-us/.

Médecins Sans Frontières. "Some of MSF's Questions in Response to the U.S. Military Investigation into Their Attack on the Hospital." April 29, 2016. www.msf.org/kunduz-some-msf%E2%80%99s-questions-response-us-military-investigation-their-attack-hospital.

CHAPTER 22

Ahmad, Jibran. "Son of Afghan Taliban Leader Dies Carrying Out Suicide Attack." Reuters, July 22, 2017. www.reuters.com/article/us-afghanistan-taliban-son/son-of-afghan-taliban-leader-dies-carrying-out-suicide-attack-idUSKBN1A707K.

Donati, Jessica, and Habib Khan Totakhil. "Afghan Government Secretly Fosters Taliban Splinter Groups." *The Wall Street Journal*, May 22, 2016.

Entous, Adam, and Jessica Donati. "How the US Tracked and Killed the Leader of the Taliban." *The Wall Street Journal*, May 25, 2016.

CHAPTER 24

Afghanistan Bureau. "Afghan Forces Fight to Regain Northern City of Kunduz from Taliban." Reuters, October 2, 2016. www.reuters.com/article/us-afghanistan-taliban/afghan-forces-fight-to-regain-northern-city-of-kunduz-from-taliban-idUSKCN123086.

CNN staff. "Comment: Was MOAB a Message to North Korea?" CNN clip, April 15, 2017. https://edition.cnn.com/videos/tv/2017/04/15/comment-was-moab-a-message-to-north-korea.cnn.

C-SPAN. "Military Operations in Afghanistan." February 9, 2017. www.c-span.org/video/?423552-1/general-john-nicholson-tells-senate-we-stalemate-afghanistan.

Department of Defense Press Briefing by General Nicholson via teleconference from Kabul, Afghanistan. Transcript. November 28, 2017. www.defense.gov /Newsroom/Transcripts/Transcript/Article/1382901/department-of-defense -press-briefing-by-general-nicholson-via-teleconference-fr/.

European Council. "Brussels Conference on Afghanistan: Main Results." Press release, October 5, 2016. www.consilium.europa.eu/en/press/press-releases/2016 /10/05/bca-main-results/.

Feith, David. "H. R. McMaster: The Warrior's-Eye View of Afghanistan." *The Wall Street Journal*, May 11, 2012.

Gul, Ayaz. "US Military Rejects Russian Claims About Number of IS Fighters in Afghanistan." Voice of America, February 24, 2018. www.voanews.com /east-asia-pacific/us-military-rejects-russian-claims-about-number-fighters -afghanistan.

LoBianco, Tom. "Donald Trump Backtracks on Afghanistan War: Not a Mistake." CNN, October 20, 2015. https://edition.cnn.com/2015/10/20/politics /donald-trump-afghanistan-war-not-a-mistake/index.html.

Watson Institute for International and Public Affairs at Brown University. "Costs of War." September 2019. https://watson.brown.edu/costsofwar/figures/2019 /us-war-spending-afghanistan-2001.

CHAPTER 25

Donati, Jessica, and Ehsanullah Amiri. "At Least 90 Killed in Blast Near Embassies in Afghan Capital." *The Wall Street Journal*, May 31, 2017.

Office of the Inspector General. "Audit of Cost Management of Embassy Air in Afghanistan and Iraq." United States Department of State, AUD-MERO-19-33. September 2019. https://www.stateoig.gov/system/files/aud -mero-19-33.pdf.

US Air Forces Central Command. Airpower Summaries: Monthly Data. Accessed July 6, 2020. www.afcent.af.mil/About/Airpower-Summaries/.

Wolff, Michael. *Fire and Fury: Inside the Trump White House*. New York: Macmillan, 2018.

CHAPTER 26

Jones, Timothy, and Massod Saifullah. "Afghanistan: Ghani Announces Ceasefire with Taliban for Eid al-Fitr." *Deutsche Welle*, June 7, 2018. www.dw.com /en/afghanistan-ghani-announces-ceasefire-with-taliban-for-eid-al-fitr /a-44106896.

CHAPTER 27

Abed, Fahim, and Taimoor Shah. "Taliban Overrun Afghan City, Kill 30 People and Leave." *New York Times*, May 16, 2018.

Azadzoi, Nesar, and Rod Nordland. "After Ghazni Attack, Taliban Still in Afghanistan City." *New York Times*, August 11, 2018.

Hennigan, W. J. "Exclusive: Inside the US Fight to Save Ghazni from the Taliban." *Time*, August 23, 2018.

Rempfer, Kyle. "Air Force A-10s Called in to Hold Off Taliban Attack on Major Afghan City." *Air Force Times*, May 15, 2018.

CHAPTER 29

Clark, Kate. "The Afghan Territorial Force: Learning from the Lessons of the Past?" Afghanistan Analysts Network, January 15, 2019. www.afghanistan -analysts.org/en/reports/war-and-peace/the-afghan-territorial-force-learning -from-the-lessons-of-the-past/.

INDEX

JUAN GAMBOA

JESSICA DONATI covers foreign affairs for *The Wall Street Journal* in Washington, DC, and has reported from over a dozen countries in the role. She joined the paper as the bureau chief in Kabul in 2015 and lived in Afghanistan for over four years. Previously, she worked for Reuters in Europe, the Middle East, and Asia, covering the conflicts in both Libya and Afghanistan. Her work on a series on the war in Libya was chosen as a finalist for the Pulitzer Prize for International Reporting in 2012. She is British-Italian and grew up in Italy. She lives with her husband and son in Washington, DC.

PublicAffairs is a publishing house founded in 1997. It is a tribute to the standards, values, and flair of three persons who have served as mentors to countless reporters, writers, editors, and book people of all kinds, including me.

I. F. STONE, proprietor of *I. F. Stone's Weekly*, combined a commitment to the First Amendment with entrepreneurial zeal and reporting skill and became one of the great independent journalists in American history. At the age of eighty, Izzy published *The Trial of Socrates*, which was a national bestseller. He wrote the book after he taught himself ancient Greek.

BENJAMIN C. BRADLEE was for nearly thirty years the charismatic editorial leader of *The Washington Post*. It was Ben who gave the *Post* the range and courage to pursue such historic issues as Watergate. He supported his reporters with a tenacity that made them fearless and it is no accident that so many became authors of influential, best-selling books.

ROBERT L. BERNSTEIN, the chief executive of Random House for more than a quarter century, guided one of the nation's premier publishing houses. Bob was personally responsible for many books of political dissent and argument that challenged tyranny around the globe. He is also the founder and longtime chair of Human Rights Watch, one of the most respected human rights organizations in the world.

·   ·   ·

For fifty years, the banner of Public Affairs Press was carried by its owner Morris B. Schnapper, who published Gandhi, Nasser, Toynbee, Truman, and about 1,500 other authors. In 1983, Schnapper was described by *The Washington Post* as "a redoubtable gadfly." His legacy will endure in the books to come.

Peter Osnos, *Founder*